94131

338.4
768872
0973
Ste

Stern, Sydney La-
densohn

Toyland

DUE DATE	BRODART	01/94	19.95

TOYLAND

TOYLAND
The High-Stakes Game of the Toy Industry

SYDNEY LADENSOHN STERN
AND TED SCHOENHAUS

CB

CONTEMPORARY
BOOKS

CHICAGO

94131

Library of Congress Cataloging-in-Publication Data

Stern, Sydney.
  Toyland : the high-stakes game of the toy industry / Sydney Stern
and Schoenhaus.
    p.   cm.
  Includes bibliographical references.
  ISBN 0-8092-4520-5
  1. Toy industry—United States.   I. Schoenhaus, Ted.   II. Title.
HD9993.T693U67   1990
338.4′768872′0973—dc20   89-71198
                                                              CIP

Published by Contemporary Books, Inc.
180 North Michigan Avenue, Chicago, Illinois 60601
Manufactured in the United States of America
International Standard Book Number: 0-8092-4520-5

COPYRIGHT AND PHOTO ACKNOWLEDGMENTS

CONTENTS

Amy Binder, William Birnbaum, Jerry Blatt, Margie Blatt, Helen Boehm, Alan Bohbot, Spencer Boise, Howard Bollinger, Jeff Breslow, Paul Brichta, Nolan Bushnell, Beverly Cannaday, Dave Capper, Bill Carlson, Al Carosi, Sharon Carpenter, Tim Cawley, Wayne Charness, Peggy Charren, Jack Chojnacki, Jerry Cleary, Margie Cleary, Phil Cohen, Victor Cole, Andrew Cornell, Steve D'Aguanno, Donna Datre, Garth DeCew, Josh Denham, George Ditomassi, Jerry Dunne, and Harvey Dzodin.

Also Peter Eio, Pat Feely, Ellen Feig, George Fink, Rita Fire, Mari Forquer, Jack Fox, Renee Fraser, Bob Fuhrer, David Fuhrer, Jay Garfinkel, Bill Garrity, Manny Gerard, Laurel Gilbert, Rick Gitter, Eddy Goldfarb, Michael Goldstein, Barry Golombik, Pat Green, Arnold Greenberg, Tom Griffin, Elliot Handler, Ruth Handler, Alan Hassenfeld, Don Heckman, Faith Heckman, Patrick Henry, Andy Heyward, Loren Hildebrand, Jack Hirsch, Shelly Hirsch, Jill Himonas, Ed Hjelte, Candace Irving, Bob Jackman, Jeremy Jacob, Gary Jacobson, Betty James, Bob Jezak, Saul Jodel, Al Kahn, and Tom Kalinske.

Marvin Katz, Michael Katz, Lauren Kellachan, Ed Kelly, Larry Killgallon, Paul Kirchner, Thomas Kully, Melvin Lachman, Peggy Lane, John LaPick, Ray Larsen, David Leibowitz, Kenny Lewis, Laurie Lively, Aaron Locker, Bernie Loomis, Bruce Maguire, Kim Maguire, Joe Mantegna, Joe Marino, Dave Mauer, Ian McDermott, Sean McGowan, Arthur Melin, Joe Mendelsohn, Les Mendelsohn, Isabel Miller, Marty Miller, Tony Miller, Joe Morrison, Thomas Murdough, Tom Murn, Arthur Nadel, Jan Nowak, Dave Okada, Phil Orbanes, Kimerlea Osborne, Mike Phillips, Paul Pressler, Paul Rago, Larry Ramsey, Joe Rein, Xavier Roberts, and Patty Root deserve our gratitude.

Also contributing were Jack Ryan, Richard Sallis, Roger Schlaifer, Cy Schneider, Steve Schwartz, Dick Schwarzchild, Mark Setteducati, Judy Shackelford, Ralph Shaffer, Steve Shank, Roger Shiffman, Wendy Shugarman, Tom Shure, Ira Smith, Marvin Smollar, Maurene Souza, Arthur Spear, Sid Spielvogel, Bruce Stein, John Sterner, Scott Stillinger, Ned Strongin, Judith Sussman, Ed Swartz, Arnold Thaler, Paul Valentine, George Volanakis, Richard Weiner, Lionel Weintraub, Rita Weisskoff, Stan Weston, Howard Wexler, Michael White, Jim Willcox, Fred Zant, Jane Zimmy, and Sy Ziv.

The staffs at *Toy & Hobby World* and *Playthings* magazines generously made their back issues available as well as space to inspect them. The NPD Group patiently answered our questions and calculated new figures for us from the voluminous data they collect for the toy industry.

Special thanks must go to our agent, Michael Cohn, who suggested this book because he wanted to read about toys; Corky Stern, who was first to read portions of the manuscript; Jon Stern for his full-court press of editing at the last minute; and our two product consultants. Lizzie Friedland taught us that modern girls don't play with one Barbie doll and lots of clothes; they play with lots of Barbie dolls and lots of clothes. Toby Stern's opinions guided us on everything from which Nintendo games were radical to which kids' commercials were nerdy. Representing 43.6 million American children was a tough job, so we picked a tough kid to do it.

Thanks, all of you.

WINNING THE GAME

. . . When the last player has completed his final
month of play, each player totals his cash (after all
bills have been paid up) and adds his savings or
subtracts his loans. The player having the greatest
total is the winner. If all players are in debt, the
player who is least in debt is the winner!

Instructions for PAYDAY
Parker Brothers

1

PROLOGUE
February 8, 1988

6:00 A.M.

A BATTERED TAXICAB HURTLES THROUGH dark
New York streets and halts in front of a canopied office building.
Two men, obviously in a hurry, leave the cab and hasten inside.
Too restless to ride the elevators, they mount the stairs, punc-
tuating their conversation with snorts of nervous laughter.

On the third floor they emerge and turn left. The door they
seek is a few steps away, and one of the men already has his keys
in his hand. He unlocks the door, and they step quickly inside.

Once across the threshold, their urgency dissipates. They eye
each other uncertainly, ruefully. Now that they have achieved
their objective, they begin to wonder why it was so important.
Their hesitation is short-lived. In silent accord they turn and
head through a warren of rooms. When they reach their desti-
nation, the one nearer the switch flicks on the light.

Plastic objects, ranged around the room on tables, stare silently at the intruders. The two men stare back. They approach
the tables, unable to resist touching the objects. They move one
a quarter of an inch to the left, push another a quarter of an
inch to the right.

The changes are minuscule, imperceptible. The men are obviously trying to reassure themselves—as if they suspect the objects of moving when no one is there to watch. They cannot stay away. Just nine hours ago they left the company party to come to this room and do exactly what they are doing now.

Finally the men fuss and fidget so much that they begin to annoy even themselves. They stop moving the objects and begin to pace.

They act as if they were a pair of expectant fathers, except that they seem to be the ones about to give birth. Perhaps they are playwrights, hours before the opening of their first play.

They are both.

These two have spent the last two years creating something. Now it is time to let go, and they are feeling powerless. Their creation no longer belongs to them alone. It never did, really, but now its fate is completely out of their hands. All they can do is stand back and watch.

The curtain is going up, and the public will be the judge.

Hit or flop?

They are about to find out.

8:00 A.M.

The sun radiates through the cold, blue sky. For February in New York, the weather is better than cheerful; it is resplendent.

The lobby at 200 Fifth Avenue is already packed. Buyers pour in. Shills head out. Old comrades greet one another, hugging and kissing. "You owe me twenty-five dollars," one announces, shaking hands with a friend he hasn't seen for a year. A few sleepy buyers pass through the lobby into the Hickory House for a quick cup of coffee. A man strolls toward the elevators with the three-foot-tall head of a toy soldier under his arm.

A young woman in pigtails and a child's dress leads a giant red pitcher toward the front of the lobby. She stops near the doors and takes a couple of photographs of the pitcher, then grasps its handle again, issuing a steady stream of instructions in a soft southern accent. "Now we're at the first doors. Let's see if we can get you through. If not, we'll have to deflate you a little." She is twenty-eight-year-old Kimerlea Osborne, a Tennessee accounting clerk, and she is dressed to resemble Kool-Aid Kid dolls, which she invented. It has taken two years, help from the citizens of Dyersburg, Tennessee, and all the money she could raise by selling her car and her jewelry to get her to Toy Fair. The human pitcher is the Kool-Aid Man, although the human inside is a woman.

They manage to squeeze through the doors without letting any air out of the pitcher and join the other hawkers on the sidewalk. Daffy Duck is there, wearing a sign that says, "Daffy Duck in *The Duxorcist.* First Theater Short Subject in Twenty Years." Raggedy Ann and Andy are there too, along with U. Dirty Rat and Ducksy Malone of the Touchables, Dennis the Menace, and men in caricatured heads of President Ronald Reagan and New York mayor Ed Koch. A pair of young women in medieval caps and fox-trimmed velvet capes demonstrate Blooming Dolls, stuffed flower pots that convert into dolls. Two large, green creatures hand out buttons that say, "Teenage Mutant Ninja Turtles, FRESH FROM THE SEWER."

Three grim-faced men in overcoats hand out flyers. They look so comically earnest that no one can tell if they are serious or kidding. "NOTICE OF PENDING LITIGATION," say the flyers. "January 29, 1988. U.S. Patent No. 4,022,350." They must be serious. A "BATTERY OPERATED WATER GUN" is the issue. Apparently only four companies have paid for the right to manufacture the battery-operated water guns protected by Patent No. 4,022,350, and the inventor has already filed lawsuits against five companies for making copies, as well as Child World and Woolworth for selling them. He warns anyone else even thinking of copying him to forget it. "Further lawsuits seeking maximum damages and injunctive relief from those who produce, import, distribute or sell counterfeits or knockoffs, covered by Patent No. 4,022,350, will be filed," threatens the flyer ominously.

Toy Fair 1988 has begun.

Inside the building the morning wears on. A public relations agent with a cowboy ventriloquist and dummy in tow wanders downstairs to the basement press room. "Wouldn't anyone like to talk to Buffalo Bob?" she asks the room brightly, but no one replies. Howdy Doody is back, but the reporters are too busy stuffing press kits into shopping bags to notice.

Upstairs the registration lines lengthen, as TMA (Toy Manufacturers of America) staff members carefully type each color-coded badge. Buyers wear fuschia, purple is for manufacturers' representatives, gray for exhibitors, gold for trade guests, blue for reporters, and green for advertising salespeople. Beside the counters a carousel of trade publications needs constant replenishment as passersby grab Toy Fair editions of *Toy & Hobby World, Playthings, The Toy Book, Children's Business,* and a host of others.

The elevators are filled beyond capacity. At least one breaks down every year, and attendants hired for the week make the usual jokes about fourth floor, ladies' lingerie. Midwesterners look uncomfortable in such close quarters and vainly attempt to maintain their distance. Northeasterners, accustomed to intimacy with strangers on the subway, jam themselves in. Including those who will show elsewhere, there are 1,101 exhibitors.

Even the stairs are crowded. Two Hundred Fifth Avenue is officially the Toy Center South, but everyone calls it the Toy Building or just 200 Fifth. The other eleven months of the year the Italian Renaissance–style building is practically deserted.

Packed with permanent showrooms, the Toy Building was officially recognized as The Toy Center of the World in 1925. It is connected to 1107 Broadway, the building next door, by a ninth-floor bridge built in 1968 especially for Toy Fair traffic. Lining the bridge are plaques that make up the Toy Industry Hall of Fame. Established in 1984 by the Toy Manufacturers of America, the exhibit originally honored only deceased toy luminaries. They ran out of deserving candidates sooner than they expected, so this year the TMA board has voted to admit one living inductee a year.

For many years most of the manufacturers or importers who wanted to exhibit during Toy Fair did not show at the Toy Building. They rented rooms at nearby hotels, covered the furniture with sheets, and displayed their wares on top. Never a sophisticated group, the exhibitors were as importunate as merchants in a Third World bazaar. "Why is it that a buyer who calls at one hotel should be warned against going to another hotel and filled full of gossip about buttonholing, bodysnatching and other fearful things?" asked the editors of *Playthings* magazine in 1918. No one paid any attention. In 1959 the magazine was still admonishing exhibitors to stop soliciting customers in the hallways and corridors, and its complaints were still ignored. "We used to turn our name tags upside down so that they were harder to read," recalls a buyer who worked for Sears, Roebuck in the 1960s, when Sears was the largest account in the toy industry. "Otherwise everyone was always grabbing at us. We didn't like to refuse them, because we wanted to be polite, but it was very embarrassing."

A much-heard refrain is that Toy Fair is not what it used to be. Nothing is, of course, but Toy Fair really has changed. In the old days it was three weeks long and served as the major buying period for the industry. Today, one veteran observes, "the halls are filled with reporters, television producers looking for tie-ins, authors writing books, licensing agents, and television camera crews. Every once in a while you may spot a buyer—hallelujah—but even he's probably not writing any orders. He's just coming back to check on what he already saw at pre–Toy Fair. He'll buy later on."

Toy Fair may not be the buying show it once was, and now

that it follows toy fairs in London, Hong Kong, Milan, Toronto, Nuremberg, and Paris, some of the novelty is gone as well. But the American International Toy Fair is still the annual gathering of the clan. Everyone complains about it, but no one would miss it for the world.

Toy Fair is the time to see and be seen. To look for another job. To show product lines to peers. To make deals with licensers and licensees for everything from lunch boxes to pajamas. To meet with inventors. To sell inventions. To meet with advertising agencies, syndicators, network officials. To talk to Wall Street analysts. To be interviewed by the general press, the trade press, the financial press, the parenthood press, and every other kind of press. To check out the competition, both openly and by spying (which is less effective but more fun). To catch the latest trends. To gossip.

Bernie Loomis is here, with an aching back. He can hardly walk and will go into surgery soon, but he would never miss Toy Fair; this is his thirtieth. A legend in the industry, he has worked for Mattel, headed Kenner, started two licensing and design companies called MAD and GLAD, and now consults under his own name. He is known for his marketing prowess, his astute product sense, and his loquaciousness.

Artie and Judy Albert have been coming to Toy Fair for even longer than Bernie Loomis. The couple met at Ideal Toys, where Judy was a doll designer and Artie became the vice president for dolls. Now an independent team, they come to check on their latest creations. Judy adapted Coleco's Cabbage Patch Kids from the Georgia originals, invented Puffalumps for Fisher-Price (stuffed creatures made from parachute nylon), and designed Maxie, Hasbro's newest challenge to Barbie. The Alberts chuckle about how glitzy everything is today compared with the old days.

Not everything has changed. Artie remembers when he started working at Ideal a month before Toy Fair. He sat in a new-product conference watching Ideal's president try different doll heads on different doll bodies and assumed he was helping to choose new products for the following year. Slowly it dawned on him that these were the new products for the next month's

Toy Fair. Many of the products the Alberts see on display today are clearly just as fresh out of the workroom.

David Fuhrer paces the Random House showroom. He will be demonstrating a game he, his brother, and a game inventor created, based on his unusual talent. Fuhrer, who has appeared on "Late Night with David Letterman" and "The Tonight Show," can talk backward. Won eh si gniog ot ekam yenom morf ti. The three of them spent over a year perfecting Backwords, and he doesn't want to let his partners down.

All the inventors with products at the fair come to check on their inventions—and on the competition's. Even one of the most successful, California veteran Eddy Goldfarb, worries about what he will see. "Every year I go to Toy Fair with a light heart and a heavy heart," he explains. "I'm excited to see my inventions as products, but I dread seeing things others have made that I just started working on." One of Goldfarb's inventions this year is an electronic game called Babble, which records a phrase and repeats it backward. Goldfarb and Lewis Galoob Toys, the San Francisco company that produced his game, are dismayed when they learn about the board game Backwords.

The duplication at Toy Fair surprises the uninitiated. The appearance of two independently conceived games based on the idea of talking backward seems too coincidental. But dolls that talk intelligently (forward) appear in every showroom. Two major manufacturers introduce die-cast cars that change colors. Even packaging seems repetitious. A number of competing products are housed in white boxes trimmed with gray grids and geometric splashes of hot pink and turquoise. This phenomenon, "parallel development," is a fact of life in Toyland. Spying, copying, and downright stealing are not unknown, and there are always plenty of lawsuits in progress, but much of the duplication is innocent.

The culprit is groupthink. Inventors, marketers, designers, packagers, art directors all read the same material, see the same movies, listen to the same music, watch for trends in all the same places, and they all ask themselves the same question: what does the public find appealing or exciting, and how can I turn it into a toy, a package, a marketing concept that will sell?

Some of the duplication is not so innocent. A Tyco salesman walks out of the Tyco showroom without his badge, and a sneaky-looking character sidles up to him and beckons. Curious, the salesman follows him to a far corner of the hall, where the furtive stranger opens his coat to display pictures of Tyco's brand-new plastic dinosaurs, part of an action-figure line called Dino-Riders. The salesman asks the man to send him samples so that he can get a closer look. Tyco just began shipping the line in December, so if Dino-Riders is being knocked off before it even proves itself, someone must think it is going to be a hit. He can hardly wait to tell Tyco's marketing men. They are so obsessed with the product that they have been in Tyco's showroom since six in the morning, just walking around.

Among the showroom visitors are a number of Wall Street analysts who evaluate the products as seriously as if their business were blocks instead of stocks. They would deny that they judge companies more by their products than by their financial performance, but they cannot ignore the toys themselves. As they say in the toy business, "Product is king." As the analysts would put it, the toy companies' success is largely product-driven. Besides, product lines are more fun than bottom lines, at least once in a while.

As usual, there are demonstrators in front of the building protesting war toys. Someone is always criticizing the toy industry. The toy industry is regulated for safety by the Consumer Product Safety Commission, for advertising fairness by the Federal Trade Commission, for television programming and commercial content by the Federal Communications Commission. TMA members voluntarily submit their advertising to regulation by the Children's Advertising Review Unit of the Council of Better Business Bureaus. All of the industry's television-related activities are monitored by Action for Children's Television. Activists from the Americans for Democratic Action evaluate toys every year and hold a big press conference to announce their findings. Ad hoc organizations protest everything from television violence to racism. Toy people complain frequently that regulators and "do-gooders" watch them more closely than other industries. They cannot understand why the rest of the world does not view them the way they view them-selves—as responsible businesspeople.

While selling seems almost incidental to all this other activ-ity, selling does remain the point of Toy Fair. Eighteen or twenty thousand buyers register, and many of them are there to write orders. They buy for museum shops, drugstores, super-markets, variety stores, wholesale distributors, general-merchan-dise chains, mom-and-pop toy stores. The TMA estimates that toys are sold at about fifty-seven thousand retail outlets, al-though many of the smallest deal only with wholesalers.

At the top are buyers for the big, national accounts. Buyers and merchandise managers from Wal-Mart, K mart, Target, and the major toy chains—Lionel Leisure, Kay-Bee Toys, Child World—have already been shown many of the product lines, but they come anyway, because the manufacturers are always mak-ing last-minute additions, subtractions, and adjustments. Be-sides, they like to see all the products at once to compare them with one another. They also view many of the commercials for the first time at Toy Fair, and they evaluate them as carefully as the toys themselves.

In a class by itself is Toys "R" Us, or simply, Toys. Accounting for about a fifth of total domestic retail toy sales, Toys "R" Us is intimidating. Like the proverbial eight-hundred-pound go-rilla (Where does an eight-hundred-pound gorilla sit? Anywhere it wants), wherever the buyers from Toys "R" Us walk, the ground trembles; sometimes manufacturers clear whole rooms just so they can view the line undisturbed. "Toys "R" Us is coming through," an exhibitor tells a group in the middle of its showroom tour. "You'll have to wait outside," Mattel even sets aside the last day of Toy Fair exclusively for Toys "R" Us.*

The displays in the showrooms range from straightforward and simple to elaborate and expensive. The smaller companies array their products neatly on shelves. Buyers may be shown

---

*Estimates of the Toys "R" Us share of retail sales range from 16 percent (NPD market research) to 22–27 percent (financial analysts) to 30 percent (some toy manufacturers). Whatever the reality, the chain is the largest, or the second largest, customer of many toy manufacturers, and its predominance as a customer is unprecedented.

through by salespeople, owners, members of the owners' families, or manufacturers' representatives. Reps are independent operators who represent a number of different companies. Some of the large reps maintain their own showrooms; if not, they may travel with a customer from room to room to show their different lines.

The smallest entrepreneurs, along with foreign companies and children's book publishers, exhibit at the end of the week in temporary booths at the Javits Convention Center. Many of them sell exclusively to small businesses such as museum shops, educational toy stores, and gift shops, because their products are too expensive or too specialized for mass markets. Some of them just want to stay small. "I won't sell to the mass merchandisers because they cut the prices and hurt my smaller customers," one explains. Most would be thrilled with a big order. "The buyer from Toys "R" Us came through and said he'd like to try again even though we had supply problems last year," a vendor exclaims when her partner returns from lunch.

The showrooms of the large corporations are worlds in themselves. Every year the companies spend hundreds of thousands—and in some cases millions—of dollars on specially designed sets, lighting, and costumes, professional demonstrators, multimedia presentations, and even built-in television sets beside each display to show their commercials. The largest few, Hasbro, Mattel, and Coleco, have moved out of 200 Fifth Avenue to buildings nearby because they need so much space to display and demonstrate their hundreds of products.

The showrooms are arranged into series of areas devoted to a product or product line that is demonstrated by professional actors or models in costumes. The demonstrators know how to make their voices last for ten full days without growing hoarse, and they seem to enjoy hamming up their roles as vampires, monsters, bratty children, or honorable fighting men.

In these showrooms a buyer does not generally approach a shelf full of dolls and pick up one that interests her. Considerate buyers do not touch anything unless it is handed to them. Many of the items displayed at Toy Fair are not factory-made, because the companies have not begun production. Often they are handmade prototypes worth thousands of dollars; sometimes they have been flown in the night before. Alert buyers take note of which products are shown in prototype. Handmade items not yet in production may mean late deliveries—or they may be product ideas that will not be manufactured at all unless the company receives enough orders. Some companies inform the buyers when they kill an item a buyer has ordered, and some never bother.

A visitor seeing Mattel's Barbie doll line will be led, room by room, through the entire Barbie section. Music plays, doors open automatically to reveal the latest Barbie creation, and young women dressed to duplicate Barbie's clothes or echo a theme—Perfume Pretty Barbie, Island Fun Barbie—talk about the product and the trends that inspired it: "Fifty-five percent of girls use fragrance. Perfume Pretty Barbie comes with her own specially created perfume which can be worn by the little girl."

Fisher-Price's Fun With Food demonstrator, a burly man dressed as a butcher, jokes about keeping his thumb on the scale as he shows off the company's highly successful line of fake food. His acting ability attracts the envy of Fisher-Price's competitors, although what he says is less important than what follows. The commercials are an integral part of the show, frequently serving as the introduction or finale to the live product demonstrations.

Toys advertised on television compete largely with each other, so the strength of the commercial and the size of the advertising budget may be the most important factor determining the product's sales. Unfortunately, the information about the size of the advertising budget—how many millions of dollars will be spent buying television time—is often subject to inflation. It consistently places first among the three biggest lies told at Toy Fair, and in an industry characterized by excessive optimism, that is no small feat. Toy people joke that if all the advertising dollars promised were actually spent, there would be no time on TV for the programs. Even companies honest enough to say "large budget planned" or "millions of dollars for television," rather than promising a specific number, may change their plans without notice. Advertising allocations are shifted around to follow the sales. If a product begins to exceed expectations, the manufacturer will usually boost its exposure, and if sales are sluggish, ad dollars may be cut.

Most of the major companies, the predominant users of television, lost money in 1987, so their mood is more chastened than cheery. The words "back to basics" are heard with irritating regularity. Translated, that means with no major hit toys on the horizon we know orders are going to be conservative; so we'll sell the old favorites and make a virtue of it at the same time.

Even the industry leader takes a conservative line. "We're not going out to try to hit home runs. We're a singles and doubles team," Hasbro's chairman and chief executive officer Stephen Hassenfeld tells the *Wall Street Journal*. With 1987 sales flat at $1.3 billion, Hasbro eked out $48 million in profits, down from $99 million the year before. That measly 3.6 percent return on sales (and 7.9 percent on equity—barely better than the bank) is extremely low, given the amount of risk in the toy business. But at least the numbers are positive. The only other large, independent, publicly held company in the black for the year is Tyco Toys, which has been selling the right product—radio-controlled cars—at the right time. Fisher-Price and Little Tikes, both makers of preschool toys, had record years, but one is a subsidiary of Quaker Oats, the other of Rubbermaid.

For the rest, the color for 1987 was red. Mattel lost $113 million on sales of $1.02 billion, Coleco lost $105 million on sales of $504 million, Tonka lost $10.5 million versus $22.3 million profits a year before, and Lewis Galoob plummeted from 1986 profits of $5.8 million to 1987 losses of $24.6 million. Sadly, the swings surprise no one. That is the toy business. Most dramatic is Worlds of Wonder. A year ago it generated $18 million in profits. In the next three quarters it lost $182.8 million on sales of $109.8 million, and now it is in Chapter 11 bankruptcy proceedings.

Despite Stephen Hassenfeld's low-key predictions, Hasbro comes on strong with its latest assault on the lucrative fashion doll market. Mattel's Barbie doll, clothes, accessories, and furnishings (like ice cream parlors, saunas, and Ferraris) generated about $360 million in 1987, over 90 percent of the category. According to Mattel, 98 percent of the little girls in the United States have a Barbie doll.

Hasbro is just aching for a piece of that market. Maurene Souza, Hasbro's marketing vice president for girls' toys, does not want to be greedy—just a portion will do. She figures her California teenager, Maxie, may have a chance. Maxie shares Barbie's busty body and vacant, starry-eyed smile, but Hasbro has positioned, or defined, Maxie as "much" younger than Barbie. She is only a sixteen-year-old high school girl, but she will be backed by a $7 million promotional budget.

Hasbro fell on its face the last time it took on Barbie. In 1986 the company produced the "truly outrageous" Jem, a record executive by day and a rock star by night, complete with her own rock group, the Holograms. In two years Hasbro sold about five million dolls to its customers, counting Jem, the Holograms, her boyfriend, Rio, and their enemy rock stars, the Misfits. But they sold through too slowly at retail. Jem is a good example of what may happen when the market leader gets a little arrogant. Although her critics said that Jem was ugly and hard-looking and that her identity as a rock star was too limiting, Hasbro really went too far when it made Jem taller than Barbie. That meant the twelve-and-a-half-inch rock star could not borrow eleven-and-a-half-inch Barbie's clothes.

Since more than twenty million Barbie fashions are sold each year—more than 250 million have been produced since 1959 and at least one hundred new outfits are designed annually—designing a fashion doll who could not wear Barbie's clothes was like producing a computer with a unique disk size. The fashion doll software was already out there, and it was called clothes. Hasbro is ordinarily considered a superb marketer, and it is ready to show Toyland what it can do with Maxie.

At Mattel's showroom a few blocks away, the employees who remain wear the brave smiles of survivors. The company laid off five hundred employees at its headquarters in 1987 and reduced worldwide manufacturing capacity by 40 percent. Chairman John Amerman is ebullient as usual, but buyers wonder if he went too far in his reductions. They understand that Mattel had to take fewer risks, but they have trouble finding interesting new products in its line this year.

Barbie enjoys the usual royal treatment. She is known around the company as the Queen, and the title is not much of an overstatement, since all of Mattel's employees are her dependents. Barbie accounted for about 35 percent of 1987 sales, and without her earnings losses would have been much heavier. Souza's counterpart at Mattel, who bears an equally rousing name, Rita Fire, knows she must protect Mattel's most valuable property. In dealing with Maxie, she will be merciless.

Mattel's salespeople arrived from all over the country before the weekend and have spent the last few days in sales meetings. They relieve their tension by touring the showroom and preparing pitches they cannot use. Their favorite target this year is a doll sitting inconspicuously in the corner. Li'l Miss Makeup, the company's new temperature-sensitive makeup doll, becomes quite vivid when cold water is applied to her skin. Her lips, cheeks, fingernails, and toenails turn bright red, and a beauty mark appears. The salespeople dub her Little Baby Hooker.

The third-largest company in the industry is new to its position. Toyland spent the previous fall following the proceedings of the industry's first and only foray into the exciting, high-stakes arena of hostile tender offers, unfriendly takeovers, and white knights. Kenner Parker, public for less than two years, had just become profitable when New World Entertainment, a producer of grade-B movies and Marvel Comics, decided to acquire it. The press had been full of stories with headlines like "Can Monopoly Find Happiness in Spiderman's Arms?"

Tonka Corporation bought it instead for $548.8 million (plus another $61.2 million in associated costs), and chairman Stephen Shank has been roundly criticized ever since. Wall Street analysts complain that he overpaid, that the deal lacks the synergy that made Hasbro's Milton Bradley acquisition work, and that Shank bought Kenner Parker to cover up a bad year. They are convinced that Tonka will never be able to service the debt load.

All the employees at Tonka, Kenner, and Parker are highly conscious of that debt. They know that this year's products have to succeed—there is little room for error. They have high hopes for Parker Brothers' Starting Lineup Talking Baseball, an interactive electronic baseball game, and Kenner's Starting Lineup collectible plastic statues of major league baseball, football, and basketball players. Kenner is also betting on a group of dolls based on a trend: the return to old-fashioned, fundamental values. Its four Special Blessings dolls, Christina, Abigail, Angela, and Matthew, can kneel and pray with the aid of Velcro tape, and they come packaged with a book of poems.

Coleco is a disaster area. Riddled with debt, the company has lost over $100 million two years in a row. Coleco can always be relied on for good products and bad management decisions. Cabbage Patch Kids are appearing at their sixth Toy Fair, this time "with Growing Hair." Two of the previous year's introductions, Alf and Couch Potato Pals, are still very popular, and Coleco has added new spuds: Sweet Couch Potato Pal, who megadoses on soap operas, and Small Fries, who watch only the best in children's programming. The company has discontinued two unsuccessful action-figure lines, Rambo and insect-based Sectaurs. Buyers hesitate to order anything, wondering how Coleco will come up with the money to produce it.

Worlds of Wonder's fortunes have shifted so dramatically that it has managed to astonish even an industry that considers peaks and valleys a normal condition of business. The company produced the number-one toy two Christmases in a row, Teddy Ruxpin in 1985 and Lazer Tag in 1986. Four days before Christmas in 1987, Worlds of Wonder declared bankruptcy. Teddy Ruxpin is appearing at the company's temporary show space at the Waldorf-Astoria, and so is Julie, "the world's most intelligent doll." If only the investors in WOW had been as intelligent as Julie. WOW's stock hit a high of twenty-nine dollars on its first day as a public company. The week before Toy Fair, the highest bid was fifty-six cents.

Those corporations are the giants. The vast majority of the toy manufacturers never buy a minute of television time, measure their sales in five to eight figures, and display their products in showrooms, not fantasylands. The industry trend toward consolidation is irreversible, but the toy business always has room for the entrepreneur and the small operator with a good product.

One pair of newcomers exhibits a strange-looking object with an even stranger name. It is a Koosh Ball, made by OddzOn Products. Looking like a porcupine made of brightly colored rubber bands, the Koosh Ball was invented to help young children learn to catch. It is heavy enough to throw easily, but soft enough that children will not shy away from it. It is also fun to hold, and the company has captured that quality with its tagline, "Easy to Catch . . . Hard to Put Down!" OddzOn was formed in April 1987 by two men in their thirties, and it just began shipping Koosh Balls in October. The men are parsimonious with details about their technologically sophisticated manufacturing process. "Rubber goes in one end," they explain, "and Koosh Balls come out the other."

Betty James is approached every week by potential buyers—for her company, not just for her product. She has one of the classics in the industry. James Industries has been turning out Slinky, the metal or plastic coil that can travel down stairs, since 1945. Her husband invented the device, she chose the name from the dictionary, and the first time they showed it to the public— demonstrating it one night in Gimbel's in Philadelphia—they sold out their entire stock of four hundred Slinkys in ninety minutes. Mr. James eventually ran off to South America, leaving behind Mrs. James, six children, and the Slinky factory. Betty James made sure the children and the factory all grew and flourished over the years, and today she runs three shifts a day, turning out two thousand Slinkys every shift.

Goldberger Dolls, which features Dolly Parton and Charlie McCarthy dolls along with Kool-Aid Kids, is seventy-two years old. Ninety-five-year-old Mr. Goldberger still goes to work when he is not in Florida.

Playmates Toys has blanketed both buildings with late-breaking editions of the *Toy Times*, emblazoned with the headlines "TURTLES SAVE TOY FAIR" and "Mutant Amphibians Uncover Devious Plot." The tabloid features stories about the Teenage Mutant Ninja Turtles who foil a plot by a Japanese manufacturer to take over the American toy industry.

In response to a series of tragic accidents, Daisy Manufacturing of Rogers, Arkansas, the world's largest and oldest manufacturer of BB guns, is leading the industry's effort to "de-replicate" toy guns that look too realistic. Several children brandishing realistic toy weapons were recently shot with real guns by adults who thought they were defending themselves. Henceforth, the company announces, the barrels of all Daisy toy guns will be marked with an orange tip.

The Lego showroom always attracts extra visitors, who come just to admire the intricate constructions its professional sculptors erect, take down, and reerect all over the country. This year, spectators take in a Greek temple complete with Ionic columns, a tree with giant branches, and horses whose heads move.

Atari's showroom is always crowded. It looks like a public arcade with television monitors lining the walls. In front of each monitor is at least one grown man intently taking his turn. Atari used to be the leader in home video games, before the games' market crashed spectacularly in the early 1980s. Nintendo, a Japanese company, has almost single-handedly revived the product, and its success has cast a pall over the rest of the industry. Apparently afflicted with selective blindness, buyers and manufacturers have bemoaned the lack of a hit toy all through 1987, while simultaneously complaining that Nintendo was pulling so many dollars away from other boys' toys. Nintendo sold 4.1 million systems in 1987—200,000 fewer than demand, but all it could make—which helped to generate about $750 million for the company and its game licensees in U.S. sales alone. There was a hit toy in 1987; it just wasn't their hit toy.

This year's TMA press conference is fairly uneventful. Tom Kalinske, the incoming TMA chairman, wonders why he seems to be answering so many of the questions. Perhaps it is because he is used to the spotlight. Passed over for the chairmanship of Mattel, he left to head Matchbox Toys. He also has a famous past. He worked in advertising before he started in the toy business, and Tom Kalinske is the man who inspired the famous Mennen's Skin Bracer commercial by saying, "Thanks, I needed that" when someone slapped him to wake him up.

He can hardly wait to get through with the conference to see how his company's Pee-wee Herman doll and color-change Matchbox cars are doing with the buyers. Dealing with the real Pee-wee is a pain because he is such a perfectionist, but he is one of the year's hottest licensed characters and Kalinske considers him well worth the trouble. Kalinske smiles when he thinks about Matchbox's new Super Colorchanger cars. Mattel had financed the research on color-change technology, but after Kalinske moved to Matchbox, Mattel canceled its exclusivity agreement with the Japanese developer of the process to save fifty thousand dollars. That error enables Matchbox to launch color-changeable die-cast cars this year at the same time as Mattel.

At the end of the press conference, about thirty reporters proceed to the next dining room. There will be parties and media events all week, but Tonka has scheduled the first, a junior power breakfast for children. The breakfast guests, who have just toured the company's showrooms, are finding their seats around a linen-draped table. The six females stick together on one side, while the males gravitate to the other. As they drink their milk, they eye the table decorations, samples of Tonka's newest products, including a summer water game called Splash Darts, Dress 'N Dazzle accessories for playing dress-up, figurines based on the upcoming George Lucas movie, *Willow*, Real Racer cars, and Sega video game cartridges.

The children ask who has the ideas for making toys, and Tonka chairman Steve Shank, who has been introduced to them as "the boss," tells them the truth. "A lot of people make a living thinking up the ideas. Then we first ask adults about the new toys and they're usually wrong. So then we take models and ask children to compare them with other toys."

Psychologist Helen Boehm, author of a book on choosing toys for children, interviews the group for the benefit of the audience. Boehm, who likes to call herself a toycologist, has served as a spokeswoman for several toy companies and currently works with FAO Schwarz. The participants in the press conference, handpicked by their teacher as the most extroverted eight-year-olds in her Connecticut, third-grade class, wave their hands to be recognized. After a minimum of prompting, the girls adorn themselves with the Dress 'N Dazzle gear strewn across the table. The most assertive female quickly appropriates the lavender gloves with pink bows, a boa, a turquoise hat with purple veil, and turquoise sunglasses. "How do you feel, Lauren?" Boehm inquires.

"I'm not done yet," replies Lauren, as she snatches a purse from the girl sitting beside her.

Holding up a *Willow* figure, Madmartigan ("the greatest swordsman who ever lived"), Boehm asks who will buy them.

"Boys," the group choruses.

"Boys like violence more than girls," one adds.

"If you had one, would you let your sister play with it?" Boehm asks one boy.

"If I had more than one," he replies honestly.

The group also takes questions from reporters. At least one member of the audience is concerned about the socially redeeming value of Tonka's products. Tonka distributes video game equipment and cartridges made by a Japanese company, Sega. "Do you learn anything from video games?" asks the unwary adult.

"Yes," replies Scott. "You learn how to stab people."

Even the educational toy business has its hazards.

1

TOYLAND

You got to know when to hold 'em,
Know when to fold 'em.
Know when to walk away,
And know when to run.
You never count your money
When you're sittin' at the table.
There'll be time enough for countin'
When the dealin' is done.

Don Schlitz—"The Gambler"

THE TOY BUSINESS OPERATES ON a few generally
accepted principles. Listen to your gut. Don't fall in love with
your product. Research is better at predicting failure than success. Don't show girls in commercials for boys' toys, and vice
versa. Product is king.

Every rule but the last has been broken successfully, at least
sometimes, and the rewards of a hit are tempting enough to
make the risk worthwhile. Many of the most wildly popular
products are so bizarre that no rational businessperson would

invest a cent in them. There were the funny-looking dolls that men, women, and children solemnly swore were their real babies. There is a game that has lasted fifty years even though it takes so long to complete that it is often abandoned. There is a simple plastic hoop that children rotate around their waists, wiggling and gyrating for hours. There is a metal coil whose most exciting accomplishment is going down stairs.

Toymakers always say that they have the next Cabbage Patch Kid, Monopoly, Hula Hoop, or Slinky right there in their showrooms, and sometimes they even believe it themselves. Once their product is in the stores they always say it is "flying off the shelves." The most optimistic of industries, the most anxious of industries, toymaking is also the most fun. Unpredictability prevails, and silliness is a valuable asset.

The secret of success lies inside the head of an eight-year-old child. That is the eternal paradox of the toy industry. Adults running multimillion-dollar toy companies are always trying to climb back inside that eight-year-old head. Creative people in the industry love to boast that they have not grown up, that they have retained enough youthful enthusiasm to know what children will consider fun. They, like Tom Hanks in the movie *Big*, think that they are really still kids, trapped inside men's bodies (this is a male belief—the women *know* they are grown up). The men think they are Peter Pan.

Their belief in their powers of transgenerational communication is touching. Many of the citizens of Toyland are actually lunatics or masochists, and proud of it. They like to explain that running a toy business is like driving down the highway at ninety miles an hour—while looking in the rearview mirror. They make more decisions in a week than managers in other industries make in a year, and all on the basis of what has been. They shift production targets and advertising dollars among their products on a week-to-week basis, whenever they sense a shift in market conditions. They thrive on the pace, and in spite of the practically impossible operating conditions, they manage to create and sell more than $8 billion worth of toys a year.

Toy people describe their industry as a fashion business like the apparel industry; as a fad business that thrives on novelty;

as an entertainment business similar to the motion picture business. They are all right: the toy business manages to combine the problems of all three.

As in the apparel business, toys follow trends and fashions. Children are tuned into the popular culture to a degree that astonishes adults. Tiny children seem to know the lyrics to the latest hits, the newest expressions, which way to wear their socks, and generally what is in, out, or totally gross. Since children emulate their peers even more slavishly than adults— or at least they are more obvious about it—a new toy can sweep through the world of children like a tornado.

Another unpleasant fact of life toys share with apparel is seasonality, except that in the toy business it is worse. Apparel manufacturers and retailers usually have two or more seasons to capture their sales for the year. The toy business has one. Christmas-season buying has always accounted for the bulk of toy sales, and it still does. About 60 percent of the toys sold at retail are sold in the fourth quarter. That is an improvement; it used to be 70 percent.

Waiting for that burst of buying at the end of the year is nerve-wracking. Volume is unpredictable, and so are choices. Sophisticated computer information systems at the large retail chains alleviate some of the uncertainty, because early-year purchases can predict buying trends—but never with comfortable accuracy. The manufacturers are just as concerned about retail sales as the retailers. If their products do not "sell through" at retail, the manufacturers may not be able to "sell in" more merchandise. They may have to wait until their customers' old inventories are cleaned out.

The faddish nature of the toy business leaves the companies extremely vulnerable to inventory risk. When it's over in the toy business, it is truly over, and every manufacturer has been caught at some point with a warehouse (or two or three) full of unsaleable merchandise whose market just died one day—or dropped off a cliff, as they like to say in Toyland.

It is also an entertainment business. Like movies, the products must entertain to succeed, and marketing promotional toys is very much like marketing motion pictures. Movie companies

invest millions of dollars in individual movies; toy companies
have to invest in product development and special tooling—
molds—up front. Motion picture companies use actors and actresses they expect to draw at the box office; toy companies often
use licensing to create brand recognition. If a film proves successful, moviemakers slavishly churn out sequels and imitations; Toyland is the me-too capital of American industry.
Movie companies back up their efforts with multimillion-dollar
advertising campaigns; so do toy companies. Movie companies
never know what they have until they get it in front of the
audiences at the theaters; toy companies know that if the kids
say "yuck" the product is history.

For an industry whose products are in so many homes,
$8 billion is tiny. Fifty-four companies of the 1988 *Fortune* 500
industrial corporations had sales exceeding $8 billion.* The toy
industry is often described as a family, and its relatively small
size has allowed it to remain one—complete with bickering and
backbiting. It is also very much an industry of family businesses. Most toy companies are privately owned, and even some
of the publicly held ones remain closely identified with one
family.

Two companies, Hasbro and Mattel, have sales that hover
around $1 billion a year. Two foreign corporations have huge
American subsidiaries: the Japanese company Nintendo sells
over $1 billion worth of video game equipment (projected 1989
sales, $1.8 billion), and Lego, whose parent company is Danish,
sells about $600 million worth of blocks. The other large public
operations are Fisher-Price, a subsidiary of Quaker Oats; Matchbox Toys, owned by Hong Kong–based Universal Matchbox;
Tonka Corporation, which combined in 1987 with Kenner
Parker; Western Publishing, which publishes Little Golden
Books as well as more puzzles than any other manufacturer; fast-
growing Tyco Toys; Little Tikes, a preschool manufacturer
owned by Rubbermaid; Lewis Galoob, a California company;

---

*Home video game hardware and software have traditionally been excluded from
industry figures, and we do not include them here. Home video game volume has
fluctuated from zero to a peak of $3 billion in 1982. In 1988 wholesale video game
sales were about $2 billion. See Sources for more on industry figures.

LJN, a subsidiary of the entertainment conglomerate MCA (which also owns Universal Studios); and Ohio Art, maker of Etch A Sketch. There is a smattering of large private or foreign-listed companies such as Kransco, which owns Wham-O, and Playmates Toys, and hundreds of smaller operations, many brand-new and some quite well established.

A number of companies specialize in one type of toy. Stuffed-animal companies come in small, medium, and large, just like their animals. The industry term for stuffed toys is "plush." One of the leaders in plush is Dakin, whose operators answer the telephone, "Dakin, make a friend." The company started as an importer of shotguns and toy trains, but some stuffed animals used as packing in one of the shipments proved more popular, and today Dakin enjoys one of the best licenses in the business: it manufactures the incorrigible cat Garfield. Gund, established in 1898, is another family business, the first plush manufacturer to take some of the stuffing out of its animals to make them squishier.

Like General Motors and Ford, many of the toy-vehicle companies are in the Midwest, including Strombecker, Ertl, and Tonka. Many of the doll companies are clustered in New York, including the famous Madame Alexander, Effanbee, and Gold-berger. There are companies that specialize in games, like Pressman, Cardinal, and International Games; legitimate knockoff houses like Blue Box and Marchon; preschool specialists like Today's Kids; electronics manufacturers like Tiger Electronics; educational-toy manufacturers like Creativity for Kids; and electronic-learning toy producers like Connor Toys and Video Technology.

Consolidation has steadily reduced the number of large companies over the years, as many of yesterday's industry leaders, such as Ideal, Marx, and Knickerbocker, fell on hard times. The ten largest manufacturers account for about 60 percent of the sales volume. The toy industry remains far more fragmented than many other American industries, however, because of the constant stream of new entrants. Despite the risks in Toyland, the opportunities always attract entrepreneurs, and the idea for a hit toy can come from anyone—neophyte as well as established player.

Toy manufacturing is fairly easy to enter because it is not capital-intensive. Entrepreneurs usually start with a cottage industry or hire an established manufacturer to make their products; it can cost as little as $25,000 to make up some plush animals. Printers can manufacture games, and the Far East is full of contract manufacturers who make toys. A twenty-four-year-old waiter invented a game called Pictionary and personally promoted it in his native Seattle before he could find a national company to back him. Then The Games Gang, a new games company formed by Selchow & Righter veterans (who nicknamed themselves The Over the Hill Gang), took on Pictionary as its first product, sold 300,000 in its first six months (July–December 1986), and more than thirteen million by the end of 1988, making it the bestselling game and one of the top-selling toys for two years. Many of the so-called megahits of the early 1980s came from outside the industry. Trivial Pursuit was invented by three Canadians, Cabbage Patch Kids were conceived by a rural Georgia artist, and they in turn inspired a Ford assembly-line worker from Cincinnati to create Pound Puppies.

Although even the largest toy companies are dwarfed by major American consumer-products corporations like Procter & Gamble and RJR Nabisco, those giants do not face the fundamental challenge the toy companies confront every year. The life span of many toys is so brief that toy companies typically have to replace a large portion of their sales each year with totally new products. Makers of promotional toys consider themselves fortunate if they can produce a toy that sells for one year, and if they make a product that lasts three years, they consider it practically a classic. It is also almost certain to be copied or knocked off—which in many cases is legal—or even counterfeited—which is not. Duplication is one of the reasons toys have such short life spans. Since it is easier to copy a good idea than to create one, imitations constantly flood the market, tiring the public with their repetition.

The larger the hit, the more new sales the company will have to generate to replace that volume when the hit is finished. Replacing lost sales is more difficult than it sounds. The failure rate of new products is quite high—probably 80 percent fail—

and sometimes a particular company will come up with 100 percent losers. Consequently, sales and earnings can fluctuate wildly from year to year, and there are always a few companies in Chapter 11 bankruptcy proceedings.

Coleco's Cabbage Patch Kids generated $540 million in 1984 and $600 million in 1985. Coleco forecast a 25 percent decline in sales for 1986 and geared its manufacturing capacity for what it thought was a conservative $450 million. Actual 1986 sales turned out to be $230 million, an error that pushed Coleco into a $111 million loss for the year. The decline in Cabbage Patch Kids sales for the year exceeded the total sales of any other toy line in the industry. Coleco's swings were extreme because of the dimensions of its hit—which is why toy people say a hit can be more disastrous than a flop.

The need to replace sales is challenge enough, but the natural volatility of the business places the publicly held toy corporations under additional pressure. Public corporations in all industries are required to report to their stockholders every three months, preferably showing consistent profits and steady growth. That is extremely difficult for toy companies, and their attempts to superimpose this unnatural pattern have led to a number of disastrous decisions. More typically, toy company earnings may quadruple one year and plunge into the red the next. That is the nature of the promotional toy business.

Promotional toys are the toys that are heavily promoted on television, and most of the large toy companies sell them. Promotional toys create the booms and busts; it is the promotional toys that make the industry a fashion and entertainment business. There are fashions, fads, hits, and then next year they are forgotten.

Manufacturers try to guess what their public would like, make it, and then advertise incessantly to whip up demand. The process, the products, and the commercials often reflect the lowest common denominator of public taste: sensationalism, commercialism, hyperbole. Like commercial television programming, promotional toys and their commercials are often disappointing to those who believe children deserve better. In some cases they are even deplorable. Each company makes its own choices about what it will and will not do to generate sales.

Promotional toys could be considered the junk food of the toy world. They are products that are not necessarily constructive, and in some cases parents consider them harmful (sexist, violent, expensive for what there is, exploitatively advertised). Sometimes, like junk food, their only ill effect is that they crowd out some of their more wholesome competition.

They are not usually the toys parents would choose for their children. They are the toys children choose for themselves. Children want the products they see on television, and if their friends have them, they want them even more. The urgency with which their children insist that they "need" these heavily promoted products is one of the reasons parents dislike them. And when, as is often the case, the products do not do very much and their appeal quickly fades, the children soon focus on the next exciting product they see on television. The toys' lack of play value thus encourages an acquisitive, throwaway mentality, which earns them further parent enmity.

Another parental complaint about promotional toys is that the commercials promise more than they deliver. Not all television-advertised products are disappointing, but in commercials the bad toys are indistinguishable from the good. Toy people like to say that a good commercial cannot make a bad toy a hit but that it can sell the first million dollars' worth. After that the toy has to be good or the junior grapevine will kill it. Even so, many of the heavily advertised toys leave a trail of disappointed children in their wake.

Some of the toys adults consider "good" toys are also advertised on television, but they are more likely to be what are called classics, staples, or basics. Generally adults consider "good" those toys that are tried and true (whatever they had as children); toys made of natural materials, particularly wood; board games; stuffed toys; activity toys (arts, crafts, hobbies); building toys; toys that seem to require more creativity from the child; nonviolent, nonsexist toys; educational toys; low-technology toys.

Manufacturers whose products fall into these categories almost automatically make toys that adults consider "good." Preschool toys, for example, are usually wholesome, charming, and nonsexist. They also tend to be plastic, but the durable, easy-to-clean material is so obviously practical for preschool toys that it is forgiven for being synthetic. Fisher-Price, Playskool, Little Tikes, and other makers of preschool toys enjoy an excellent reputation with adults, who typically consider them more virtuous than the manufacturers who make those shoddy, faddy, sexist, violent toys that are advertised so exploitatively on children's television.

In fact, their supposed virtue is just good business. There is no point in advertising preschool toys on children's television, because their target market is adults. Adults, not children, buy preschool toys, so if the manufacturers advertise preschool toys on television, they buy time on adult programs. The companies advertising the shoddy, sexist, violent toys are selling to elementary-school-age children, and children's television is where to reach them.

Besides, the virtuous Fisher-Price is trying to increase its promotional toy business and advertises those products for older children on kids' shows. The wholesome Playskool advertises, too, and is owned by Hasbro, the heaviest user of both television advertising and toy-based programming—as well as the maker of that perennial fighting man, G.I. Joe. With the exception of Little Tikes, whose products are all for preschoolers, all of the large toy companies beam their commercials at children. That is how they generate hundreds of millions of dollars in sales. There is no other way to do it. For years Lego saw no need to advertise to children. Then Tyco came into Lego's market with television advertising, and now Lego uses television, too.

Some advertise tastefully, some do it exploitatively, but as long as they are allowed, they are all going to do it. A company in the promotional toy business promotes on television—that is the definition of a promotional toy. The only makers of promotional toys that do not buy television time are the knockoff companies, or, as they define themselves, parallel marketers. They benefit from the market leaders' advertising and compete on the basis of price and availability: when the promoted item runs out, the customer may buy their product instead.

Ironically, the industry shares many of the public's definitions of "good toys" and "bad toys," albeit for different reasons. All corporations would love to produce the staples or basic toys so admired by adults, especially the ones so well known that they generate healthy sales without costly advertising campaigns. Manufacturing can be planned more accurately because those toys sell at predictable levels every year. Their sales do not have to be replaced. Their names may be recognizable enough to be expanded into entire product lines or brands. There is nothing toy manufacturers, promotional or otherwise, like better than a staple. Some staples are heavily promoted, like Barbie dolls. Others are very old classics—games like Clue or Scrabble, which are found in the average American home. Staples are the family jewels of toy corporations.

No one was more adept at assembling a collection of staples than Stephen Hassenfeld, Hasbro's chairman from 1980, after his father died, until his own untimely death nine years later at the age of forty-seven. Hassenfeld began when he bought Milton Bradley in 1984 for $380 million. Ridiculed at first for overpaying, he was later admired, and finally feverishly imitated— feverish imitation is one of the things Toyland does best. In buying Milton Bradley, he bought a library of classic games like Chutes and Ladders, Candy Land, and Go to the Head of the Class and acquired at the same time Bradley's Playskool subsidiary. One of the industry's preeminent preschool companies, Playskool provided Hasbro with another group of steady sellers.

When Hassenfeld bought Milton Bradley, the industry was in an era of megahits, so the wisdom of his acquisition was not immediately apparent. Toy-based television programs seemed capable of turning hits into megahits, and many in the industry thought they had at last found the formula for producing a blockbuster when they needed one. They were encouraged in this belief when they watched industry sales jump 51 percent in just one year, from $5.3 billion in 1983 to $8.3 billion in 1984. It was not until 1985 sales rose only to $8.7 billion and 1986 sales actually dropped, to $8.3 billion, that Toyland finally understood that even television was not a magic ingredient that could produce megahits with any degree of reliability.

That was when the beauty of Hasbro's strategy finally came to be appreciated. During the lean years, in the absence of big hits, Hasbro could enjoy a steady stream of earnings from staples, which would cushion the peaks and valleys of its promotional toy business. Industry people always claim to be in some cycle or other, and in lean periods they usually announce that they are in a "back-to-basics" phase. They explain that the consumer has grown tired of big hits and wants the high quality of proven staples. The fallacy, of course, is that the consumer always buys the basics—that is why they are basics. That is why they are so valuable.

While toymakers aspire to create toys that will sell forever, they are realistic enough not to expect it. Whether they set out to create a classic or just a one-year wonder, many new toys take years to develop, cost millions of dollars, and employ the latest technology. Others are just simple, good ideas. Neither route guarantees success: every new product is a gamble. Many of the offerings are so ill-conceived, offensive, ugly, or just plain dumb that it is hard to imagine how anyone could have thought they might succeed. They are all repositories of their creators' hopes and dreams, however.

The toy business is a very personal, emotional business. Most toys emerge from group efforts. Designers, artists, engineers, marketers, even the people at a toy company's advertising agency contribute their ideas along the way. Through that process they all acquire a proprietary interest in the project that sends them into the toy stores, wandering through the aisles saying, this is mine, or I did that.

Even the new products that fail are successful compared to all the ideas and half-formed products that never make it to Toy Fair. Of the select few that reach the manufacturers' showrooms, even fewer win a place on the retailers' shelves. Many of the rejects along the route to the marketplace die quietly, expected casualties of the odds against success. Some sell, but not nearly enough. A few fail spectacularly and drag entire companies down with them.

The promotional toy business as it exists today is only thirty-five years old, but the American toy industry has been growing steadily throughout this century. There have been toymakers in America for as long as there have been children; native American children were happily playing with dolls, balls, and other typical playthings before and after settlers began coming from Europe. That might have been the end of it, in fact, if the Puritans had had their way. They tried to ban playing.

They failed, and once New Englanders accepted the idea that fun might have redeeming value, they settled down and made the area an important center of toy production. One of the earliest products manufactured specifically for children was a book, *Spiritual Milk for Boston Babes, Drawn Out of the Breasts of Both Testaments*. The *Poky Little Puppy*'s 1641 predecessor was apparently very popular, because it went through many editions—products had a longer life span in those days.

By the nineteenth century, toys reflected the increasingly complex adult world around them: village carpenters, glassmakers, tinsmiths produced miniature versions of trains, clocks, and crockery. Factories grew, enhancing the productivity of individual toymakers. Two of the most inventive toymakers of the century both turned modest family businesses into large, successful operations. Cousins, both were named Crandall.

Jesse Crandall invented the spring horse. Then, for children too small to stay on a spring horse, he invented the shoo fly, a seat connected by two horse shapes set on rockers. Anticipating the modern practice of squeezing every possible application out of an invention, he expanded into a shoo-fly cradle, a rock-and-rolling high chair, and a folding nursery chair. In his ultimate multipurpose contraption he offered a combination go-cart, sleigh, swing, hammock, baby jumper, stepladder, and rocking chair.

The most famous invention of Jesse's cousin Charles Crandall was an 1889 game called Pigs in Clover, and the speed with which it swept the nation proves that crazes need not rely on electronic transmission. It was distributed by a firm called Selchow & Righter, which went on to turn out games like Parcheesi and Scrabble for almost a century, until success in the form of Trivial Pursuit killed it. Pigs in Clover required players to drive four marbles, the pigs, through a maze of concentric circles into the center, the pen. Within three weeks of its introduction, the factory was turning out eight thousand puzzles a day and was already four weeks behind on its orders. The national mania even reached Congress, where, according to the *New York Tribune*, "five dignified senators sat down in a circle and began a pig-driving match. They worked for half an hour at it and finally Senator Vest announced in a triumphant tone that he had driven his last pig into the pen."

In the early years of the twentieth century, American toy production expanded, but imports, particularly from Germany, grew faster. Two companies that became prominent in the industry for many years were founded during this period. One was the Ideal Novelty and Toy Company, whose owner supposedly named the teddy bear in honor of President Theodore Roosevelt. The other was A. C. Gilbert. Besides inventing the Erector set (and probably chemistry sets), A. C. Gilbert was an Olympic gold medalist in pole vaulting, a trained magician, and a Yale-educated doctor. He was also a visionary. One of the first toymakers to advertise extensively, Gilbert took the lead in founding an industry trade organization, Toy Manufacturers of the United States of America (later shortened to Toy Manufacturers of America) in 1916.

Gilbert was also the industry's first and most successful lobbyist. In order to save materials and encourage the spirit of wartime self-denial during World War I, the government began to consider imposing an embargo on the buying and selling of Christmas presents. The toymakers were alarmed, and Gilbert led a delegation to Washington, D.C. The group took along a number of their wares that so enchanted the Scroogelike Cabinet secretaries that they changed their minds. The TMUSA prevailed and saved Christmas for American children.

American toymakers benefited from anti-German sentiment, as toy imports dropped precipitously in the years surrounding the war, but imports rebounded by 1921. Gilbert and his group and their samples went back to Washington, this time to the House Ways and Means Committee to seek protective legislation. Again they were successful. The group went in requesting a 60 percent tariff on imported toys, but after the legislators carefully tested their products, they came away with 75 percent.

The same year Gilbert and his cohorts were protecting the American toy market from foreign incursions, the young man who would be known as the king of the toy business struck out on his own. Louis Marx was only twenty-five years old when he and his brother began manufacturing toys similar to those already on the market and underpricing their competition. That tiny operation grew into a manufacturing empire that spanned the globe and became the largest toy company in the world.

Louis Marx liked to say there were no new toys, just old toys with new twists, but many of his twists accounted for the enduring appeal of his products. They were filled with the detail that fascinated adults as well as children. His 1951 dollhouse had a baby's playpen, a vacuum cleaner, a French poodle, and a Rolls-Royce; a wind-up Little Orphan Annie had a jump rope.

Although brilliant and clever, Marx could also be tough, boorish, and crude. In 1955 *Time* magazine ran a cover story on him, the only toymaker so honored, and described him as a "roly-poly, melon-bald little man with berry-bright eyes . . . America's toy king and cafe-society Santa." In vintage *Time*-ese the magazine called him a toycoon, and informed its readers that he frequented the "21" Club. Marx loved to entertain luminaries such as ventriloquist Edgar Bergen and Prince Bernhard of the Netherlands and never went anywhere without pockets full of toys to hand out to friends and acquaintances. Even adults must have enjoyed the replicas he had specially made, depicting himself as a samurai, Napoleon, Mao Tse-tung, and Buddha—all short, bald, and rotund like Marx himself.

After his first wife died, Marx married a twenty-one-year-old starlet. The couple surprised their acquaintances with an enduring union that added four sons to Marx's four children from his first marriage. Marx had a penchant for befriending generals, and he named each of his last four boys after two military heroes, including Dwight Eisenhower, George Marshall, Omar Bradley, and Curtis LeMay. Perhaps it was hanging around with generals that led to Marx's own battle of the bulge—he fought his girth by jogging on the roof of his office building. A dedicated autodidact who hated to waste time, Marx read as he

ran. He memorized poetry, read philosophy, and added words to
his vocabulary—he worked his way through *Webster's* in twelve
years, then started over. He also attended classes at New York
University after work, went on learning crazes with his wife, and
invited professors to his office to lecture his employees.

Louis Marx kept himself somewhat aloof from most of the
industry and encouraged a mystique by hiring Junoesque female employees, often over six feet tall, who were variously
described as unemployed actresses or secretaries who couldn't
type. He always liked a crowd, and in the Far East would tear
around in an open car surrounded by a bevy of beautiful young
Asian women. Elliot Handler, whose Mattel, Inc. eventually
dethroned Marx Toys as industry leader, remembers his last
glimpse of Louis Marx, in Hong Kong. The open car remained,
but the Occidental potentate and his exotic entourage were
gone. In their place sat a quiet old man, perched sedately in the
backseat, accompanied only by his wife.

When the toy business began to change, Louis Marx did not.
His emphasis on individual products and low-cost production
began to seem dated when all around him competitors were
applying the sophisticated marketing techniques of consumer
packaged goods to the toy business. In 1955 Marx, with about
$50 million in sales, spent $312 on advertising. Mattel, the
upstart competitor from the West with $6 million in sales, spent
$500,000 on television advertising alone.

None of Marx's children or grandchildren were interested in
taking over the business, so he sold Marx Toys to Quaker Oats
in 1972 for $51 million. In 1971 Marx Toys had earned
$3 million on sales of $67 million. A year after he sold it, the
operation began to lose money. Quaker poured $48 million into
the company over the next three years but could not turn it
around and finally sold it to a British conglomerate, Dunbee-
Combex-Marx, for less than $18 million. D-C-M, which had
distributed Marx products for many years, could do no better.
After four more years of losses, D-C-M folded Marx Toys.

Louis Marx outlived his company, dying in 1982 at the age of
eighty-five. A quarter of his obituary in the *New York Times* was
devoted not to Marx but to his son-in-law Daniel Ellsberg, who

had leaked the Pentagon Papers to the *Times* a few years earlier. The once-proud industry giant, friend of generals and presidents, would not have been pleased.

The industry Louis Marx dominated had really begun to change after World War II, when the development of high-quality plastics stimulated an explosion in the invention of new products. At the same time, the postwar baby boom provided an unprecedented expansion in demand. Moving en masse through the economy, the baby boomers, whose effect is often compared to a pig in a python, began to enrich Toyland in the 1950s and early 1960s.

As children, baby boomers received more toys than their predecessors, and now that they are parents themselves, this ample group is once more stimulating the baby- and childhood-goods sectors of the economy. The boomers do their part in quality as well as quantity: they are not only numerous, they are spenders. Unhampered by puritanical convictions about the evils of pleasure, or dreary Depression-era thinking about the benefits of saving, Americans in the second half of the twentieth century have elevated consumption to a philosophy and made shopping a national pastime. Annual spending on toys is about two hundred dollars per child.

A number of other demographic trends benefit Toyland. The fact that so many baby boomers postponed parenthood means that a greater percentage of recent births has been first children, who traditionally generate higher levels of expenditures: the money spent on toys for subsequent siblings is only about one-fourth as high. These parents also tend to have higher income levels, because they are older and further along in their careers and because more of the mothers are working outside the home.

One of the bleaker trends to benefit the business is the high divorce rate. With parents in two different places, the number of households stocked with at least a few toys increases as well. When parents, as well as grandparents, remarry, children may also acquire more than the traditional two sets of grandparents. They account for about a fifth of the retail toy dollars.

Last, but increasingly important as a source of toy purchases, are children themselves. More and more products not traditionally associated with child purchasers are being marketed to children as they control an increasing amount of money themselves—children under eleven spend an estimated $5 billion annually themselves, and influence another $50 billion in family purchases.

With all the gods of demand smiling on the toy industry, Toyland should be a happy place. But about the best that can be said is that the toy business is never dull. Supplying toys is just not that easy. If it were, the manufacturers would all be rich.

2

DECEMBER 26, 1985
What Toymen Do in Bed

JIM ALLEY LAY IN BED, THINKING. Lying around in bed was an unaccustomed luxury for the father of two boys five and eight years old, but Robyn and Bryan were still happily occupied with their Christmas acquisitions.

For a few minutes he savored his solitude. Then with characteristic efficiency Jim began to wonder how he could best utilize his relaxed mental state. Mild-mannered but highly disciplined—he even sleeps in his gym shorts, as if ready to spring up for calisthenics at the buzz of an alarm—he could not resist the opportunity to find something constructive to do with what otherwise would have been wasted time.

His thoughts wandered to his work. It was not an enormous leap for a toy-company executive on the day after Christmas. While his boys had ripped open their packages the previous morning, Jim had been imagining Christmas scenes all across the country. How many boys were opening Tyco train sets? How many preschoolers were squealing over Tyco's Super Blocks? The figures would not be in for a couple of weeks, so unlike his children, Jim had to remain in a state of suspense even after December 25.

He stopped thinking about sales figures. His boss, Tyco president Dick Grey, had told him to find new products, because the company needed to diversify. As head of marketing he was expected to know what the new trends would be.

Jim shared that expectation. I ought to be able to figure out the next fad, he mused. All the clues are out there floating around. All I have to do is fit them together. He searched for a major theme. Over the last year robots had predominated. Hasbro had Transformers, Tonka had GoBots, and three companies had been tripping over each other bringing out a third line of robots called Voltron. The usual host of imitators had crowded in as well, so it didn't take a genius to figure out that robots were already entering the final stage: death by oversaturation.

Military toys were always popular, but the industry leader, Hasbro, had locked up competition with its G.I. Joe line. Magical characters like wizards with swords had had their day, so Jim, who loved that sort of thing, regretfully eliminated them. Mattel's He-Man and Masters of the Universe line had been copied enough to exhaust the superhero theme.

The only new idea Jim had heard about was a line of space cowboys Mattel was planning. What else was there? Ordinary cowboys and Indians could be due for a revival, but Jim doubted it. Robyn and Bryan had never shown the slightest interest in anything western, although Jim, who was born in 1950, had followed the adventures of Davy Crockett, Wyatt Earp, and Matt Dillon with rapt attention.

Thinking about the generation gap gave him an idea. I should be approaching this from the other direction, he told himself. What are my kids interested in? What do they like hearing about that they aren't getting enough of at school? He immediately thought of dinosaurs. He had been fascinated with them in childhood, and he still enjoyed sharing his boys' interest in the subject. It amused Jim to hear their tiny voices pronounce the long names with such authority, and he had realized long ago that they already knew far more about the various species than he did. They knew which were the biggest (size is very important when you're five or eight), which ones ate meat and which did not. They also knew that there were no cavemen living at the same time as the dinosaurs.

Suddenly Jim wanted to make a line of toy dinosaurs. It was no secret that children loved dinosaurs. Everyone in the toy industry knew it, and the market had been full of dinosaur books and models for years. But Jim believed that he could create a formidable product if only he could find a gimmick, a niche—some concept that would give Tyco a new way of using the creatures.

If he could involve the dinosaurs with people, there would be all kinds of possibilities, but when one species predeceases the other by 65 million years, the opportunities for interaction are limited. That hiatus, whose length his boys knew as well as their own ages, seemed insurmountable if he wanted to utilize the dinosaurs as real, rather than fantasy, creatures.

But why was he so concerned about realism, Jim asked himself. After all, he was only trying to invent a line of toys. He answered his own question: because the children would care. Notoriously finicky about details, children are very proud of their mastery of dinosaur names and facts, and Jim suspected that they would be scornful of a concept that tried to combine cavemen with dinosaurs. That impossibility was one of the most basic facts they were likely to know.

Suddenly it hit him. The dinosaurs could remain realistic; the fantasy would come from the people. We could bring people in from another place and another time, he thought with excitement. They could come from outer space and we could use some kind of time travel to get them to earth. Then once they reached earth they could ride the dinosaurs like cowboys and Indians.

By now his mind was racing. Maybe the people could do more than just ride the dinosaurs. Maybe they could make them into vehicles. And there could be bad guys who would do bad things to the dinosaurs.

It sounded great. He was too excited to stay in bed. By the time he was dressed he had thought of a name for the toy line, and he could hardly wait to try some market research. He approached his test population of two sounding much calmer than he felt. "I have an idea for a toy," he told them. When he explained the concept, the boys liked it, so he went all the way and tried out the name on them too. Since the people from space were going to ride dinosaurs he'd call them . . . Dino-Riders!

A casual acquaintance would find it hard to imagine Jim
Alley lying in bed dreamily conjuring up fantasies of spacemen
riding around on dinosaurs. Jim's close-cropped hair, erect
bearing, and clean-cut good looks lend him an almost military
authority—he could be Oliver North's younger brother. Younger
than Tyco's other senior executives, he radiates an affable poise.
When he has time to train, he competes in triathlons, in which
the contestants bicycle forty kilometers, run ten kilometers, and
swim one-and-a-half kilometers. The rest of the year he stops
conscientiously at the health club on his way to work.

Jim became the youngest vice president in Tyco's history
because he was in the right place at the wrong time and made
the most of his opportunity. He had been a traveling salesman
for Tyco for two years when a questionnaire seeking suggestions
for marketing strategies landed on his desk. Jim, then twenty-
eight, filled it out and returned it to headquarters. The questionnaire had been intended for sales managers only, but Jim's
response so impressed Dick Grey that he offered him the vacant
post of director of marketing. Two years later he became a vice
president.

Jim likes to say he has been in the toy business all his life. He
grew up in a suburb of Chicago while his father, B. G. (George)
Alley, traveled the world as the toy buyer for Sears, Roebuck. In
the late 1950s and early 1960s Sears was the largest toy retailer
in the country, so George Alley was what salespeople call "the
big pencil." He was courted by all the major manufacturers of
the day, and little Jimmy and his brother were bombarded with
samples from eager toymakers.

The day after his inspiration Jim Alley practically flew to
work. Tyco's headquarters are in an office park in Mt. Laurel,
New Jersey, midway between Philadelphia and Atlantic City.
Approaching Tyco from the New Jersey Turnpike is like travers-
ing a giant version of a Tyco car racing set. Heading south, one
sees the office park off to the right. Exiting, one doubles back
heading north and observes the office park on the left. After the
next turn, there it is on the right again; at least it seems to be
getting closer. By the time the buildings appear on the driver's
left again, it is finally time to turn into the parking lot. Needless

to say, the people who work at Tyco's headquarters manage to avoid this tortuous zigzagging. They know the shortcuts.

When he arrived, Jim headed straight for Woody Browne's office. One of two marketing directors reporting to Jim, Woody was contemplating his Super Blocks problem of the day. Tyco had divided the company's products into two categories, vehicles and everything else, and Woody was the marketing director for everything else.

Jim had originally offered him vehicles—train and car sets accounted for the majority of Tyco's revenues—but Woody had not been interested. At the time, he was working on trucks at Tonka, and he was tired of vehicles. The smaller nonvehicle category sounded more interesting, and since Jim assured him that Tyco was committed to diversification, Woody figured that his area would be more dynamic.

Unfortunately, blocks were Tyco's major nonvehicle product so far, and Woody had come to loathe blocks. He had never realized how many different combinations and permutations of block foul-ups there could be. Tyco's Super Blocks were very similar to the popular Lego blocks, which clamp together through an arrangement of pegs. A set of Super Blocks could contain more than one hundred blocks in many different sizes and shapes. If something went wrong with any one of them it could ruin the entire package, and something often did.

Jim's appearance offered a welcome diversion, and Woody leaned back, expecting to join in a rehash of all the little Alleys' and Brownes' Christmas antics. Instead, Jim began to recount his own post-Christmas activities, and Woody listened with growing excitement. In words that became famous around the company—they were repeated so often that everyone grew heartily sick of them—Jim described his idea. "I was lying in bed yesterday morning," he began, "and I was trying to figure out what the next big trend in the industry would be. . . ."

Jim's scenario was simple, but to Woody it seemed original and compelling. Aliens would crash to earth in 65,000,000 B.C. and ride around fighting each other, using dinosaurs as vehicles. A concept that linked dinosaurs and spacemen—the past and the future—what a powerful combination! Woody immediately

started adding his ideas, elaborating on the fantasy and speculating on marketing strategies.

What Jim was proposing was a product line of action figures,
which an older generation would recognize as descendants of
toy soldiers. They are small plastic figures two-and-one-half to
six inches high. Unlike their metal predecessors they are articulated, or jointed, so that a child can make them walk, bend, or
fall over dead in a number of dramatic poses.

They are also imaginary. Instead of the French Foreign Le-
gion versus the Royal Fusiliers, the battles of the 1980s pit forces
led by characters like Mattel's He-Man, Master of the Universe,
against the troops of his archenemy, Skeletor. Their minions
include mechanical warriors such as Roboto or villainous assis-
tants such as Leech, Evil Master of Power Suction, and the
battles are enhanced by a tempting array of accessories: vehicles
such as He-Man's Bashasaurus, weapons like the Beam-Blaster
battle pack, and play sets like Castle Grayskull.

Manufacturers and retailers particularly like action figures,
because they stimulate subsequent sales. Many toys are single
purchases—not many households buy more than one Monopoly
set, for example—but action toys encourage multiple purchases
of troops and equipment to wage battles. In war, more is better.

Also, for many of today's children accumulating is half the
fun. Product lines that promote sequential purchases are described as "collectibles," and collectibility has become one of the
most desirable features of toys in the 1980s—at least from the
sellers' point of view. Collecting treasures is as old as childhood
itself, and rock, shell, baseball card, and junk collections still
clutter the rooms of children all over the world. Savvy marketers
have managed to extend the concept to toys (preferably expensive ones) so that the initial sale will whet rather than satiate the
buyers' appetite. By 1985 action-figure products were selling at
the rate of $1 billion a year, making them the largest category
by far in nonelectronic boys' toys.

Action figures had evolved into battle troops by then, but the
earliest ones were sold individually. The first product to be
called an action figure was Hasbro's G.I. Joe, an eleven-and-a-
half-inch soldier doll issued in 1964 with a line of costumes and

accessories to be expanded annually. Although the company hoped to make Joe a Barbie for boys, it carefully avoided calling the product a doll—which real boys didn't play with—and described it as an action figure.

In the 1970s the category evolved through a variety of themes. Mattel once brought out a wholesome sportsman called Big Jim, but many of the lines were based on licensed characters that children already knew and liked. Kenner's bionic hero, the Six Million Dollar Man, proved so successful that the company offered girls the Bionic Woman. Action figures really exploded in 1977 when Kenner licensed the toy rights to the characters from *Star Wars*. Movies are ordinarily considered poor licensing prospects because they come and go within a few months, but *Star Wars* was the exception. Not only was the movie an enormous hit, but it had unprecedented staying power—what the industry calls "legs." Aided by its sequels, *Star Wars* brought Kenner over $1 billion in revenues over the next few years.

In 1982 Mattel raised the ante. The industry leader hired a television production company, Filmation Associates, to write a script for a daily animated television program based on He-Man and Masters of the Universe, an action-figure line the company had developed in-house. The product line generated about $37 million in sales in the second half of 1982. ABC turned the show down, and Mattel and Filmation undertook the unprecedented step of syndicating it (selling the program to independent stations around the country). They offered the stations sixty-five half-hour episodes, which would air every weekday afternoon for thirteen weeks and then go into reruns, in return for a fee and some of the advertising minutes on the program. Mattel and Filmation hoped to resell their time segments to other advertisers and thereby recoup their investment ($7 million each). The show began airing in September 1983 and quickly became the most popular children's program on TV. He-Man's 1983 sales were $111 million, about double what the company had forecast, and the following year sales more than doubled again, to over $250 million. "I have the power!" was He-Man's motto, and clearly he did.

Soon none of the companies thought they could sell an action-figure line without television exposure. Even with a program many of the products still failed, but enough succeeded to fuel the practice, and they crowded out other kinds of entertainment and toys.

Primarily because of the cost of television programming (sixty-five episodes cost $10–20 million), by 1985 action figures had become a huge, complex, and expensive product category. In addition to a television program, the lines were backed by multimillion-dollar advertising campaigns with licensing tie-ins such as pajamas, sheets, costumes, lunch boxes, and anything else the toymakers thought would help—in-store promotions, personal-appearance tours (real people performing in costumes), and even movies.

The action-figure arena was the big leagues. In fact, the category was one of two that Tyco's president had explicitly told Jim to avoid when he was looking for new products. (The other was large dolls, a category in which no one at Tyco had the slightest interest.) The company Dick Grey had been building for twelve years produced 1985 earnings of a little over $2 million on sales of $65 million. By contrast, the fourth-bestselling action-figure line in 1985, Tonka's GoBots, had sold twice that—about $132 million.

The top three lines were made by Hasbro and Mattel. In 1985 Hasbro had spent a total of $170 million on advertising and programming, and Mattel, $185 million. Although those dollars were spread over the companies' entire range of products, each company was spending on advertising an amount approximately three times Tyco's annual sales. To compete in this crowded, jealously protected category, Tyco would have to commit to development, production, and advertising expenditures way out of proportion to the rest of its operations. It would be the equivalent of a motorcycle manufacturer's deciding to make an automobile.

Woody had never actually worked on an action-figure line himself, but he almost had. He had been at Tonka the year the company had produced GoBots, its first (and, as it later turned out, its only) successful action-figure line, and the marketing director in charge of the product had worked in the office next to Woody's. In the absence of anyone more qualified at Tyco,

Woody figured he knew enough to function as the in-house action-figure expert.

Woody was already laying out the product line in his head when Jim called the product-development people to come join them in Woody's office. For the second time Jim told the story of his inspiration, and for the second time his audience seized it and started adding on.

Mike Hirtle, the department's chief, was so enthusiastic that he forgot to run through his usual litany of objections about how much trouble the project could cause, how much it would cost, how he could never fit it into the department's crowded schedule, and what a pain it was all going to be. Lee Volpe, the exuberant head of design, *loved* the concept and could hardly wait to get to work on all the ideas that sprang into his head as they talked. Crowded into Woody's office, the four of them began speculating on the size of the hit they could produce. They were all taken with the concept, but their enthusiasm was undoubtedly reinforced by the prospect of competing in the big leagues. The challenge was irresistible, and within minutes they all became obstinately determined to develop this product no matter how unsuitable it was for Tyco.

They eventually calmed down enough to begin formulating a selling strategy. They knew with perfect accuracy the size, age, and location of their target market. The number of people in their first market was one, and he was fifty-one years old. Without further discussion, they began brainstorming, searching for the best way to sell their ideas to their boss, Richard E. Grey.

Opinionated and accustomed to having his way, six-foot, four-inch Dick Grey dominates his creative, aggressive, opinionated subordinates. He insists on involving himself in the minutest of details, from packaging (one of his specialties) to office art (he added an etching by Graciela Rodo Boulanger so that his toy company would have art portraying children). He makes outrageous demands at inconvenient times, and no one dreams of defying him. He asks penetrating questions that his interlocutors wish they had anticipated. He uses his veto power frequently.

"Even when he's wrong, he's right," says one, meaning not that he is right because he is the boss but rather that Dick is correct with annoying regularity. He commands their trust to such a degree that they are like a group of planets revolving around the sun. They may rotate on their own axes, some with quite a few moons of their own, but the sun's gravitational pull ensures that all planetary activity will proceed within the context of its powerful force.

In short, Dick Grey has them all convinced that he knows how to do their jobs better than they do. This belief benefits the company because it stimulates the employees to do their best. They find Tyco an exciting place to work, and surprisingly comfortable, because Dick Grey's perfectionism doesn't just challenge his employees; it offers them security. His executives trust that Tyco will prosper because they believe Dick Grey really knows what he is doing.

Their respect for Dick's abilities does not mean that they hesitate to disagree with him. Tyco employees are a contentious bunch, and they all know that logical, rational arguments get a fair hearing. Dick can be convinced to change his mind, so when they feel strongly about something, they try. At times he cuts them off immediately, and that's that. At others he listens quietly, letting them go through their entire speech without offering a clue to his reactions. Sometimes they are so convinced they are right that even though he has vetoed an idea, they will keep up an argument for days. Grey tolerates it, although sometimes the process may strain his courtesy past the breaking point. "Don't you understand that you lost this argument thirty minutes ago?" he once asked, exasperated, after allowing a middle manager to lecture him for half an hour after he had said no. His subordinates also suspect that he lets them win sometimes, not because he agrees with them but just for the sake of winning.

With a general like Dick Grey, captains learn to choose their tactics with care. But as the meeting broke up, thoughts of selling to their leader were replaced by more compelling visions. As they drifted back to their offices, they all began to fantasize secretly about the way Dino-Riders was going to make their careers take off.

All they had to do was convince Dick.

3

University of Toyland

IN 1984 THE TMA BOARD INVITED Ruth and Elliot Handler to be its honored guests at the Toy Industry Hall of Fame inaugural ceremonies. The Handlers accepted, and the event was a triumphant occasion. Like deposed Communist leaders returning from exile in Siberia, they were back at Toy Fair for the first time in nine years.

Three years later they were honored again. At its Dolls Of The Year Awards (DOTY) breakfast, *Doll Reader* magazine presented the couple with its first Lifetime Achievement Award, in recognition of their contribution to the doll business in creating the Barbie doll.

Finally, in 1989, the TMA announced that Ruth and Elliot Handler themselves would be inducted into the Toy Industry Hall of Fame. Miraculously rehabilitated, their transformation from nonpersons into respected historical figures was now complete.

The Handlers created the most successful doll in history, but their importance to the toy industry far transcends Barbie. It even transcends Mattel, Inc., for many years the world's largest toy company. Ruth and Elliot Handler were the founding mother and father of the promotional toy business as it exists today. Mattel in the 1950s was where it all began.

Mattel has been called the University of Toyland. Mattel alumni are to be found throughout the entire industry. Ex-employees not only have penetrated the top ranks of virtually every major toy company; they have brought along systems, practices, even terminology created at Mattel. The Handlers were the first toy-industry entrepreneurs to transform their company, consciously and systematically, into a professional operation. Until then most toy companies were run like family businesses.

Even today there are literally hundreds of toy companies created on the basis of their founders' one good idea, and they remain very personal operations, extensions of their owners' personalities. Mattel's predecessor as industry leader was like that: Marx Toys was dominated by Louis Marx.

The Handlers were different. Part of their success stemmed from the fact that there were two of them. Extremely talented but very different from each other, they possessed between them an array of interests and abilities that made Mattel an innovator both in products and as an organization.

Ruth Handler was an outstanding businesswoman. Restless, volatile, profane, driven, dynamic, she loved marketing, selling, building the organization, inspiring the troops. The year Neil Armstrong landed on the moon, she told her managers, "The government put a man on the moon, and I believe there is enough talent in this room for Mattel to do the same thing." Her employees eyed each other nervously that day, because they knew she was ambitious enough to want to try. Intimidating as she could be, she was also a fierce mother hen, and she helped create the sense of family loyalty that pervaded Mattel for many years.

Elliot was an artist. Although he was sensitive and self-effacing, Elliot's gentle manner was never mistaken for weakness. Creative and prolific, he loved designing toys, yet he was practical enough to take pleasure in devising ways to use mechanisms invented for one toy in another. He remained intimately involved with product creation no matter how large the company grew, but he also participated in running the business. In his own way Elliot was also an extremely effective salesman, and selling was highly esteemed at Mattel. He had a way with products that made them irresistible; when he held a doll, it seemed to come alive in his arms. Everyone was always trying to imitate him, but no one ever could.

Together the Handlers were a formidable team.

When Elliot and Ruth Handler began making doll furniture in their garage in 1945, they had no idea they were founding the training school for an industry. They would not have been surprised, however, to learn that their operation was destined to grow large and successful. They had already built one business large enough to employ three hundred people.

The site of Mattel's origins was auspicious: founding a company in a garage is a venerable California tradition, perhaps because innovation and automobiles are both so characteristic of California culture. Whatever the reason, from Hewlett-Packard and Apple Computer to Mattel and Wham-O (maker of Hula Hoops and Frisbees), California garages have given birth to more than their share of American industry.

Ruth Paul and Elliot Handler grew up in Denver, Colorado, both children of immigrant families. Elliot was the second of four sons, Ruth the youngest of ten children. They were both twenty-one when they moved to Los Angeles during the Depression. Ruth had gone on vacation with a friend but decided to stay when she found a secretarial job at Paramount Pictures. Elliot, who had been working as a light-fixture designer during the day and going to a Denver art school part-time, was debating between art schools in Chicago and Los Angeles. When Ruth moved to Los Angeles, he reasoned that he might as well choose California; it was better to starve in a warm climate than in the cold.

They were married the following year, and Elliot went back to art school part-time while working during the day, again as a lighting designer. When he began to make Plexiglas furniture for their apartment, Ruth told him that if he could make more, she could sell it. That became their first business venture. Elliot left school, quit his job, bought some equipment, and set up shop in the garage of their apartment house. When their landlord complained about the dust, the pair rented space just vacated by a Chinese laundry and expanded from furniture into jewelry and novelty items. By 1943 they had a partner and three hundred employees making novelty jewelry, but wartime shortages made business difficult, and the partnership dissolved.

The Handlers, interested in expanding into other products, soon started another business with their ex-foreman, Harold Matson. They named it Mattel, combining Matson and Elliot, and began to make plastic picture frames for photography studios. They thought the studios could sell the frames to soldiers who came in to have pictures taken to send to their families or girlfriends. Ruth booked a huge order on her first call, but on her way home to share her triumph she heard on the car radio that the government was freezing all plastic supplies. Determined to salvage the order, Elliot made some frames out of second-grade lumber, covering the imperfections with flocking. Ruth secured an even bigger order, and Mattel was in business.

In his usual frugal way, Elliot tried to find a use for the scrap wood left over when they completed the frame order, and he made some doll furniture. When they earned a $30,000 profit on $100,000 worth of sales, the three decided they had found a business they liked. They never duplicated those margins, but profits were enough to finance the company's continuing growth. Matson, who was older, felt uncomfortable risking his life savings in the toy business, so Ruth's brother bought him out late in 1946. By then Mattel was known mostly as a producer of musical toys. One of its most successful products was an inexpensive jack-in-the-box that played "Pop Goes the Weasel" and timed the jack to pop out at just the right moment: when the song went "POP!"

By 1947 Elliot had designed a plastic molded ukelele, which they called a Ukedoodle. Introducing it in January, they were innocently pleased by the item's success. In March Elliot went east for his first Toy Fair and was shocked when his new sales representative took him to competitors' showrooms, where he saw copy after copy of his creation. When he protested, the competitors laughed at him. "What are you going to do, sue me?" taunted a man at Knickerbocker Toys. There was nothing he could do, but it was a useful lesson. "We learned a lot," he recalls over forty years later. "Like never introduce anything in January."

In 1955 Mattel was ten years old, and its sales had grown to about $4 million. That year the Handlers made a decision that affected the history of the American toy business the same way that the Japanese bombing of Pearl Harbor affected the history of the United States: both precipitated events that probably would have occurred anyway, but not with such dramatic suddenness.

Up to that point, toy companies generally spent their advertising budgets on catalogs and trade advertisements at Christmastime. If they used television at all, they ran commercials on local stations and concentrated on their most promising products. Hasbro claims to have been the first toy company to advertise on local television, for its 1952 product Mr. Potato Head. Mattel had used some television advertising for its products with less-than-exciting results.*

Mattel had already allocated about $60,000 of its 1955 advertising budget of $150,000 to Christmastime television advertising when a representative from the relatively new network ABC asked Mattel's ad agency, Carson/Roberts, if Mattel might be interested in national television advertising. ABC was going to run a new five-day-a-week children's program, to be created by Walt Disney's studio, and expected it to enchant the children of America. It was to be called "The Mickey Mouse Club."

There was nothing comparable on television for children, and the Walt Disney name was magic, so the success of the venture seemed assured. The cost of its advertising time was prohibitive, however. To become a sponsor for one of the four fifteen-minute segments once a week, a company had to pay $500,000 for the entire year on a noncancellable basis.

---

*For an extensive firsthand history and analysis of children's television, including Mattel's first experiences with television advertising, see *Children's Television* by Cy Schneider (Lincolnwood, Illinois: NTC Business Books, 1987). Schneider worked for Mattel's advertising agency, Carson/Roberts, from 1953 to 1980, became president of the agency in 1965, and contributed to the following account.

The offer hardly seemed worth mentioning to a company like
Mattel, which sold most of its goods in the last quarter of the
year and often lost money the other three, and whose total
advertising budget was less than a third of ABC's price. Furthermore, Mattel was doing quite nicely without it. Carson/Roberts
told the Handlers anyway, but, according to Cy Schneider, more
to warn them of what one of Mattel's larger competitors might
do than to suggest it as an option for Mattel.

The Handlers astonished their agency with their response.
They called in their comptroller and asked him whether they
could afford to invest half a million dollars in the venture. He
explained that $500,000 was their company's entire net worth.

"If it fails completely, will it break us?" they persisted.

"You'll be bent, but not broke," the comptroller replied.

They went for it.

Schneider has kept a reel of the early Mattel commercials, and
they are still entertaining. One of the first ads featured Mattel's
new Burp Gun, a cap gun modeled after World War II jungle
guns. The agency filmed Ralph Carson's son stalking around
his living room fighting imaginary elephants, which were
shown in a film projected onto the living room wall. Every time
Cary Carson shot the gun, the film was shown in reverse so that
the elephants "retreated." At that time Carson/Roberts also
invented a Mattel logo and slogan, hoping to make Mattel a
brand name children would remember. Children do not pay
much attention to manufacturers' names, but the agency did
succeed in creating a memorable slogan. "You can tell it's Mattel . . ."
can still elicit the response "It's swell" from the baby boomers
who watched "The Mickey Mouse Club" thirty-five years ago.

The show debuted in November and was an instant smash—
in the ratings. The effect on Burp Gun orders was nonexistent.
The product had been well received by the buyers, but it was
languishing in the stores. By the week of Thanksgiving, Mattel
and the agency were getting so desperate that they considered
placing ads in newspapers to alert parents to their commercials.

They had just been too impatient. The Monday after the
Thanksgiving weekend, the rush of orders overwhelmed them,
dwarfing anything Mattel had ever experienced. "We came back

after Thanksgiving and everything hit the fan," Ruth Handler recalls. "We couldn't make enough, we couldn't find enough. Everyone who had cancelled wanted to reinstate their orders, so we got rid of everything we had. Then we called all the people who had called to say they had too much and wanted help. But they all said they were out now and wanted more."

"We had a total cleanout that year," adds Elliot. "It was wonderful." They had simply underestimated the time it took for retail sales to translate into manufacturers' orders. By Christmas Mattel had shipped one million Burp Guns, and customers were clamoring for more. At four dollars each, the guns more than doubled Mattel's annual sales. As Schneider put it, "The Burp Gun had fired shots heard 'round the world."

The promotional toy business had begun.

Mattel's decision to advertise toys to children on national television fifty-two weeks a year so revolutionized the industry that it is not an exaggeration to divide the history of the American toy business into two eras, before and after television.

To begin with, television advertising profoundly altered the toy manufacturers' relationship with their ultimate customers. Before television, children generally saw what the buyers chose to stock in the stores. By reaching children directly, the manufacturers not only went over the heads of the wholesalers and large-store buyers, but they also bypassed the children's parents. Controversial though the practice has remained, advertising directly to children changed the pattern of supply and demand. The manufacturers began to stimulate the demand themselves, showing millions of children all over the country toys they had never seen before, in a manner calculated to make the toys seem as appealing as possible.

Soon children expected the stores to stock what they wanted to buy, so buyers had to guess what their customers were going to request. As television became a major determinant of what children wanted, buyers realized that they could make better guesses about which toys to buy if they knew how much television exposure a product was going to have—and how effective that exposure would be. It was by necessity, therefore, that buyers began to base their purchasing decisions as much on the companies' commercials and advertising budgets as on the toys themselves. Mattel, which understood the power of the medium quite quickly, put signs around its showroom at the 1956 Toy Fair that read, "Remember the Burp Gun" and offered buyers a look at the commercials it had planned for the coming year.

From then on, the trade went into the business of evaluating commercials as well as toys.

Television increased the total volume of toy sales, but it divided companies more sharply into haves and have-nots. Companies that could afford to advertise on television now had an opportunity to reap enormous sales that their poorer competitors could not match. Advertising did not guarantee success, but the companies able to advertise successfully grew larger and more powerful and even more able to spend more money on advertising than their smaller competitors. The predictable result has been a continuing tendency toward consolidation among manufacturers, which in turn favors toys oriented toward the mass market. Large companies need large volumes.

The industry's traditional pattern of sales shifted as well. By stimulating demand, national television made toys more a year-round business, although never to an extent great enough to satisfy the industry. The bulk of the retail toy sales still clusters in the last couple of months of the year, in anticipation of Christmas. Advertising remains by far the heaviest in the fourth quarter, but toy companies now advertise more during the off-periods as well. Advertising during the first three-quarters of the year has become more important because scanning cash registers and sophisticated forecasting techniques make early sales figures increasingly reliable predictors of fourth-quarter buying patterns. Toymakers want to keep their products' sales from slipping while the buyers decide what to purchase for the rest of the year.

The most important effect of national television advertising in Toyland was not the growth of the industry or the increase in off-season sales or even the change to a demand- instead of a supply-driven market. It was more subtle than any of these, but at the same time more profound: the growing importance of television advertising changed the nature of toys themselves.

Not all toys. There have always been blocks and balls and dolls and miniature versions of everything from cars to tea sets, and there always will be. But the audiovisual nature of television enabled manufacturers to sell toys they could never have sold before, because it allowed them to demonstrate all kinds of interesting features in a way that had not been possible when the toys just sat on the shelves.

Toys had been doing things for years (Thomas Edison invented a talking doll around 1890), but complicated products were hard to sell. Special features often required an explanation or a demonstration, which was impractical in the stores. Toy companies sometimes hired demonstrators to exhibit their products in major department stores during the holiday shopping season, but this was expensive and reached only the adults or children who happened to be in the toy department during the demonstrations, a tiny fraction of the potential market.

Once they could demonstrate a toy on television to millions of children, the manufacturers began to create products that could do all kinds of things: dolls that talked, walked, and crawled, cars that drove at high speeds and crashed spectacularly. Toymakers who could afford to buy advertising time were limited only by their imaginations. The products' functions became more important than their appearance, because they were competing on television, not on the retailers' shelves.

As television began to affect the products, advertising agencies increased their influence on product design. By the time he became creative director on the Mattel account in 1968, Russ Alben was already a veteran of children's advertising; he had written commercials for cereal, candy, toys, and magazines, and programs for Bozo the Clown. He remembers how they began to reverse the original product-development process. The agency people, recalls Alben, "were shaping products to the needs of the television eye and ear . . . [based] not so much on what inventors call 'hands-on' experience with the toys but more on what a successful plaything must be able to do to 'perform' in the commercial to sell itself at its best. . . . We strove to identify the single-minded preemptive qualities which would distinguish our toys from those of our competitors. At the moment of deciding which feature would be featured as the most important element we often sent the Mattel R and D guys to *their* drawing boards."

When Mattel contemplated a Golden Dream Barbie, the agency people tried to discourage the idea, since there is no natural yellow on color television, only red, green, and blue. Yellow is obtained by subtracting blue from green, and the results are unreliable and often unattractive. "You'd better be sure of what you want," Alben warned the designers at the time, "or what you'll get is Gangrene Barbie."

The commercials themselves often created the toys' play value through their presentations. Although extrinsic to the products, the fantasies in the commercials sometimes became more important in giving the toy meaning than any feature added by the toy engineers or designers. This was not a new phenomenon. Shirley Temple dolls, Buck Rogers paraphernalia, and other licensed products had been popular for years because of what they represented, not because of what they actually were. Television, however, enabled the manufacturers and their advertising agencies to create their own fantasy concepts, which could be communicated to children as part of the toys themselves. Guns and dolls soon became more than simply guns and dolls. Fantasy could be used to make the sponsors' gun or doll seem unique and special—to differentiate it from other guns and dolls.

As time went on, fantasy evolved into an increasingly important element of many toys advertised on television. By the 1980s some of the toys promoted on television simply represented concepts; they didn't do anything at all. The commercials were better than the products, and the marketing strategies substituted for product development in making saleable toys.

Back in the 1950s and 1960s Mattel and its competitors were just beginning to explore the uses of television. The medium had begun to shape, but not replace, product innovation and development. At the end of the 1950s Mattel introduced its most successful product ever, and though the product was introduced on television and relied on television to promote it, Mattel's Barbie doll has survived more than thirty years because, ultimately, it is an outstanding product.

Barbie was invented by Ruth Handler. Elliot invented many of Mattel's toys, Ruth only one. But since she invented the most popular doll in history, she was wise to stop when she did.

Just before the 1959 Toy Fair Mattel announced that it was allocating an extra $125,000, over and above the $1 million it had already earmarked for the year's television advertising, to promote a new product line. The company was entering the doll business. Ruth Handler described Mattel's Barbie Teenage Fashion Model as "the only anatomically perfect doll manufactured today." If she had known what an issue Barbie's anatomy would become over the years, she might have talked about Barbie's wardrobe instead.

The eleven-and-a-half-inch doll could be dressed in twenty-two different costumes, each with its own accessories. Its advertising agency had convinced Mattel to call Barbie a teenager, but if she had been a real teenager her parents would never have let her out of the house. Hoop earrings hung from her ears; her lips, fingernails, and toenails were bright red; her eyebrows were pointed, her mouth pouty; her eyes were heavily outlined and her expression seductive. She came dressed in a striped jersey swimsuit, accompanied by sunglasses, shoes, and a special stand with two prongs upon which to impale her hollow, metal-lined feet. Like Oriental women whose feet were bound, Barbie never stood very well on her own.

Her wardrobe also allowed Barbie to range far beyond teenage activities. She could attend slumber parties in her Sweet Dreams outfit ("tricot baby doll pajamas, matched hairbow, bedroom scuffs, diary book, apple, and an alarm clock"), but she could also go out on the town in Evening Splendour, a gold-brocade strapless sheath dress with matching coat trimmed with fake mink cuffs and hat, "pearl" necklace and earrings, evening bag, shoes, handkerchief, and gloves. Barbie could be a Sweater Girl, Plantation Belle, Barbie-Q chef, or a Commuter. Or, of course, a Bride. Barbie's wedding gown came equipped with every accessory except a groom.

Barbie's Toy Fair reviews were mixed, and Ruth Handler was bitterly disappointed. "We knew we had a great toy," she recalls. "We had poured a fortune and three years of our lives and our hearts into it. Then we got to Toy Fair and most of the buyers, who were men, looked at it and said, 'Oh, fashion dolls are dead. We can't sell them, we're loaded with inventory,' or 'American mothers are not going to buy a doll with breasts.' " The Sears buyer refused to carry the doll, insisting that she was much too sexy. About half the buyers at Toy Fair agreed with him; the other half were willing to order the doll, but cautiously.

The Handlers telephoned their representative in Japan, where they had arranged to manufacture the doll and her clothes, and lowered production targets. They figured that their H_2O Missile—a water-powered ICBM that shot a second-stage rocket two hundred feet into the air—would be the company's winning product that year. (It is a measure of Mattel's extraordinary creativity at that time that it could come out with two such innovative products in the same year.)

Half the buyers were very wrong. The ICBM is long gone, launched into obscurity, and as everyone in America knows, Barbie became as much a cultural icon as Mickey Mouse. She flew off the shelves from the start, and because Mattel had cut production, the company spent the next three years catching up with demand.

Barbie was successful then for the same reason she is successful now. She never was sixteen, or twenty-one, or even an ancient twenty-four. She was any age little girls wanted her to be, so that they could project their fantasies about their futures. Barbie's 1987 slogan, "We girls can be anything!" encapsulated Barbie's enduring appeal perfectly.

Barbie was originally inspired by paper dolls, which, not coincidentally, began to decline in popularity the year Barbie appeared on the market. Ruth Handler had noticed that her daughter, Barbara, always preferred the adult or teenage paper dolls to the babies or little girls. When Barbara and her friends played with them, Ruth was struck by the endless hours they would spend and with the variety of situations they would create. If we were only in the doll business, she would think, we could three-dimensionalize that play pattern and we would really have something.

The model for the first Barbie doll was a German doll, which, although Ruth did not know it when she first saw it, was a three-dimensionalized version of a German cartoon character named Lilli, a prostitute who was always having adventures with men.

Barbie's wardrobe was more important than the doll. Clothes were always the point of Barbie, because they were to be the girls' vehicle for projecting the doll, and themselves, into all the situations they imagined. Because she wanted authentic style and fashion and detail, Ruth began to look for someone who designed clothes, not toys. Elliot called a local art school and found Charlotte Johnson, a fashion designer who taught at the school and worked as an in-house designer at a women's clothing store. Johnson agreed to design the clothes if she could do it from her home, so Ruth and Elliot drove to her apartment two or three times a week to review designs and samples. When they went into production, Johnson flew over to Japan to supervise the clothes manufacturers, who were mostly women sewing the little garments by hand in their homes. She stayed for a year, and the results were exquisite: trimmings, real buttonholes, bust darts, tiny zippers, accessories to be used as props.

Today Barbie's clothes are not as finely handcrafted as they were thirty years ago; if they were, they could not sell at popular prices. But they are still an elaborate, accurate reflection of the popular culture of the moment. In fact, Barbie's wardrobe over the years is an archaeological treasure, a perfect record of fashion and female life in America as viewed through the eyes of little girls. Over the years Barbie has gone from flight attendant to astronaut, from garden parties to workouts, from nurse to doctor to rock star. A thirty-plus-year-old fashion doll should be an oxymoron, but Mattel surrounds Barbie with an entourage rock stars and royalty would envy. The job of all those artists, sculptors, engineers, and fashion designers is to maintain Barbie in the style to which her audience has become accustomed.

Barbie follows the styles, she does not lead them. She personifies what little girls want, not what adults want them to want. She has a dress-for-success suit and briefcase, but they are pink. Her audience unwaveringly prefers the fancy to the plain, and Barbie is, after all, supposed to appeal to her audience. Although she has changed her clothes, her body, her friends, and—once—her boyfriend (Barbie two-timed Ken for Derek when she became a rock star in 1986), Barbie has remained constant in two respects. She is always beautiful and glamorous. And she is always controversial.

Thirty years of Barbiephobia reveals as much about American culture as thirty years of Barbie fashion. As the ideals and ideas about women's roles have changed over the years, so have some of the objections to Barbie. One complaint has remained constant. Barbie is the ultimate material girl, in both senses. She is acquisitive because Mattel has provided an unending parade of costumes so appealing that Barbie's owners never have quite enough. And she is defined by her possessions—Barbie is what she wears.

"Anyone looking for deeper values in the world of Barbie is looking in the wrong place. With its emphasis on possessions and its worship of appearances, it is modern America in miniature—a tiny parody of our pursuit of the beautiful, the material, the trivial." The world the writer describes had witnessed neither the self-absorbed yuppies of the 1980s nor the possession-hungry success seekers of the 1970s; the complaint is from the *Saturday Evening Post*, December 1964. Like many critics of the nature and extent of Barbie's wardrobe, the writer would prefer that Barbie instruct rather than reflect. Mattel would not mind doing both, but most of all it wants to sell, and it designs Barbie accordingly.

The complaints about Barbie's materialism have remained, but the objections to Barbie as a role model of womanhood have completely reversed. In the 1960s Barbie's principal critics were men who saw her as a predatory female. Even the *Nation* worried about Barbie (on the same page as an essay on Khrushchev). "Teen-focused play-fantasies are rearranging the souls of girls between the ages of 6 and 15," it revealed. "Barbie threatens to make a generation of vipers that will cause men to plead for the return of momism." The ideal woman was a happy homemaker, and Barbie was just too independent. Besides, Ken was obviously just a sex object, a face-man to accompany Barbie wherever she wanted to go.

Today Barbie's biggest critics are women. Now that independence is valued, Barbie is disparaged as too passive, too interested in her possessions at the expense of her career, and too beautiful. Barbie's body has always disturbed adults. Her breasts are often described as gravity-defying, and her measurements are frequently transposed into impossible life-size statistics (which are always different because everyone gives Barbie a different real-life height) to prove that she promotes an unattainable physical ideal that will leave little girls feeling inadequate when they grow up and cannot look like Barbie.

Barbie has come a long way. In the 1960s she was considered a perfect bitch. Today she is regarded as a complete bimbo.

Whatever she is, Ruth Handler's creation is endlessly fascinating, and she has generated more coverage than any other toy in history.

When actress Jessica Lange, evidently thinking she was a trailblazer, announced in the pages of *Esquire*, "I'm NEVER going to let my daughter have a Barbie," she was promptly chided by Judy Markey in the *Chicago Sun-Times*:

> Listen, Jessica. Don't you think the millions of American women who purchased the nearly quarter of a billion Barbies sold made this speech, too? And we all have succumbed. Better women than I have succumbed. And, dare I say it, it's possible even better women than you have succumbed. In fact I once heard a rumor that Vanessa Vadim (daughter of you-know-who Fonda) once even had a Fashion Photo Barbie. If that's true, what chance do you think you have?

4

SIC TRANSIT GLORIA MATTEL

Mattel was like the Christmas star, formed by the convergence of three planets. There will never be another Elliot Handler. There will never be another Ruth Handler.

—Jack Ryan

MATTEL HELD ITS ANNUAL SALES dinner in New York during Toy Fair, and for several years the elegant Essex House hotel witnessed spirited, if unmusical, performances when Mattel's top management put on shows complete with songs, piano accompaniment, skits, costumes, props, and in-jokes for the entire assemblage. Increasingly elaborate as time went on, the shows were written by Mattel's advertising agency, and the songs were based on popular musicals ("Toys and Dolls" was one). By the end of the evening the audience was usually gasping with laughter, calling for the author, and carrying someone around the room.

The enthusiasm of the audience members was not entirely due to the copywriters' witty lyrics—or even to the pleasure of seeing their bosses make spectacles of themselves. They were shouting

64

and laughing because they knew that their turn was next. The original cast appeared for a one-time-only New York premiere, and then the parts were given out to Mattel salespeople from all over the country. After Toy Fair they went home and held a few rehearsals. Then they invited their regional customers to a party, where they re-created the show they had seen in New York and showed them Mattel's new product line. A gregarious group to begin with, they all vied with one another for the parts they wanted, especially the ones in drag.

Mattel grew rapidly throughout the 1950s and 1960s. Even in the 1970s and 1980s, when it began to have severe legal and financial problems, Mattel remained an exciting, fast-paced place to work, sparkling with creative ferment. Jealousy and competitiveness were not unknown, and sometimes they were even encouraged. But many in Toyland continued to believe that anyone serious about a career in the toy industry should, at some point, work for Mattel.

There was a glamour about the company. Managers were told to look for a certain kind of personality, one that combined enormous aggressiveness with an attention to detail, and Mattel employees considered themselves an elite group within the industry. The Handlers wanted strong personalities, and the company attracted a number of strange characters who were allowed the freedom to indulge their eccentricities as long as they produced. No one was more eccentric than Jack Ryan. Ryan could never be described as typical of anything, but he is illustrative of the mixture of talent and weirdness the Handlers assembled and tolerated at Mattel.

A brilliant, puckish engineer, Ryan had been working on the Sparrow and Hawk missiles at Raytheon when he left at the age of twenty-nine to head Mattel's design department. Ryan had met the Handlers while he was accompanying an army general to California to test Raytheon's missiles out in the desert. He had watched the general sell the Handlers a toy invention every time they made the trip and soon decided he could do better. He began offering them inventions such as a toy radio, and the Handlers were so impressed that they spent the next few years trying to lure him away from Raytheon.

Although he liked California, Ryan had no interest in working for a toy company, and he responded by making impossible demands. The Handlers were so determined to hire him that they kept meeting his terms. Finally their offer was too rich to refuse, so he went to Mattel and spent the next nineteen years accumulating more than a thousand patents and over $2 million a year in royalties. He was the only employee to receive royalties from Mattel, and he made sure that every patent granted to a Mattel employee—on everything from Barbie's flexible interior knee joint to the talking mechanism for its Chatty Cathy doll—included his name as well.

Ryan was an important contributor to Mattel (his opinion of his role can be found at the beginning of this chapter), but he became a Mattel legend for his eccentricity, standing out even among the zany cast of characters who inhabited Mattel in those days. Ryan has married five times. Starting with his children's mother, who became mentally ill, the parade of wives has continued with Zsa Zsa Gabor; his Mormon secretary, who subsequently became an alcoholic and died of cirrhosis of the liver; a German actress who was being groomed to be the next Marilyn Monroe; and currently, a beautiful Polish attorney who could not return to Poland because she had worked for Solidarity.

There were also many mistresses. According to Ryan, one was a morphine addict whom he cured by sex ("the endorphins in her brain from sexual activity made it so she didn't need drugs"); she repaid him by hiring a twice-indicted murderer to crack his safe. Another was a Miss World who had been jilted by Bob Hope. One of his favorites was the estranged wife of the platinum equivalent of Goldfinger (the real-life gold magnate whom Ian Fleming immortalized in a James Bond adventure). "She was French royalty, although she was raised in Germany. I lived with her on Park Avenue while her husband paid all the bills so he could spy on her. She had three sable coats and drove a Porsche especially built for her in Germany."

The Porsche must have appealed to Ryan, who loves improving on cars. He has the front passenger seat on his Mercedes Benz backward so that he can face his conversational partner while he drives. Between wives he used to go nightclubbing in his 1935 Reo fire engine, and he lived for many years in an enormous house in Bel Air that had belonged to Hollywood actor Warner Baxter. When his first marriage began to fail, he brought his parents to California to help him raise his children and renovate the house into a castle. In the meantime he staffed his establishment with college students, gave dinner parties in a tree house, and worked quite productively at Mattel.

When he left in 1974, Ryan sued Mattel for back payments on royalties and eventually collected $10 million. By that time, he needed the money for another lawsuit, also for back royalties, against Ideal Toys in New York, for whom he had created a trackless car racing set.

Jack Ryan arrived at Mattel in 1955, the same year that Mattel advertised on national television and gave birth to the promotional toy industry. When *Time* magazine ran its cover story on Louis Marx that December, the piece was already out-of-date, because the predominance of Marx Toys was about to end. Mattel, with its tiny $6 million in sales, was not even mentioned.

That was also the year that the professionalization of Mattel began. Once she witnessed the extraordinary increase in sales produced by the Burp Gun commercial, Ruth Handler realized she needed a system that would help her predict sales on every product. She wanted to be able to produce enough of each product so that Mattel would not miss many sales if the toy took off, and at the same time hold down inventories in case the toy bombed—inventory losses could be even more costly than missed sales. Buyers customarily set their orders for each product at the beginning of the year, but they did not want the entire quantity delivered then. Instead, they would wait to see how the product sold; if it did well, they expected the manufacturer to supply them with the balance of their order. If it was a poor seller, they would cancel the undelivered portion of the order and the manufacturer would be stuck with all the unsold inventory.

Manufacturers eager to ship their inventories also had to be

careful not to load their customers with too much stock. "It was
very important to forecast as efficiently and carefully and correctly as was humanly possible," explains Ruth. "In those days
a million pieces of anything was a great deal—the equivalent
today would be 5 or 6 million. But if at that time, you shipped
150,000–200,000 more than the end customers bought, chances
were that the next year you might only sell 100,000 of that item
or less. Then the product would be dead and you'd spend all the
next year cleaning up inventory, both yours and your customers'."

Because so many of the products were new each year, Mattel
could not use past sales figures as guidelines in setting production targets. One answer, they decided, was to analyze current
retail sales figures in their customers' stores. Mattel sent people
out to count actual shelf stock and inventory of each product in
a selected sample—a practice it still follows, though customers'
computer information systems and professional tracking services now provide the same sort of information.

Mattel designed a set of reports that are still used in some
form all over the industry. Besides the reports generated by the
market research department, the company relied heavily on the
"W," or weekly report. This report, which was issued for every
single product, tracked actual weekly and year-to-date quantities
produced, sold (to the trade), and shipped. It also projected the
final quantity that would be manufactured if the current rate of
production were maintained, so that the managers could compare that with the product's projected sales. The production
quantities for each product were really moving targets, reviewed
every week and changed when necessary.

These figures were "the numbers," and they were more than
simple tools. They became a company cult. Reported weekly,
they forced everyone to watch the sales patterns and to be ready
to make far-reaching decisions on a daily basis. That is why
employees who come from other industries consider one year in
the toy business like five years anywhere else. Patrick Feely, who
later became president of Tonka Toys, went to Mattel from RCA
in 1977 after spending four frustrating years developing products that never went into production. He was amazed and then

exhilarated by the atmosphere. "I came from a giant *Fortune* 25 company, afraid of its shadow, unwilling to invest in all these wonderful new things we had come up with. At Mattel, here were these guys, knowing nothing about electronics, forging their way into the video game business that we had closed at RCA. I fell in love with the idea of doing that: running at high speed and without fear. I thought, This is where the entrepreneurial spirit lies."

Feely was also fascinated by the company-wide preoccupation with "the numbers." "When I arrived at Mattel and began going to the weekly meetings, I found that everybody lived and breathed the numbers. People seemed to like to show off to some extent that they had them memorized. They knew exactly what a certain Barbie doll was doing—they would quote the exact number at a meeting. Coming from a large company, I thought this was crazy. But after I was there a year, I realized that the business needed to be lived on a minute-to-minute basis. If you don't make the decisions today, then tomorrow it might be too late."

He never completely forgot how strange it had all seemed, and it amused him to watch new people from other industries take it in. "People who came in from outside thought we were a bunch of lunatics. I could see the looks in their eyes. I'd say to them, 'Look, I came out of another industry, just like you did. But this is different.' "

Ultimately, it was "the numbers" that led Mattel into trouble, trouble so serious that Ruth and Elliot Handler had to leave the company they had founded. They took the first step in 1960, when they sold shares of Mattel on the Pacific Coast Stock Exchange. Sales had already reached $25 million, and they needed money to finance expansion. Besides, going public was the only way to realize some of the gain in the value of their company. By 1963 Mattel was listed on the New York Stock Exchange and in 1968 joined the ranks of the *Fortune* 500. Its stock climbed right along with its sales. When it peaked in 1971, an original $10 share was worth $522.50.

Sales had grown from $18 million in 1960 to $211 million in 1969. The Handlers knew they could not continue at that rate indefinitely, but public companies are expected to sustain growth. Acquiring other toy companies was not a viable option because of the strict enforcement of antitrust laws. Diversification was very popular at the time, however, and it made good sense: through diversification Mattel could acquire companies that would cushion the shocks of the volatile and seasonal toy business.

The Handlers hired several outsiders in preparation for diversifying. Arthur Spear, an eight-year Revlon veteran, arrived in 1964 to run Mattel's operations, distribution, and purchasing. Seymour Rosenberg, a financial expert from Litton Industries, was brought in to raise Mattel's level of financial sophistication and improve its image and relationship with the Wall Street community. He would also seek out acquisitions. The Handlers and other employees who had profited over the years from the gains in Mattel's stock had always cared about the shares' price. Now the company's stock price became more important than ever, for acquisitions then were typically purchased with stock.

Mattel had never completely ignored Wall Street. When it first went onto the New York Stock Exchange, it changed some of its accounting programs in an attempt to even out some of its earnings fluctuations. It already offered discounts to customers who bought early, in an attempt to boost sales in the first half of the year, the period when production expenses typically outrun sales and toy companies lose money. To help its quarterly figures, it also began to defer some products' expenses to later quarters when the products would be sold, a perfectly legal accounting practice called annualization.

In 1970 Mattel issued an anniversary publication, "Mattel, Inc., 25 Years of Growth." Reviewing the company's progress from a fledgling mom-and-pop business in a converted garage to an industry leader controlling 11½ percent of the toy market in 1969, the book explained that the company was now more than a toy company. Mattel was expanding into a range of products "to fill the educational and recreational needs of young people." Its future looked as rosy as its past.

The acquisition program seemed to be succeeding. Between 1968 and 1971 Mattel bought five companies: Monogram Models, which made plastic hobby kits; Metaframe, a manufacturer of aquariums, gerbil and hamster houses, pet food, and pet accessories; Turco Manufacturing, a playground-equipment and wheeled-goods company; Audio Magnetics, which made blank audiotapes, cassettes, and cartridges; and the Ringling Brothers–Barnum & Bailey Circus. The company had even coproduced a movie, the Academy Award–winning *Sounder.*

During the same period Mattel introduced one of the most successful product lines in its history. Still around today, its Hot Wheels line of die-cast cars continues to compete with the original in the field, Matchbox cars, as well as a number of other imitators. With their hot California colors and styling, Hot Wheels cars looked much more exciting than the Matchbox cars, and their frictionless wheels enabled them to go much faster than their dignified competitors. Launched in 1968, the Hot Wheels line generated over $25 million in the first year compared with $23 million for the entire category the previous year.

It is often said in Toyland that success is harder to manage than failure. The success of its Hot Wheels line set the stage for the company's near-destruction. In 1970 Mattel added Sizzlers, a motorized version of Hot Wheels. The buyers were enthusiastic, but the demand for Sizzlers at retail was cool. Mattel's customers, who had ordered heavily after experiencing short supplies in Hot Wheels' first two years, began coming back to the company asking for help in getting rid of their excess inventory. Furthermore, with Sizzlers clogging the pipeline, Mattel began to have trouble selling its other merchandise. Customers demanded relief on Sizzlers first.

That was when, to sustain its outstanding record of sales growth and high profits, the company began to cross the line and manipulate figures. By using annualization accounting, it deferred expenses from the early quarters into the later quarters, where the charges would supposedly be offset by the expected sales. But because Sizzlers had been overshipped, the projected sales did not materialize.

Determined to report the sales it had projected for the later quarters, the company went further. It took a bill-and-hold program—like annualization, a perfectly legitimate accounting practice—and expanded it to inflate revenues. The company billed customers for products they did not want and did not have to take, simply to inflate its volume. Pushing products onto customers at the end of the year is not unknown in the industry; customers will accept some merchandise early because they can defer payment. But Mattel was borrowing so heavily from future sales that it would have been impossible to catch up unless it hit upon a miracle. It was not even bothering to ship the merchandise.

At the same time it was inflating sales figures, Mattel refused to write down its inventory sufficiently, because the charge would depress earnings too much. Instead, it used its earnings target to determine the size of the inventory deduction it could afford. The accounting system was so far divorced from reality by this time that the company kept the classic two sets of books. The company kept borrowing sales from the next quarter, hoping that actual sales would rise enough to fulfill the numbers it was reporting. But with the pipeline full of cars, it was not likely.

The following year a West Coast dock strike held products offshore until after Christmas, costing the company millions of dollars in lost sales. By March 1972 Mattel finally had no choice but to admit that it was losing money—an after-tax loss of $29.9 million for the fiscal year that had ended January 31. Still unwilling to untangle its web, Mattel accompanied the announcement with a cheery prediction: "We have every reason to believe that the troubles of last year in our toy business are behind us. . . . We are anticipating a healthy turnaround. . . ."

The web was tightening. Seymour Rosenberg was fired that summer, although the company continued to pay him. Most of his acquisitions were losing money, and the accounting contortions he had encouraged were not working. In October the first of many shareholder suits was filed against Mattel, the Handlers, other executives, and the company's accounting firm, Arthur Andersen, alleging insider selling before the company's March announcement of bad news.

In December Mattel's bankers, who were worried about their

$200 million in short-term financing, began to close in on the company. They forced the Handlers to turn control over to Arthur Spear, by now executive vice president of operations. The Handlers were allowed to retain the titles of president and chairman, but the bankers passed the authority to Spear, who had begun talking to them independently earlier that year.

What finally brought in the Securities and Exchange Commission (SEC), along with five class-action shareholder suits, was a pair of press releases about Mattel's financial performance for fiscal 1973. Issued eighteen days apart, they directly contradicted each other. It was like a sick corporate version of a good-news, bad-news joke. The first announced that preliminary estimates indicated a "definite turnaround from the unprecedented $30 million loss . . . and . . . the Company will report satisfactory earnings from continuing operations." The second explained that "the Company now expects to incur a substantial operating loss for the fiscal year ended February 3, 1973, rather than a profit as previously anticipated." The loss turned out to be $32 million.

Mattel's managers had issued the first release genuinely believing that fiscal 1973 was going to be profitable—barely—but the about-face was the final blow. Even before the $32 million loss was announced, shareholders brought suit for reporting false and misleadingly positive information, and there would be other suits over the next few years. Eventually Mattel and assorted executives faced five class-action suits and three private actions. Ruth Handler was forced to resign as president, although she joined Elliot as co-chairman of the board.

The SEC studied Mattel for about a year and then filed a complaint alleging that while it found no evidence of material trading in Mattel stock or of any mishandling of funds, the company had filed deliberately false and misleading statements in order to maintain the appearance of corporate growth in fiscal years 1972 and 1973.

On September 6, 1974, Mattel announced that it had "discovered" possible financial inaccuracies for fiscal years 1971 and 1972 and was requesting that trading in its stock be suspended. A few weeks later Arthur Andersen withdrew as Mattel's accountant, and the two companies sued each other. The SEC went back to court and stiffened its demands on the company. In an unprecedented request, the commission asked the federal court to order Mattel to revise its board of directors so that a majority of the directors were from outside the company. Even some within the SEC considered this a usurpation of stockholders' rights, but Mattel acceded. The SEC also called for the appointment of a special counsel and a special auditor to investigate the possibly inaccurate financial statements. Arthur Spear chose the new directors.

On October 2 the company issued a press release which explained the judgment in detail and reported sales and earnings figures for the first six months of fiscal 1975. The fourth paragraph of the eleven-page document noted simply:

> Mattel announced that on September 6, 1974, Arthur S. Spear was elected by the Board of Directors as Chief Executive Officer in addition to his position as President and Chief Operating Officer of Mattel, Inc. and that the Company's By-Laws have been amended to eliminate the position of Chairman of the Board of Directors.

So departed Elliot and Ruth Handler from the company they had founded in 1945. Not with a bang. Not even with a whimper. Without, in fact, even a whisper: the chairmanship disappeared along with the Handlers.

In November 1975, the court received the special counsel's report, which confirmed that Mattel had in fact published false and misleading statements that overstated one year's sales by $18.3 million. Instead of $17.4 million in fiscal 1971 earnings, the company should have reported a $900,000 loss. That day Mattel settled its shareholder suits for $30 million, at the time the largest settlement ever for a shareholder suit against a company.

On February 16, 1978, Ruth Handler and Seymour Rosenberg were indicted by a federal grand jury for conspiracy, mail fraud, and making false financial statements to the SEC. The ten-count indictment also charged that the two falsified internal records to influence the market price of the stock in order to acquire assets of other companies, obtain bank financing for the business, and sell Mattel stock for their own benefit. Also indicted were a former financial vice president, a former comptroller, and an accounting-staff supervisor. In accordance with the Handlers' nonperson status, Mattel issued a statement noting, ". . . neither the Company nor any of its current Directors or Officers are named as defendants in the Grand Jury indictment reported today by the U.S. Attorney in Los Angeles. Accordingly, the Company said it would have no comment regarding the indictment."

Once the indictments were issued, the cloud finally lifted from the others who were potentially indictable. Among them were division vice presidents Joshua Denham (toys), Ray Wagner (dolls), and Bernie Loomis (wheels), who had admitted that, under orders, they had executed bill-and-hold transactions but said they had not participated in devising the policies, and Arthur Spear, who had insisted all along that he had known nothing of what was going on.

Spear and the Handlers do not talk about each other in public, but others recall those days bitterly. The whole company knew, they say. Recalls one, "We used to spend hours talking about it—we were all under suspicion. How Art Spear walked through the raindrops all those years and never got wet always amazed us."

Ruth Handler and Seymour Rosenberg pleaded no contest and were found guilty in December 1978. Ruth Handler received a forty-one-year suspended sentence, a $57,000 suspended fine, and 2,500 hours of community service, which she performed. "The crimes each of you committed," the judge told them, "in the opinion of this court are exploitative, parasitic, and I think disgraceful to anything decent in this society."

The Handlers quit the toy business completely when they left Mattel, turning their backs on the industry that they felt had turned its back on them. They had to surrender some of their Mattel stock for the shareholders' settlement and ultimately sold it all. Ruth Handler, who even her friends concede is not likely to admit to errors, insisted she was misled about what was

appropriate accounting procedure. Some close to them agree
that the Handlers were in over their heads in the financial
world, adding that figures are manipulated to yield desired
results as a matter of course in American industry and that the
Handlers were unfortunate because Mattel did not hit a good
year in time to pull them out of the trough. Nevertheless, there
was a line between massaging figures and manufacturing them,
and Mattel crossed it.

Elliot returned to painting, his lifelong avocation. Ruth
started another business. A cancer victim in her fifties, Ruth had
a mastectomy in 1970. She was dismayed when she saw the
artificial breasts that were available, so she moved to fill a need
in the market. With a sculptor, she founded a company to
manufacture breast prostheses, and her product, Nearly Me,
became the "Cadillac of the business," generating several million dollars a year.

Arthur Spear spent the first few years after the Handlers left
meeting with three sets of lawyers—criminal, tax, and SEC—
and restoring the company to financial health. He left the toy
business to the toy people, and it flourished, but the MIT engineer never stopped trying to transform Mattel from a toy company into a less volatile, less cyclical, consumer-products company.

He also wasted little time. Six months after the indictments
were issued, Mattel issued a press release. It said, in part:

Hawthorne, California, August 7, 1978—Mattel, Inc. announced
today that Arthur S. Spear, formerly President and Chief Executive Officer of the Company, has been elected Chairman of the
Board of Directors, a position which has been vacant, and continues as Chief Executive Officer of Mattel, Inc.

5

JANUARY–MARCH 1986
How Toymen Deceive Their Boss

"JIM'S IDEA!" LEE VOLPE WROTE IN HIS record book the day he heard about Dino-Riders. "Boys category—Dinosaurs stuff. Dinoriders = tauntauns . . . Good = Plant, Bad = Meateaters . . . Naugahyde animals . . . Action tails . . . flying."

The words and sketches Lee scribbled in his notebook were more than casual reminders to himself. All creative professionals in the toy industry keep logbooks to record and date their ideas. Lee's books are bound in hard cover and embossed "Tyco Industries, Inc. Product Development" on the outside. Sewn inside are two hundred pages of blank graph paper with page numbers printed in boldfaced type at the top, outside corners.

The notebooks are not frills; Tyco is a no-frills operation. Product-development notebooks are designed to make fake insertions practically impossible, so that they can be used as evidence of the progression of ideas. They often serve as a company's first line of defense against the patent-infringement suits that proliferate in the industry. Tyco may never make Naugahyde dinosaurs, but if someone from outside shows Tyco the idea and Tyco later does make them, Lee's notebook constitutes proof that he had already thought of the concept on December 27, 1985.

As soon as they left Woody's office, Mike and Lee headed back to the product-development offices to tell their designers, Warren Bosch and Jack Lovewell, about Jim's idea. By the time they finished, Warren and Jack were just as excited. The fact that they were all already overextended bothered none of them. They were used to it.

Like the rest of Tyco, the product-development staff was lean; Mike always said he had just enough personnel for last year's needs. That meant they were usually behind, but they all preferred it that way. Aware of the industry's cyclical nature—busts follow booms as surely as Tyco's coal cars follow the locomotives—they considered overwork during the good times a small price to pay for the security of knowing they were not likely to be laid off in the bad times.

The department relied heavily on outside design firms, and the arrangement had worked well so far. Instead of expecting one group of employees to be all things to all people, Mike and Lee could select artists, designers, sculptors, and modelmakers for each assignment on the basis of their individual strengths. When they found people they considered exceptionally talented, they had no compunction about trying to steal them. That is how they had hired Warren.

The dinosaur project offered quite a change from their normal work. At that time electric truck, train, and car racing sets accounted for over 60 percent of Tyco's sales. Its only other product line besides blocks was novelty telephones, led by a Garfield phone with eyes that opened when the receiver was lifted.

Mike was too busy to take on any part of the project, although he and Lee loved to sit around at the end of the day and talk about the line and the characters and the background story: the opportunity to create an entire universe does not come along often. Of all of them, Mike had the most experience with large toy companies. He had surprised himself by going to work for Mattel after earning a master's degree in aerospace engineering from Stanford. He had expected to take a "real" job, but after embarrassedly sneaking in for an interview with Mattel's recruiter, he could not resist joining the company's preliminary-design group.

Preliminary design was Mattel's prestigious blue-sky research area; even getting onto its floor required security clearance and special badges. After working there for a few years, Mike had decided that the tight security was not really to keep the competition out; it was to keep the rest of the world from seeing how bizarre the inventors really were. In his three years at Mattel the group's activities included

- staging frequent water-gun fights
- rigging up boots and pants in every booth of every men's room at Mattel, so that there was a line at the gas station across the street by 10:30 in the morning
- putting bottomless Kentucky Fried Chicken containers filled with ball bearings on people's desks and waiting for them to get back from lunch and pick them up
- convincing their department head that they had created a urine-acid battery (a Ziploc bag with yellow fluid and two wires) that caused a propeller to rotate. (The real reason the propeller moved was that it was strategically placed to catch the breeze from the air conditioner.)

Mike had moved from Mattel to Fisher-Price to Tyco. As head of the department he was too busy to do any hands-on work, but everyone else had an assignment. Warren researched the dinosaurs, Jack dreamed up weapons and accessories, and Lee appointed himself chief story editor.

Lee Volpe's industrial design background complemented Mike's technological expertise. Tall and bearded, Lee favors aviator sunglasses and flights of verbal fancy. Away from work he zooms around on his motorcycle in a Darth Vader–like helmet he designed himself. He once tried to interest fellow motorcycle enthusiast Steve McQueen in manufacturing the helmet, but the actor turned him down.

Warren Bosch, whose father had been a tin-toy designer, was

delighted with his assignment. Warren assumed he had been the only child in America not interested in dinosaurs, and when he began reading up on them, he was fascinated. He had thought dinosaurs were sedentary, gray, lifeless reptiles, but he learned that many paleontologists now suspect they were much more energetic; some believe they were brightly colored, like birds.

Warren quickly became attached to the dinosaurs, and early in his research he suggested that Tyco aim for museum-quality accuracy in its products. The others liked the idea and agreed immediately. They all understood that attempting scientific accuracy would almost certainly create problems, but they considered it worth the effort.

Soon the idea became the centerpiece of the Dino-Riders concept, providing it with an integrity, at least in the minds of its creators, that they had an obligation to protect. Through all the months that followed, Warren or Lee or Woody or Jim would frequently argue against an idea if he thought it violated the dinosaurs' authenticity. "That's not accurate" or "Dinosaurs didn't do that" or "They didn't look that way" or "These are supposed to be museum quality, guys" was always reason enough to reject suggestions that would make the product too cute or too fierce or too stylized in any way.

They often assured each other that authenticity was going to be an important selling point for the product: when children grew tired of playing with the dinosaurs as toys, they would still have good-looking, high-quality replicas. Adorable beasts would not appeal to their target market, five- to ten-year-old boys, anyway. But their reasons were really just rationalizations. The truth was, they had fallen in love with the idea of scientifically accurate dinosaurs, though none of them ever admitted that the decision was anything less than cold, logical reasoning. A decision based on emotion is a pitfall feared by everyone in the industry.

Eventually they became so obsessed with scientific accuracy that in their minds it became *the* defining characteristic of their product. Every time they heard about a new dinosaur-based product—which happened too frequently for comfort—they would worry until they could get a sample. Then they would inspect it, scornfully point out all its scientific inaccuracies to one another, and sigh with relief. Any product that looked more like a toy than a dinosaur they did not consider competition.

Warren pored over his dinosaur books while he waited for Woody to send him a marketing plan. The job of the product-development department is to design the products defined by marketing. The marketing people generally give the designers a target market, a list of products, and prices for the items. The list Woody sent down sounded like an order at a Chinese restaurant: "I'll take two assortments of three dinosaurs each that we can sell for $6.25, a mid-price assortment of two at $12.99, and a deluxe *Tyrannosaurus* at $21.99." Woody was most concerned about the department's ability to deliver a product that could retail for under $10.00 and still give the customer some value.

Determining price points is no small feat. Woody looked at the two ends and came up with the middle. He was squeezed from above, because he had to keep Tyco's selling price low enough to leave room for retailers to sell the items at prices their customers would consider reasonable and still make a profit. At the same time he was pressed from below, because Tyco had to keep production costs low enough to allow for the expenses of advertising, promotion, and shipping and still make a profit itself.

The retail price that the consumer will consider reasonable is a function of many variables, not the least of which is the price of the competition. If action-figure vehicles on the toy-store shelves cost $3.98 and Tyco wants to sell a dinosaur for $8.00 to $13.00, the company will have to make its product seem two to three times as valuable. Value is difficult to define and impossible to predict, and it can be created by something as simple as an effective commercial. That is why pricing products is neither art nor science. It is gut feel, sometimes accompanied by a little testing.

In addition to the products' selling prices, Woody gave Warren target costs, which he derived from his gross-margin target of 55 percent. He wanted to be able to produce low-end dinosaurs costed at $2.82, which Tyco would wholesale for $6.25. The gross margin, which often shrinks during the development period anyway, is further reduced by the advertising (which Woody set at 18 percent of estimated sales), plus sundry other marketing and administrative costs. Promotional toys traditionally have what one successful practitioner calls "sinful" margins. They have to, in order to make up for all the failures. (Contrary to the popular assumption, promotional toys are no worse a deal than nonpromotional toys. They simply enrich different parties. They may deliver sinful margins to the manufacturers, but not to the retailers. Retailers have to meet their competitors' prices on heavily advertised products, so the popular toys often become loss leaders used to build traffic. Retailers compensate by taking higher markups on nonpromotional toys. The public, therefore, pays for manufacturers' profits and advertising expenses on promotional toys and for manufacturers' profits and retailers' profits on nonpromotional toys.)

Warren marked the price points on a chart on the wall and examined the range of dinosaur species to find appropriate candidates for each. From a product point of view dinosaurs were perfect: nature offered him an enormous variety of sizes and shapes. He decided to start by listing the most widely known species. When a kid thinks of dinosaurs, he asked himself, what comes to mind? He did not want to select anything too obscure. The last thing Tyco wanted, he explained to the others, was some kid saying, "I don't know what that is, but it sure doesn't look like a dinosaur to me." He checked with his six-year-old son, who confirmed the obvious ones, and he perused comic books and watched the news media to see what dinosaur species were prominent.

He estimated the cost of an eight-inch dinosaur and put it in the middle price range. That set the low-end products at about six inches and the high-end ones at about a foot. Next he had to determine the scale. Since he wanted all the components accurate in relation to one another, he had to consider the human action figures. They had to be large enough to look and feel like something worthwhile but small enough so that he would not have to make the dinosaurs huge. He would never be able to make huge dinosaurs at the price points Woody wanted.

Tyco's timing was fortuitous. Kenner Toys had recently established a new scale for action figures with its MASK line. Matt

Trakker, leader of the Mobile Armored Strike Command peace-keeping unit, and his archenemy, Miles Mayhem, head of VENOM (the Vicious Evil Network of Mayhem), were about two-and-three-quarter inches high. If Warren used that size for the human figures, he could portray the dinosaurs fairly accurately in relation to the humans and stay in the right price range. He realized that taking a few liberties was going to be unavoidable. The *Diplodocus* was so large in proportion to the others that if they wanted one, they would have to make it a baby *Diplodocus*.

Warren already had a favorite dinosaur, a fairly new discovery called the *Deinonychus*. Nike, as Warren promptly dubbed him, was mean, nasty, full of personality, and very fast. Warren wanted the Dino-Riders to use him as an all-purpose vehicle, a sort of cross between a quarterhorse and a jeep, and when they needed extra speed, they could add a high-tech touch by attaching a jet pack.

Meanwhile Jack Lovewell, probably the most mild-mannered, self-effacing person in the entire company, turned into a one-man armaments factory. Page after page of weaponry came flying off his desk: laser guns and missiles for firing from the dinosaurs, saddles and sidepods for riding them, maces and swords for hand-to-hand combat. The entire group believed that the innate appeal of dinosaurs was the project's strongest feature, but they considered the combination of the past—dinosaurs—with the future—spacemen—almost as powerful. By bringing technologically sophisticated people back from the future, they could arm them with any weapon used throughout history, from clubs to maces to laser guns, or anything else they cared to invent.

One day in January, Jim, Woody, Mike, Lee, and Warren met in the downstairs cafeteria to plan their presentation. The situation was ticklish. Dick had specifically told Jim to stay away from action-figure products, so they were going to be saying, in essence, Here's what you told us not to work on. But Dick had also said he wanted strong diversification opportunities, and they concluded that if they could convince him that Dino-Riders was a strong concept, he would not care about the category.

They considered a tightly planned presentation essential to

outflank a very powerful personality. "We know how Dick can take over a meeting," Jim pointed out, "and we have to do everything we can to prevent it. We've got to structure the meeting so we can get out everything we want to say in one shot. We don't want him jumping to the back page of a report when we're only halfway through, or interrupting us, or leaving to take a telephone call."

They planned a multimedia approach. Warren would open with the histories of dinosaur and action-figure products. Then someone would read a background story about the Dino-Riders. After that they would show Jack's drawings of dinosaurs, heroes, and villains and follow them with slides of more elaborate renderings of three dinosaurs and accompanying figures. All of this would culminate in an exciting climax. "Dick reacts better to 3-D [three-dimensional objects] than 2-D [two-dimensional drawings]," they agreed, "so let's show him three dinosaur models and three figures." They eventually scaled down their rather grandiose plan.

They knew they had to control the cost of the presentation, because Dick was a notorious tightwad. "We've got to spend just enough to sell it to Dick, but not a penny more," Jim reminded them. If Dick liked the idea, they would all be heroes; if he didn't, whatever they had spent would be too much. To minimize their risk they aimed for a level that might be criticized as "overenthusiastic" (an offense they figured Dick would forgive) but not "irresponsible" (a capital crime, at the least).

Throughout this flurry of clandestine activity, the target of imminent assault went serenely about his business. Like Jim Alley and Warren Bosch, Dick Grey is the son of a toyman. Even better, he is a second-generation Tyco man. His father, Milt Grey, ran a highly successful national sales and marketing operation for hobby products and directed Tyco's marketing activities for many years.

Tyco was founded by John N. Tyler in his Mantua, New Jersey, garage in 1926. Originally called Mantua Metal Products, the company produced H-O model trains, tracks, and accessories for model-railroad buffs. Assembling models from hobby kits was a popular activity in those days, although the kits were a small category compared with the electric train market as a whole.

The earliest electric trains were made in several different sizes, but as they increased in popularity they became more standardized, ultimately converging on the O-gauge design, which made a circle of track six feet in diameter. Over the years, hobbyists became interested in running their models as well as assembling them, so the models also began to become standardized. Hobbyists found that the smallest practical size they could build models and still have enough room for details was approximately half the width of the O-gauge track. They called it half-O and then simply H-O.

Preassembled electric train sets, bought usually for children (at least ostensibly), have been around since the nineteenth century. Mantua Metal Products is an unfamiliar name, but anyone who has heard of electric trains has heard the name Lionel. Joshua Lionel Cowen turned the electric train into an American toy classic. Born in New York City in 1877, Cowen always liked to tinker and developed a fuse used by the U.S. Navy to explode mines. Bored with that, he experimented with battery and light bulb combinations and invented a device for lighting plants in hotel lobbies. Bored again, he gave the idea to a salesman who was peddling the product for him. The salesman applied the device to a wider range of uses and eventually made his fortune founding the Eveready Battery Company.

Meanwhile Cowen constructed a small electric motor and, looking for something to do with it, built a small train. Displayed in a novelty shop, the first model sold immediately, and by 1903 Cowen was issuing a catalog and adding increasingly accurate miniature versions of railroad stock.

Lionel Trains eventually fell on hard times and passed through a series of owners, including notorious attorney Roy Cohn. A few years ago it was bought by an avid model-train collector, Michigan real estate magnate Richard Kughn. Kughn's friends used to tease him about the size of his collection and ask him why he didn't buy the entire company. In 1986 Kenner Parker put Lionel up for sale, and he did just that.

If it were not for Milt Grey, Mantua would probably still be placidly turning out meticulously detailed kits for dedicated hobbyists. Hobby products were traditionally sold in department stores and hobby stores, but shortly after World War II Milt Grey had noted the growing importance of discounters and national chains, and he began urging Tyler to offer ready-to-run H-O trains instead of kits. He believed that the smaller H-O trains would attract toy buyers for the same reason they appealed to hobbyists: they took up less space than the O-gauge trains without sacrificing accuracy of detail.

Others agreed with him, but the idea was controversial. Some members of the industry thought the little trains would be too fragile for a mass-market toy, and others feared they would cheapen the image of the model-making kits. Tyler overrode all objections and followed Grey's advice, although he found the transition more difficult and more expensive than he had anticipated. To make money on a product that had to be assembled in the factory instead of by a hobbyist, the company had to revamp completely both its product and its production process. But ready-to-run H-O trains were immediately so successful that it was worth it. Everyone who could make them jumped in, including Lionel and Louis Marx. The competition led to price wars that drove several of the operators out of business, but Mantua was among the survivors.

Mantua waited over ten years before diversifying again. Then, in the 1960s, Mantua not only added electric road racing sets, it also changed its name to Tyco, which was what everyone had called the company for years.

In 1970 the Tyler family sold Tyco to Consolidated Foods, a conglomerate that eventually changed its name to Sara Lee Corporation. Within two years the manager Sara Lee had hired was running Tyco into the red and lying about the figures. Sara Lee's managers were astute enough to realize that they needed someone with some industry experience, so in 1973 they hired thirty-nine-year-old Dick Grey as president and twenty-nine-year-old Harry Pearce as chief financial officer. Grey had been running Tyco's marketing with his father since 1958, and Pearce had been the company's auditor. At that point Tyco's sales stood at $25 million and the young Sara Lee executive in charge had to decide whether to order the two to close it down or give them a chance to rescue the company. John Bryan, who went on to become chairman of Sara Lee, decided to give Tyco a chance.

In two years the pair turned the company around, but by 1981 Sara Lee was selling off subsidiaries, and it sold Tyco for $18.6 million. Tyco's new owner was Savoy Industries, a small, publicly held corporation that acquires companies in leveraged buyouts, restructures them, and sells them to the public. The new owners kept Grey and Pearce on and let them operate fairly autonomously.

The overall size of the electric train market had been declining for years, and Tyco's sales eroded further when electronic toys became popular in the late 1970s. Worried about Tyco's dependency on trains, Grey searched for ways to diversify. Popular wisdom attributed the fall in train sales to the diminishing importance of trains in everyday American life, so by 1981 Tyco thought it had the answer: trucks. Children saw trucks all the time, so Tyco introduced U.S. 1 Electric Trucking sets as the "trains of the eighties." The product succeeded immediately, and they congratulated themselves on their ability to create a new classic.

They were a little premature. About two-and-a-half years later the trains of the eighties began to lose their momentum, and the group at Tyco was mystified. After spending months searching for the flaw in their theory, they finally concluded that they had not created the next electric train; they had caught the crest of a wave of interest in trucking. CB radios and *Smokey and the Bandit* movies had been popular at that time, and Tyco had benefited from the fad. They had not been as smart as they had thought, just lucky.

In January 1983 Dick Grey led his group to the annual hobby show in Dallas. Unlike the New York Toy Fair, in which the showrooms are closed except by invitation, the hobby show is supposed to be open, so when Tyco's president saw curtains around Aurora Toys' booth, he went straight to the show's management to protest. Aurora was Tyco's archrival in racing car sets, and he wanted to see what it was hiding behind the curtains. When Aurora was forced to open its booth, Tyco was stunned. Aurora had attached track to the walls vertically, and its racing cars traveled straight up, at a ninety-degree angle.

Dick had to have it for Tyco. He turned to Mike Hirtle. "Can you make a car do that?" he asked. Mike suspected he could. Dick told him to get it ready for Toy Fair—which was only nine days away.

When Toy Fair 1983 opened in New York, Tyco had a vehicle, a package, and a commercial. Cliff Hangers sold strongly at Toy Fair, and Tyco delivered its product earlier than Aurora did. Aurora sued Tyco, lost, and went bankrupt shortly afterward. Tyco extended the line year after year to include Cliff Hangers with Nite Glow, Super Cliff Hangers with Nite Glow (they race upside down and go through the Giant Loop), and Daredevil Cliff Hangers (they include the Daredevil Jump). By 1986 Tyco was running out of Cliff Hanger car embellishments, so that year Mike's group started making trains that could run up the walls.

After Toy Fair 1986, the Dino-Riders plotters were so preoccupied with their secret that they paid little attention to an important milestone in Tyco's history: on February 20 Tyco went public. Savoy sold its shares over the counter for $13.4 million, not a bad return on a 1981 cash outlay of $3 million. Although Savoy relinquished its ownership, the Savoy investors retained tight control of Tyco's board.

There was little time to savor Tyco's status as a public company. Jim had set March 7 for the meeting with Dick, and the next few weeks flew by.

No one awaited that meeting with more excitement—and anxiety—than C. Woodrow Browne. Woody, who looks like every other Woody in America—fair, with a bony face and rapidly receding hair—has always been ambitious. At the same time, he treasures his reputation as the corporate wild man. He scowls frequently, complains at the slightest provocation, and never hesitates to take on Dick Grey, although he esteems him highly. Woody delivers his best lines in perfect deadpan. "I have a mole at Tonka," he amiably tells a reporter while everyone around him freezes. "He talks only to me, and very few people at Tyco know about him. He tells me everything he knows and

I give him advice. . . . His name is Steve Shank." Everyone relaxes—sort of. Steve Shank is chairman of Tonka.

Woody saw Dino-Riders as the opportunity of his career and threw himself into every step of the project. "If Dick doesn't like it," he told Jim often in the weeks preceding the presentation, "you and I are going to quit and take this to Hasbro." He never doubted that he could manage the product, even though it was far more complex than the Tonka trucks or Thermos lunch-boxes in his past. It's complicated, but it isn't brain surgery, he reassured himself.

The meeting date finally arrived. This was supposedly a normal new-products review meeting, so the chiefs of sales, manufacturing, engineering, and advertising would all be there. The only member of top management not usually at the new-products meetings is Harry Pearce, head of finance and second in command of the corporation, although he is shown the products eventually as a courtesy.

The excitement of the presenting group, which was unusually large, was obvious. Jim, Warren, Lee, Mike, and Woody had speaking parts, and Jack Lovewell and another artist were hanging around the hallway. Once everyone was seated (as they say at Tyco, "everyone" means Dick), Jim stood up and said simply, "We have something to show you." He sat down, the lights were turned off, and Warren began.

"Dinosaurs have been a popular theme for toys for many years," he began nervously. Then the weeks of preparation took over, and he relaxed. He interspersed slides of every dinosaur toy he had found with newspaper quotations and polls attesting to the undying appeal of dinosaurs. Woody narrated the second part of the slide show, on the history of action figures. After that the lights went on and Mike tied the two strands neatly together by reading a short, simple background story. The essential facts were as follows:

> Far in the future, some aliens from Sauresia fight for their lives against evil invaders called Rulons. The Sauresians escape through a time warp with no control over where they will come out. When they emerge from their spaceship they find themselves on earth 65,000,000 years ago.

The planet is full of dinosaurs, and they begin to make friends with them. The evil Rulons also land there, so the Sauresians have to keep fighting, and both sides utilize the dinosaurs as mounts, weapons-carriers, and vehicles. The Rulons enslave the dinosaurs with Brain Boxes that turn them into automatons, while the Sauresians work with the dinosaurs as partners and communicate with them telepathically.

The Sauresians, who realize they have left their planet behind forever, rename themselves Dino-Riders in honor of their reptilian comrades.

When the story ended, Warren and Jack marched into the room carrying a stack of Jack's drawings and began tacking them up on the walls. The centerpiece was a large pastel battle scene depicting nine different species of dinosaurs and one woolly mammoth. Each was loaded with individually tailored battle regalia and labeled with a name and price. Lee described the individual items in the prospective line.

In the center of the conference table in front of Dick, they carefully placed a small object covered with a draping cloth. When they felt Dick had absorbed the two-dimensional renderings, they drew the cloth away with great flourish to reveal . . . a *Deinonychus*. Warren, an exceptional modelmaker, had lovingly sculpted and painted the first three-dimensionalization of their concept.

Michelangelo admiring his David could not have looked prouder than did the members of that presenting group as they gazed reverentially at Warren's homely little six-inch sculpture. Like kindergartners proudly pushing their "art" toward their parents, they eyed Dick hopefully.

Woody wound up by describing the product line they proposed; the spin-offs, such as licensing, movies, and books; and a marketing plan for years one, two, and three of the product's life.

Then they waited.

This was one of the times Dick remained totally impassive. He sat there wearing his poker face throughout the entire performance, letting the speakers say their parts without giving them the slightest hint of what he was thinking.

Not until they were completely finished did he allow his biggest smile to break through, the one that lights up his entire face. Then he stood up, all alone, and applauded. Finally, he gave them his highest accolade:

"Guys," said "everyone," "that's goddamn sensational!"

6

TOYLAND CASHES IN ITS CHIPS

Parents Fear Games Turn Their Kids into Zombies
Wall Street Journal, March 8, 1988

PARENTS CAN BE IMPOSSIBLE TO PLEASE. First they complain that heavily promoted toys lack play value. They say that television toys are so functionless that the only thing their children can do with them is possess them. Then, they say, the kids quickly tire of them and move restlessly on, wanting the next toy they see on television.

Then, when a product comes along that really holds children's interest, parents complain about that too. It seems that too much play value can also be a problem. The games described in the *Wall Street Journal* headline (above) are Nintendo video games. Nintendo is a Japanese electronics company whose American subsidiary has been infiltrating American homes with its little gray boxes—an estimated 21 percent of American homes by the end of 1989. The little gray boxes hook up to a television set, enabling children to play a variety of intriguing, fascinating, mesmerizing games. In fact, the games seem to be habit-forming to the point of addiction.

"Mom can't get me out of my room," explained a fourteen-year-old boy to the *Journal's* reporter. He heads the neighborhood club Fanatic About Nintendo Games (FANG). An eleven-year-old's mother did more than get him out of his room: she banned the game completely when she learned that her son played for fourteen hours straight at a friend's house. "It's like I want to stop, but I can't help myself," he told her.

These game addicts, mostly boys eight to eighteen years old, cannot resist the pull of one of the most compelling forms of entertainment ever invented. Television proved its power as an advertising medium for toys in the 1950s. In the 1970s television became a toy itself. By attaching video game hardware to their television sets, the players became participants in the action, able to interact with the vivid audiovisual images on their screens instead of just viewing them passively. No longer must they simply watch a chase scene, an athletic contest, or a fight; now they can be the pursuer, the track star, the pugilist.

The zombification of their children dismays parents, but evidently not enough for them to ban the games. In 1986 new video game sets entered 1.4 million American households. Nintendo's share was 1.1 million. In 1987, 4.1 million more were sold; Nintendo sold 3 million, and the rest were sold by Atari and another Japanese company, Sega. In 1988 Nintendo enjoyed $1.2 billion in sales in the United States alone. By comparison, Hasbro, the largest American toy corporation, with hundreds of different toys, generated $1.3 billion in total sales worldwide. Many of Nintendo's dollars were dollars diverted from Hasbro, Mattel, Kenner, and other toy companies that hoped to sell several hundred million dollars' worth of boys' toys. Action-figure product shipments dropped from $702 million in 1987 to $523 million in 1988, and the age span of the figures' market seemed to shrink, leaving mostly the younger boys. Many of the eight- to ten-year-olds abandoned action figures to plug into Nintendo.

Hit toys are regarded as generally helpful to the industry because they generate more year-round traffic in the stores, but video games are "selfish" toys: customers who cannot find the game cartridge they seek will not spend the forty dollars (or even twenty dollars) on something else. Nintendo's success, therefore, is viewed more as a curse than a blessing in Toyland, and the manufacturers cannot wait for the games' hold to weaken so that some of those dollars will flow back in their direction. Meanwhile, they try to make the best of it by licensing the right to make Nintendo game cartridges or turning more of their efforts to girls' toys. Nintendo was one of the reasons the 1989 Toy Fair looked like a hospital nursery; the manufacturers created a baby-doll boom because they were temporarily giving up on the boys.

The craze for Nintendo is really Video Game Madness, Part II. The industry has been there before. Only the name of the leader has changed.

Part I, 1978–1983, was one of the most dramatic episodes in the history of the toy business. It rearranged the landscape of Toyland as effectively as an earthquake. Some companies went out of business. Hundreds of people lost their jobs. Mattel was superseded as industry leader, possibly forever.

There were tremors beforehand. Video games—the electronic games that hook up to a television set—were just a part of the industry-wide electronics revolution. The story is not a simple boom-and-bust chronology; it is a welter of many boom-and-bust stories, and they overlap one another. Demand for individual products came and went. Markets for whole categories exploded and then evaporated. Fortunes of companies rose and fell, sometimes more than once.

The era began in 1976 with simple products like air hockey and self-enclosed, arcade-style shooting games like Star Trek Electronic Phaser Battle and Tin Pan Alley. The manufacturers called them family entertainment to justify the high prices and were startled when they immediately sold out at retail.

The race to get into electronic products soon became a stampede. The manufacturers and their customers could not believe their luck. They were selling their products at price points they had never seen before. After spending years debating the existence of magic price points like $9.95 (they did not believe the consumer would pay more than $10.00 for a doll, for example), they were selling items for $20.00, $40.00, $100.00. They seemed to forget that the demand would not go on forever. They also forgot that as the level of competition grew, everyone's profit margins would shrink, squeezed by higher promotional expenses as well as price wars.

Mattel entered the fray cautiously. The company was profitable but still mired in legal problems. Its managers knew they wanted to get involved in electronics, but they were not sure how. They put several people to work on it and came up with a new kind of product, self-enclosed, hand-held electronic games. The first two they made were Auto Race and Football, and both sold out immediately. In 1977 the total hand-held electronics market was $22 million.

Within two years the total market was about $375 million, and Mattel had grown less cautious. In 1977 the demand for its games exceeded supply by 100,000 units. In 1978 the company sold 2 million units and still came nowhere near meeting the demand. It sold $93 million worth of electronic products in the United States alone in 1979 and another $10 million overseas. In its 1980 annual report (which covered most of 1979, since Mattel's 1980 fiscal year ended February 2, 1980) the company modestly explained to its shareholders that it had everything under control. "At Mattel, successes such as these do not come by chance. They come as a result of the experienced managing of a broad range of creative and marketing resources, considerable pre-introduction product and market testing and constant post-introduction evaluation."

The entire industry was infatuated with the microchip. Coleco had announced that it was going to be "number one in electronic fun," and its president, Arnold Greenberg, proclaimed electronics "the greatest thing for our industry since the development of plastic." In 1978 a Milton Bradley executive told *Newsweek*, "In the future all games will probably be electronic." In fact, Milton Bradley had one of that year's most successful products. Simon was a follow-the-leader game in which players had to press its panels to duplicate a series of sounds that Simon emitted. It resembled a small flying saucer and beeped in four different tones, depending on which of its four panels was pressed. The game was introduced at a celebrity-filled party at a New York discotheque, Studio 54, and sold out quickly when it went on the market.

Milton Bradley tried to duplicate Simon's success with Milton, which played almost the same game as Simon, except that Milton used words instead of beeps. Players who failed to recall the third word of an expression such as "pluck your turkey" in time would hear "Ha ha ha" or "Garbage." Perhaps Milton was too hostile, for it failed abysmally. Simon is still around, and Milton Bradley still does not know the secret of its success.

Everyone wanted an electronic product in spite of all the risks. Getting stuck with too much inventory was the most obvious danger, but there were others. Microelectronic chip shortages occurred periodically, so the manufacturers had to stock up early. That meant they had to carry large chip inventories and commit themselves to larger production runs than they ordinarily did with toys. Developing electronic products also required longer lead times and cost more. In 1979 a typical board game could be developed for $200,000–$350,000, versus $750,000–$1 million for a simple electronic item. As the competition heated up, the cost of promotion increased dramatically, cutting into profits. Technology also threatened current products. Technological innovation progressed rapidly, and the manufacturers and retailers lived in fear of waking up one morning and finding that their products had become obsolete.

By 1979 the toy industry, in its usual frenzy of feverish imitation, was offering consumers about one hundred different electronic products. In the area of sports alone, there were enough electronic games to occupy fans for the next ten years. Consumers had a choice of at least ten football, eight baseball, seven basketball, four hockey, three soccer, three bowling, two horse-racing, and two auto-racing games, plus golf and boxing. For the less athletically inclined, manufacturers offered one poker and four blackjack games and battle games that featured war in space (nine), at sea (three), and on land (even a gunfight in the old West). There were pinball games, follow-the-leader games, multi-game devices such as Parker Brothers' Merlin and Ideal's Wizard, musical toys, and a multitude of others ranging from Safari to Zap. For the budding intellectual there was Challenger Chess, Amazatron, and Texas Instruments' line of educational toys, including Speak & Spell and Little Professor. Just before Christmas, Russell Baker could not resist offering his idea for a sure seller: "Much, much fun can be had with your new miniaturized electronic MOMMY AND DADDY due to the alacrity with which it responds to your remote-control command module. . . . Unlike your old cumbersome U.S.-made mommy and daddy, MOMMY AND DADDY does not shout and abuse you when you wish to open it and reorganize its miraculous contents more to your liking."

In 1980 the market for hand-held electronic games collapsed. With so many suppliers, the number of products had quadrupled in a year. Retailers had ordered heavily to assure themselves of stock, so they had to slash prices to move it off the shelves. Manufacturers had to advertise heavily to help them, and as a result, everyone's profits disappeared. Retail sales actually rose in 1980, although the retailers had cut or canceled many of their orders by midyear. A few items did very well, including Mego's Fireman Fireman, in which players maneuvered an on-screen fireman to catch babies falling from a burning building in a safety net. If the fireman missed, the baby went "splat" on the ground, and an angel appeared in the corner of the screen. Three angels and the game was over.

Mattel's 1980 operating profit (fiscal 1981) dropped to $16.7 million from $61 million the year before because of high expenditures in electronics, but the company did not seem overly concerned. Mattel had entered the newly emerging video game market in 1980, and its Intellivision system (named for intelligent television) had already generated $21 million in sales. The rage for electronics looked like Mattel's big chance to turn from a toy manufacturer into a consumer-products company. Mattel had already segregated Mattel Electronics into a separate division, and the company planned to move from video game hardware into home computers within a year or two.

It was unfortunate that Mattel passed through the hand-held electronic-games crash of 1980 without paying much attention, because the same sequence would by replayed just two years later with video games. The second time around, the stakes were much higher.

During the same period Coleco, a Connecticut swimming-pool company on its way to becoming a major toy company, experienced not one but two boom-and-bust cycles of electronic products. Coleco also learned nothing. Boom-and-bust was the way Coleco operated. The company would overextend itself and then, on the brink of disaster, another hit product would rescue it just in time.

The Connecticut Leather Company was founded in 1932 by Maurice Greenberg, a Russian emigrant, to sell leather and other supplies to shoe repairers. The year he tried to diversify by selling rubber snowboots, the snow failed to appear. By the 1950s the company had expanded successfully into Mickey Mouse moccasin kits—and then Davy Crockett kits, Howdy Doody Bee-Nee kits, and Chief and Princess handbags. In 1956 it moved into plastic with space helmets, wading pools, and sleds. Plastic was so much more profitable than leather that in 1961 the company sold the leathercraft business, changed its name to Coleco, and went public. Several of the company's acquisitions were successful, but when Coleco again tried to exploit its New England climate by buying a snowmobile company, it again encountered a series of practically snowless winters. Coleco did better with summer: in 1980 it sold $68 million in above-ground swimming pools.

In 1976 Coleco produced Telstar, one of the earliest video games, and watched its sales double from $71 million in 1975 to $137 million in 1977. In 1977 a microchip shortage delayed production until late in the year, however, and then an East Coast dock strike tied up supplies until after the Christmas selling season. By the time Coleco was ready to ship Telstar again, in 1978, the demand had died, and the company had to write off the product for $26.9 million.

Coleco in 1978, like Mattel two years later, was not particularly interested in finding out what had gone wrong with its old product, because it had an exciting new product. Its Head to Head line, hand-held games that could be played by two people, increased the company's sales by 42 percent, and made Coleco one of the few winners in 1980 when the hand-held market was going through a shakeout. By 1981, however, not even the most popular product could penetrate the retailers' overstocked inventories, and Coleco joined the hand-held games bust. Its electronic-product sales dropped to $58.1 million (from $90.4 million in 1980), and the following year looked even worse for hand-held games. Again, Coleco ignored the losses. Its attention was back on video games.

Nolan Bushnell is usually called the father of the video game, but he did not really invent it; he adapted it. The first video game was designed in 1962 by MIT undergraduates for a mainframe computer. Space War allowed two players to maneuver spaceships and fire missiles at each other on a screen, and visitors to MIT were fascinated. Over the next few years Space War was reproduced in campus computer laboratories all over the country and played by thousands of college students. A commercial version was impossible because of the size and cost of mainframe computers.

In 1968 a German refugee working for a military-systems consulting firm in New Hampshire took the next step. Looking at the video display terminal of his computer one day, Ralph Baer had an inspiration. "The thought came to me," he later recalled, "[that] you should be able to do something else with television besides just watch it." By 1970 Baer had sold a video hockey game to Magnavox, and by 1972 Odyssey, the first home video game, was on the market with a retail price of one hundred dollars. Players could play twelve different games, but to do so they had to place different plastic overlays on their television sets. Magnavox threw in cards, dice, and play money and sold 100,000 units.

Meanwhile, on the other side of the nation, in a valley once filled with fruit, thousands of computer scientists worked far into the night. They dream, in Silicon Valley, not of curing cancer but of becoming millionaires. Their heroes are David Packard of Hewlett-Packard or Steven Jobs and Stephen Wozniak, who founded Apple Computer.

Among the night toilers was the man who later became known as King Pong. Tall, bearded, brilliant, and eccentric, Nolan Bushnell had been doing weird things all his life. As a teenager he had attached a one-hundred-watt light bulb to a kite to convince his Utah neighbors they were under attack from enemy aliens. He could not have imagined then how important alien attacks would be in his future. Bushnell had played Space War in college, and now he worked at night to construct a freestanding version of a game that players would pay to play, like coin-operated pinball machines. He called the game Computer Space and designed it to simulate a dogfight between a spaceship and a flying saucer. He was able to get it produced, but it was a commercial failure. It was much too complicated, too geared to the mentality of other computer hackers.

Bushnell realized that a coin-operated game needed to be simple and quickly understandable so that a casual player could start playing without reading complicated directions. In 1972 he and a friend each put up $250 and founded a company they called Atari, and within three months they had Pong, a game that resembled Ping-Pong. Unable to interest pinball manufacturers in making it, Bushnell decided to make it himself. He rented an old roller-skating rink, hired engineers to design more games, and set up a production line. Atari quickly became a Silicon Valley legend, as much for its corporate culture as for its immediate success. The assembly-line workers were 1970s hippies; hot tubs were installed as "think tanks" for the engineers; drugs and sex were rampant.

In three years the company grew from zero to $40 million in sales, and Bushnell wanted to put a home version of Pong up against Odyssey. Sears, Roebuck had helped him manufacture Home Pong in 1975 in exchange for a year's exclusivity, but to expand Home Pong production beyond Sears's market he needed a much larger cash infusion. He tried to sell Atari to Walt Disney, but he settled for Warner Communications, which agreed to buy the company for $28 million, half of which was to go to him.

The deal took longer than expected, because of Bushnell's marital problems. During the negotiations with Warner, an article appeared in a San Francisco newspaper, accompanied by a photograph of Bushnell in a hot tub with a woman friend. Shortly thereafter the ex-Mrs. Bushnell announced that she was going to sue for recision of the divorce settlement, claiming she was entitled to half of Bushnell's stock in Atari (California is a community-property state). Warner had no interest in owning only 75 percent of Atari, so the corporate lawyers spent the next few months helping to renegotiate Bushnell's divorce settlement with his ex-wife's attorneys.

Over the next two years Warner poured millions into Atari to develop and manufacture its Video Computer System (VCS), a home video game system that could play different game cartridges. In 1977 Atari sold about 340,000 units. Its coin-operated video games sales rose 48 percent, and Warner told its shareholders that pinball machines were its next great growth opportunity. At the same time, Warner suggested that Atari might benefit from some professional management, and Bushnell acceded. Once there, Warner's man tried to rein in Atari's freewheeling ways. He tightened the financial controls, instituted regular hours, removed the hot tubs and other perquisites for the engineers, and overrode many of Bushnell's decisions.

After that Bushnell, who was ready to move on anyway, managed to get himself "fired" early in 1979. It was an amicable firing; Bushnell's contract stipulated that if he quit, he would lose his $100,000 salary, so his boss obligingly fired him. He has gone on to make an entire career of entrepreneurial peaks and administrative valleys. As he admits, "I enjoy most the thing I'm working on next. Almost at the time something goes into production I'm ready to turn it over to someone else, because that's when I lose interest—even though there can be a lot of life left in the product."

First he started a chain of restaurants/game parlors called Pizza Time Theaters, built around the idea that the twenty-minute wait for pizza could be utilized to generate profits for the restaurant if the customers spent the time playing coin-operated games. He helped pull the customers in by engineering some electronic robots, including Chuck E. Cheese, a rat with a New Jersey accent. By 1983 the company's sales were up to $150 million but it was expanding too rapidly, and by March 1984 Pizza Time was in Chapter 11 bankruptcy proceedings.

By then Bushnell was on to his next project. He entered the toy business and over the past few years has tried to enrich the world with A. G. Bear, a teddy bear that talks "BearTalk"; Petsters, sound-activated electronic plush animals; Rude Ralph, a vinyl head that makes gross sounds when its eyeball is pulled; and Tech Force and the Moto Monsters, creatures that interact with the television. He also sold Hasbro an interactive game system called N.E.M.O. for Never Ever Mentioned Outside, but after spending $10 million to develop it, Hasbro found that N.E.M.O. would be too expensive to produce and had to write it off.

Warner had owned Atari two years when, in 1978, video games really took off. The catalyst was Space Invaders, a coin-operated arcade game imported from Japan, where it had been so popular it had caused a coin shortage. Space Invaders generated the vogue for arcade games, which soon proliferated in other public places as well: stores, bars, bowling alleys, movie theaters, restaurants. From the beginning, adults who were not playing them were dismayed at the games' mysterious magnetism; the games pulled in customers and their quarters as if by magic. Several communities tried to pass ordinances to keep the arcades out of town. Mesquite, Texas, even took its case to the Supreme Court, but that august body zapped the case back to the lower court.

The arcade craze stimulated the home video game market, and by 1979, the rush was on. Arcade games' technology allowed them more complexity than could be engineered into a home game cartridge, but Atari licensed Space Invaders for its VCS home system, reasoning that if a home game could deliver nine-tenths of the excitement of the arcade game, it would be a winner. It was, and its success triggered the industry practice of licensing the most popular coin-operated games for home systems. By 1980 Atari's sales had more than doubled, from $238.1 million in 1979 to $512.7 million, accounting for about a quarter of Warner's total sales and almost a third of its operating income. The market was so hot that Mattel also sold all it could produce of its new Intellivision video game system, 200,000 sets.

The cartridges were much more profitable than the consoles, so as soon as Atari took off, so did some of its employees. They left and formed their own companies to make game cartridges

for the Atari system. Four Atari game designers and one marketing man from outside Atari gathered $700,000, formed Activi-
sion in 1979, and managed to sell $65.9 million worth of car-
tridges in their first year, for profits of $12.9 million. Atari sued
them but could not stop them. Even Mattel began producing
cartridges for the Atari system.

By 1980 the rage for video games had created a gold-rush
atmosphere. The market tripled in 1981. They were boom times,
and new competitors came flooding in. In addition to Magnavox, Mattel, Coleco, and a company called Astrovision, Emer-
son Radio, Milton Bradley, Commodore, and, later on, even
Atari, were working on new systems. A group of executives left
Mattel Electronics and started General Consumer Electronics
Corporation to offer a two-hundred-dollar machine with a
screen of its own.

Large corporations tried to get in any way they could. Fore-
casters were predicting that the boom would last until 1985 and
that the game systems' 10 percent penetration of American
households would grow to 50 percent before saturation set in.
Fisher-Price bought U.S. Games. CBS set up a licensing agreement with Bally and bought Ideal Toys to use as a distribution
network. Parker Brothers had a hit game when it licensed
Frogger, and its corporate parent, General Mills, pushed the
company to produce twenty more.

Every major movie studio wanted in on the action, although
none knew quite what route to take. While movies were generating less than $3 billion at the box office, estimates on the
revenues from home video games and quarter-munching arcade
games ranged as high as $8 billion. Twentieth Century Fox
entered a joint venture with Sirius, a computer game manufacturer, and planned to bring out games based on some of its hits,
such as *9 to 5* and *Porky's*. MCA wanted to do the same with
Dracula, Jaws, and *Frankenstein*. Even the Children's Television
Workshop, producer of "Sesame Street," teamed up with Atari
to form the Children's Computer Workshop.

Anyone who could scrape together a few chips was fielding a
game. Games By Apollo was founded by an ex-disc jockey who
owned an educational film company in Texas. As he was look-

ing at a football cartridge for his Intellivision set, the economics of the video game business suddenly hit him. He told *Fortune* magazine a year later, "I knew what the box cost and I knew what plastic cost. I didn't know what was inside the cartridge, but it sure couldn't cost $39." He hired a computer programmer from Iowa who had reverse-engineered Atari's system (figured out how it worked by analyzing its chips) and the two of them developed a game. The day after Thanksgiving he put his film company people to work assembling the cartridges, shipped $200,000 worth of Skeet Shoot by Christmas, and by 1982 had generated $8 million by selling a dozen more games, including one called Lost Luggage, which simulated that exasperating airport experience. A company called American Multiple Industries offered something different. Its Mystique Presents Swedish Erotica line included a Swedish folk hero called General Custer, who had to dodge cacti and arrows to reach an Indian maiden. Bachelor Party and Beat 'Em & Eat 'Em were other selections from the X-rated line.

The pinnacle of madness may have been the day Pac-Man became a national hero. Bally's Midway, the coin-operated–machine leader, had licensed the maze game from the Japanese company Sega and had sold 96,000 of the arcade games in 1981, generating over $200 million. Pac-Man, which is credited with getting women interested in video games even before the addition of Ms. Pac-Man, was the first and only video game dot to become a popular personality. By 1982 thirty companies had legally sublicensed the gobbling creature, and it soon adorned pajamas, mugs, wrapping paper, and watches. Pac-Man even had his own television program. Atari bought the rights to make a game cartridge, introduced it on April 3 (which it had declared National Pac-Man Day), and eventually sold over $2 million. Coleco brought out a tabletop arcade game at $55. Milton Bradley created a Pac-Man board game, too, using marbles as the dots.

Coleco rolled out three different products for the video game market in 1982, and all were successful. It diverted its money-losing hand-held games production to what it called tabletop arcade games. These were miniature versions of arcade games, complete with tiny screens and joysticks (toggle switches). They were unique, and Coleco had managed to license four of the currently most popular games: Pac-Man, Frogger, Galaxian, and Donkey Kong (in which a monkey rescued a maiden in distress). Coleco's second product line consisted of cartridges for the Mattel and Atari systems. The most important of the new products was ColecoVision. Coleco's entry into the hardware market was positioned as the third-generation video game, supposedly superseding Atari's VCS and Mattel's Intellivision, and the company announced that ColecoVision would be expandable into a personal computer in the future.

But early in 1982 the storm clouds began to gather. No one doubted that the video game boom would continue, but there had been rumbles. A Parker Brothers study indicated that video game hardware was reaching the saturation point. The competition among cartridges had become so intense that advertising expenditures were shooting up. Some gamemakers estimated that they needed to spend $3 million per game on advertising. Mattel spent $21.1 million on advertising in the first nine months of 1982 versus $8.5 million for all of 1981—and the upcoming fourth quarter was traditionally the heaviest advertising period. A shakeout among competitors looked imminent, but everyone expected the overall demand to keep growing. New suppliers kept flooding in. In June a retailer had a choice of one hundred different game cartridges; by September, four hundred.

On December 8, 1982—the day after the anniversary of Pearl Harbor—Warner Communications dropped its own bomb. Citing a slump in cartridge sales, the company announced that its fourth-quarter earnings would rise only 10 to 15 percent. The projected 10 to 15 percent rise was interpreted by all as a disaster; 50 percent had been expected for the year. The next day investors unloaded so much Warner stock that it dropped 16¼ points in a day, the most actively traded security on the New York Stock Exchange. The stock that had risen to a high of 53⅞ on Wednesday, December 7, closed Friday, December 9, at 30¾. Outraged shareholders filed suit. They considered it inconceivable that Warner could not have known what was going on.

Warner took all the related stocks down with it. Mattel lost nearly a third of its value in heavy trading and stayed down, as did Texas Instruments and General Instruments, makers of silicon chips. Toys "R" Us, Commodore, Tandy, and Coleco also dropped, although they later recovered. A game cartridge company about to go public, Imagic, postponed its initial offering until the market conditions were "clarified."

The boom had peaked. Players were losing interest. Retail chains such as K mart, which had installed arcade rooms in two hundred of its stores, were taking them out. The average weekly income for a coin-operated game dropped from $140 in 1981 to $109 in 1982. Many thought the boom ended because the games had become boring. "Once you'd done Pac-Man, you didn't need another maze game," recalls one industry observer. "Pac-Man was the perfect maze game." Video game parlors, which had doubled between 1980 and 1982 to ten thousand, shrank by about 15 percent in 1983. Even those that kept their doors open watched their profits shrink faster than their sales as they offered special deals to generate volume.

The hardware producers were not immediately upset in 1982; they believed they were on top of the situation. They figured that consumers were getting more interested in personal computers, which could be used for other things as well as for games, and Mattel and Coleco both thought they could solve the problem of declining hardware sales with . . . more hardware. They were going into the computer business.

At the Consumer Electronics Show in June 1983, home computers were the hot product, and one of the hottest was Coleco's ADAM. Priced to sell for only six hundred dollars, the 80-K machine came equipped with its own letter-quality printer and some software. It looked like a wonderful product at an outstanding price. Unfortunately, ADAM encountered every conceivable kind of problem in its short but unhappy life. Coleco rushed it to market. The company had been working on ADAM for only nine months when it exhibited at the June show, but it promised to deliver 500,000 machines in plenty of time for Christmas. By September it had orders for 400,000, but ADAM was still not ready. To quell rumors, Coleco invited financial analysts and journalists to its Hartford, Connecticut, headquarters for a demonstration of samples, which the company insisted had been taken right off its assembly line.

Later the same month Coleco postponed shipment for the third time. Television advertising was scheduled to begin in mid-October, so the retailers were getting nervous. Their fears were not alleviated when Coleco's president, Arnold Greenberg, announced that the 400,000 machines on order were not going to be returnable. Nor did it help when Coleco sought to placate its customers by pointing out that the delay would give the company time "to run the instructions past focus groups to make sure the product's instructions are easily understood by the buying public." It seemed like a strange time to be reading the directions.

The first ADAMs finally left the factory the third week in October. Greenberg tried to gloss over the delay by explaining, "ADAM is much more than a Christmas product. Computers generally sell throughout the year, and ADAM should prove to be no exception." Faced with reports of high defect rates, Coleco (which in the past had never had much of a reputation for veracity) flew analysts and journalists back in December, this time to their Amsterdam, New York, plant to see the assembly lines for themselves. Greenberg told them that shipments were running at two thousand a day.

Nineteen eighty-three was disastrous. Coleco sold 1.5 million more ColecoVision sets, but tabletop game sales dropped by two-thirds. Its total electronics sales rose, but expenses had skyrocketed. Coleco had spent over $29 million on product development, mostly in electronics, and $34 million on capital expansion, mostly related to ADAM, and it had to carry the extremely expensive electronics inventory at all stages of production.

As a result, Coleco lost $24.8 million before taxes in 1983, for an after-tax loss of $0.48 a share versus a $2.90 per share profit the previous year. Coleco expected to make up the loss through ADAM sales, but the extent to which electronics was bleeding the company can be appreciated only if one more fact is noted: that same year the company had the most successful doll introduction in the history of the toy business.

The next year was even worse. While Cabbage Patch Kids

products generated $540 million in sales and $208.6 million in operating profits, consumer electronics lost the company $258.6 million (1984 net loss per share: $4.95) because Coleco wrote off ADAM. Toys "R" Us, Zayre Corporation, Best Products, Lionel Leisure, and Kay-Bee Toys bought the remaining inventory early in 1985 and sold the leftover ADAMs for about $300 each.

Mattel bled red ink too, and there was no Cabbage Patch Kid to soak it up.

In 1982 Mattel Electronics had practically doubled its sales, but profits sank from a quarter of sales to 12.1 percent as Mattel fought for its share of the market. The company had to boost advertising, promotion, discounts, and research and development, all in an effort to sell in to the trade and sell the products through at retail. The electronics staff had also quadrupled in one year, nearly tripling general and administrative expenses. As a result, Mattel Electronics lost $28.2 million in its fourth quarter compared with 1981 operating profits of $45.1 million. Mattel also introduced a home computer, Aquarius, at the January 1983 Consumer Electronics Show, but it never generated the same excitement as ADAM did.

Après 1982, *le déluge.* As Josh Denham, who was Mattel Electronics' president, recalls, "We never caught up with demand until it dropped dead." Consumers were buying Intellivision in the stores, but distributors and retailers had so much inventory they didn't need any more from Mattel. Only by pushing shipments overseas was Mattel able to show any sales at all. In the second quarter electronics sales slid to a miserable $3.5 million versus $124.9 million the previous year, and the operating losses for the quarter mounted to $166.7 million.

By then the company had completed massive layoffs, and it began to backpedal on the Aquarius. The electronics business was pulling the entire company into insolvency. When it announced third-quarter earnings—or, rather, losses—Mattel added ominously that it was continuing to operate under a recently negotiated interim-financing agreement with its domestic banks, which would continue "until replaced or until four or more banks holding 25% or more of the outstanding domestic bank debt demand payment."

By the end of the fiscal year, it was all over. On February 3,

1984, Mattel announced that it was selling Mattel Electronics for $20 million to a new company formed by one of the division's senior vice presidents. It also had to unload all its other subsidiaries at fire-sale prices. By necessity, Mattel went back to its roots. When its annual report appeared in April, the financial statements isolated the pathetic electronics figures like lepers and noted, "As reflected throughout this Annual Report, the story of Mattel now becomes the story of Mattel Toys." For the first time in years there were pictures of toys on the report's cover.

Mattel's chairman, Arthur Spear, had been trying to lessen Mattel's dependence on toys ever since he had taken control in 1974. It was ironic—and fortuitous—that toys had been enjoying a phenomenal run for the past six years, while the rest of the company had been mesmerized by electronics. Operating profits on toys had risen 55, 49, and 36 percent in the three previous years, and sales in the last year had increased 24 percent.

Buried at the bottom of the 1983 figures (fiscal year 1984) was the cost of all the rest, lumped together as discontinued operations. Toys: sales $633.4 million, operating profits $81.4 million, earnings per share $0.57 (and that even included some interest charges arising from electronics); losses from discontinued operations: $420.7 million, of which $361 million was attributable to electronics.

Barbie was back.

Atari, which had risen the highest, had the farthest to fall. From sales of $2 billion in 1982—two-thirds of the total market—Atari's share dropped to 40 percent the following year, and the division lost $539 million on sales of $1.1 billion. Warner laid off several thousand workers and moved production to Mexico, but combined after-tax losses for 1983 and 1984 amounted to a billion dollars. In July 1984 Warner sold Atari to Jack Tramiel, who had started Commodore Computers.

During the entire cataclysm, the conventional toy industry was enjoying some of the best years in its history. Things were looking particularly good for one company. Too poor to afford a video game or even a hand-held electronic toy, it watched the entire electronics adventure from the sidelines. Now "Has Been" was going to have the last laugh.

7

HASBRO GOES TO THE HEAD
OF THE CLASS

IN 1985 THE NATIONAL ASSOCIATION OF Investors
named Hasbro, Inc., its 1984 Growth Company of the Year. A
share of Hasbro's stock, which sold for as little as $23.88 in
January 1983, was worth $139.95 by January 1985. When he
accepted the award, Hasbro's forty-three-year-old chairman
noted that his company had just joined the ranks of the *Fortune*
500, and its sales had grown faster that year than those of the
other 499. In 1985 Hasbro's sales were going to pass the billion-
dollar mark for the first time, and it would become the largest
company in Toyland.

It was a heady moment for Stephen Hassenfeld. During the
electronic games era, he had been ridiculed for staying out of the
lucrative new category. He had protested that Hasbro chose not
to make an electronic toy because it could not find a product
that offered something unique, but his listeners knew he had
little choice. Even if Hasbro—which at that time was dubbed
"Has Been"—had found a unique product, it could not have
afforded to manufacture it. Hasbro had lost money in 1978 and
by 1979 had suspended dividends.

At the end of 1982, when the video game market began to collapse, everyone at Hasbro began to realize how fortunate they had been. By missing the boom they missed the bust, and Hasbro emerged the principal beneficiary of the entire episode. While their competitors were raking in profits and looking like winners, Stephen and his younger brother, Alan, were digesting the lessons of adversity and developing a business strategy that eventually became the industry model. During that period Stephen explained that he was looking for products with longer life cycles so that Hasbro could become a producer of staples. His "strategy" was greeted with understandable derision, since it was analogous to a record executive's saying he wanted his company to be a producer of gold records. Of course Hassenfeld wanted to produce staples; everyone in Toyland wanted to produce staples. None of them liked seeing their products die. The problem was that no one had ever figured out how to do it.

Third-generation managers in family businesses are usually presumed incompetent until they prove otherwise, and when Stephen Hassenfeld became president in 1975 he spent a few years floundering. He was willing to take chances, however. He had dropped out of Johns Hopkins University in the middle of a respectable academic career because he had known for years that he wanted to work for the family business, and by 1964 he was ready to get on with it.

Hasbro started as Hassenfeld Brothers, formed in 1923 by three Polish immigrants, Herman, Harry, and Hillel Hassenfeld, to make hat liners and cloth-covered pencil boxes out of scraps they bought from Rhode Island textile mills. The brothers were fighters. When the pencilmakers began to make their own pencil boxes, the brothers retaliated by diversifying into pencils, and their pencil business has prospered as the Empire Pencil Company. During World War II, Merrill and Harold, the second generation, took the company into the toy business by turning the pencil boxes into doctor and nurse kits.

By the time the third set of brothers, Stephen and Alan, came to work, Hasbro boasted a toy company, a pencil company, and one staple. First appearing in 1952, Mr. Potato Head subsequently acquired a Mrs. Potato Head; a son, Spud; a daughter,

Yam; Spudette Potatohead Pets; and Tooty Frooty Friends Oscar the Orange, Cooky the Cucumber, and Katie the Carrot. In 1987 Mr. Potato Head was enough of a celebrity to serve as the Official Spokes-spud for the Great American Smokeout, giving up his pipe permanently in honor of the occasion. Mr. Potato Head still generates about a million units a year—small dollars for Hasbro but steady.

For fourteen years the Hassenfelds had assumed they had another staple, G.I. Joe, which was much more remunerative than Mr. Potato Head, but in 1978 Hasbro dropped the product line because antiwar sentiment had depressed sales of all war-related toys. In response to popular demand, Joe returned only four years later, and Hasbro again began to hope G.I. Joe was a staple.

It also considers Joe a soldier. Hasbro has spent the last few years trying to convince the U.S. Customs Service, and then the U.S. Court of Appeals, that G.I. Joe is a toy soldier, not a doll. Hasbro was not worried about Joe's manly pride. As toys, toy soldiers can enter the country at 6.8 percent duty (Joe is made in Hong Kong); the tariff on dolls is 12 percent. In 1989, however, the U.S. government, in the person of a Washington, D.C., judge, declared Joe undeniably a doll.

G.I. Joe originally was conceived as a doll—a Barbie for boys. The product was the first toy developed by Stanley Weston, who is still developing and licensing properties (some of his recent products are Alf, Couch Potatoes, and Nintendo). In the early 1960s Weston was convinced that boys played with Barbie dolls surreptitiously, so he believed that a socially acceptable version of Barbie could be extremely popular. He chose a military theme because he had loved toy soldiers as a child. At the 1963 Toy Fair, Weston approached a friend at Hassenfeld Brothers, who encouraged him to show his idea to the company. For the next two days Weston hurried around New York's army/navy stores buying military insignia such as chevrons, miniature flags, and other paraphernalia. He mounted them on yellow oaktag and found a movable figure in an art store to demonstrate the way he thought the doll should be articulated (jointed). By this time Weston had invested all of fifty-two dollars.

Hassenfeld Brothers agreed to buy the idea, although the two parties did not immediately agree on terms, and the manufacturer spent the rest of the year developing the product it had named G.I. Joe. As the 1964 Toy Fair approached, Weston and Hassenfeld still had not settled. The normal inventor's fee was 5 percent of net wholesale revenues, with an advance against royalties. Citing high development costs, Hassenfeld Brothers had offered Weston only half of 1 percent. When Weston countered with 3 percent, Hassenfeld raised its offer to 1 percent. Weston finally said, See you in court.

Three days before Toy Fair, Merrill Hassenfeld (father of Stephen and Alan) intervened. He called Weston in for a private meeting and told him that half the buyers who had seen G.I. Joe liked it and the other half hated it. Because that meant the product was going to be a big gamble for the company, he explained, Hassenfeld would prefer to own the property completely so that the company could realize all the profits if it succeeded. "Would you sell it outright for $75,000?" he asked.

Weston liked the idea and countered with $100,000. Hassenfeld agreed, although he later called Weston back and offered him $50,000 plus a 1 percent royalty on all sales over $7 million. Weston considered the offer for twenty-four hours and then took the $100,000.

"When I took that check to the Chase Manhattan Bank," he recalls, "I established an $80,000 line of credit for my business, and then I walked outside and kicked up my heels. I had just made $100,000 on a $52 investment, and I knew I had found the right business."

He had found the right business, but he had made the wrong deal. In its first year G.I. Joe generated 70 percent of Hassenfeld's $25.5 million sales, so Weston's payment in the first year alone would have been over $150,000. Hassenfeld has sold the product line ever since, except for the years 1978–1981. When Hasbro reintroduced G.I. Joe in 1982, it marketed the product much more aggressively than before, and the line generated $49 million in 1982 and $250 million by 1987.

Over the years Stan Weston has undoubtedly spent and respent those millions he bargained away, but he is a philosophical man. "Even though a lot of people think I'm a fool, I'll take those odds—100,000 to 52—any day. Besides," he grins, "I've been married and divorced twice. If I'd had all that money I probably would have been divorced four times instead of two."

Merrill Hassenfeld was a shrewd negotiator, but he was also a gentle man, one of the most honorable, respected, and well-liked members of the industry. When his sons came to work for him, he gave them enough autonomy to learn on their own. "If you make a mistake, that's fine," he told them. "Just don't make the same mistake twice." They made a few. Among the many toys that did not become staples were Show-Biz Babies, five-and-three-quarter-inch replicas of the Flying Nun, Mitch Ryder, Bobbie Gentry, and the Monkees, each accompanied by its own record. Stephen also tried diversifying out of the toy business, but the day-care centers he bought lost money, and the wooden salad bowls succumbed to termite attack in the warehouse.

Even before he went to work full-time, Stephen tried to help his father with the Flubber fiasco. In a 1963 tie-in with the Walt Disney movie *Son of Flubber*, Hasbro had developed a popular product called Flubber, a substance made of rubber and mineral oil that could bounce like a ball and take imprints (similar to Silly Putty). After it had been on the market for several months, the company began receiving reports that Flubber seemed to be causing a rash. The simple Flubber formula had passed all normal tests, but the company began testing again, this time on volunteer prisoners. One prisoner developed a rash on his head, and the company learned that the hair follicles of a small percentage of the population could be irritated by the combination.

Hassenfeld recalled Flubber—thousands and thousands of balls—and consigned it to the city dump. The next day Merrill Hassenfeld received a call from the mayor of Providence. There was a black cloud over the dump because the rubber would not burn properly. Hassenfeld called the Coast Guard for permission to weight the Flubber and dump it at sea. Permission was granted, but the next day the Coast Guard called to complain that Flubber was floating all over Narragansett Bay. After paying the Coast Guard to sweep the ocean, Hassenfeld finally took the mess and buried it in his backyard. The company was building a new warehouse at the time, so he had the Flubber placed under the site of the building and the adjacent parking lot.

There lies Flubber today, gone but not forgotten. It would be hard to forget Flubber, because the irrepressible material has risen again, pushing its portion of the warehouse and parking lot an inch or two higher than the rest of the property. No one at Hasbro minds much. The ghost of Flubber offers living proof that you can't keep a good toy down.

Merrill Hassenfeld died suddenly in 1979, and the following year the two branches of the family split the corporation. Harold's family took over Empire Pencil, while Merrill's family kept the toy company. At the time, the pencil operation looked more promising than the toy division, but that changed within a year. The toy group at Hasbro began to develop into aggressive, opportunistic marketers, and Stephen found that even if he could not create staples, he could keep the company lean enough to remain profitable—and then use his profits to buy staples when his competitors had to sell.

Hasbro's sales passed $100 million for the first time in 1980, and by 1983 sales had more than doubled to $224 million. Hassenfeld had made two acquisitions that year (Glenco, an infant-care products company, and Knickerbocker Toys, which owned the license to make Raggedy Ann and Andy dolls) but the two accounted for only about $20 million of its 1983 volume. The rest was generated internally. In 1984 Hasbro's internally generated growth more than doubled again, to $514 million.

The early 1980s were bumper years for the toy business in general, and while video game sales were dropping $2 billion between 1983 and 1985, the toy industry enjoyed an unprecedented series of blockbuster hits. As a result of the huge volumes generated by those products, industry sales jumped by 51 percent in one year, from $5.3 billion in 1983 to $8.3 billion in 1984.

This was the period when the industry began to believe that a television show tie-in was indispensable to make a toy into a hit. In fact, several of the biggest were hits without it. Coleco's

Cabbage Patch Kids had no TV series, just a half-hour Christmas special, and Trivial Pursuit (1984 wholesale sales: $350 million) was sold mostly to adults, who were certainly not interested in watching a television program about the game.

Television was neither necessary nor sufficient to produce a megahit, but it had an obvious effect on some products, particularly action-figure lines and a few girls' products such as Care Bears. Hasbro was not the first to use television programming to promote its products, but at the same time Stephen Hassenfeld was proclaiming the virtues of staples his company became the most aggressive and effective utilizer of television in the industry.

Hasbro's marketing prowess first became apparent when the company reintroduced G.I. Joe in 1982. Though the new G.I. Joe had been scaled down to three-and-three-quarters inches, G.I. Joe's sales rose 76 percent in 1983 and another 53 percent in 1984. Hasbro freshened the line every year with new characters, vehicles, and accessories and kept supplies tight instead of flooding its customers with too much merchandise. It also hired Marvel Entertainment to license the line to over fifty licensees, thereby increasing its exposure, and created a very popular daily television program. (The program has lasted for years in spite of frequent criticism from adults that it is a prime example of how plot or character development can be subordinated to the company's desire to maximize the number of characters, vehicles, and weapons shown in every episode.)

In 1983 Hasbro showed that it had also developed the flexibility to exploit an unexpected winner. Hasbro went to Toy Fair that year with one major product line in its girls' toys area, a line of floral-scented "collectible jewelry playmates" that could be used as charms on necklaces, bracelets, or barrettes. Maurene Souza, vice president of Hasbro's girls' toy division, recalls the company's enthusiasm. "We thought Charmkins were the cure to the ailments of the world. We had a huge licensing program, a press conference, everything. The whole room was full of Charmkins—we had even built them a special gazebo."

Stuck over in the corner of the Charmkins room was Hasbro's extra girls' line, a group of six small ponies. While conducting some blue-sky research, Hasbro had asked little girls, "What do you see when you go to bed and close your eyes?" and the answer was often "Horses." The company had produced a brown plastic horse in 1982 and to its surprise sold half a million without any advertising. The six ponies in the corner were the marketing department's rather casual expansion of the product. Instead of natural colors they had decided to use "fantasy colors," so the ponies were blue, pink, and yellow, and Hasbro targeted them to school-age girls rather than to toddlers. The company expected the product to last about one year and sell about 450,000 units.

By the end of 1983 Hasbro had sold $10 millon worth of Charmkins—and $25 million worth of My Little Ponies, which was all it could produce. The company boosted production and marketing efforts as quickly as it could and sold $85 million in 1984 and $100 million in 1985. By mid-1989 My Little Ponies were still galloping off the shelves, a total of 100 million ponies worldwide.

Because the product combines such traditionally popular elements, My Little Pony has often been called the perfect girls' toy. Girls' interest in horses is well known, but as Hasbro explained to its shareholders, its Ponies are more than mere horses. "Although not dolls per se, their popularity derives in large measure from two traditionally important doll features, hair care and fashion," the 1986 annual report revealed. Available in a great variety of characters, each Pony comes with its own personal comb to groom its long mane and tail.

What the annual report neglected to mention in its psychological market analysis was Hasbro's attention to detail. The company has added new generations of ponies (Princess Ponies, Gossamer Winged Flutter Ponies, Watercolor Baby Sea Ponies) every year and has kept the price down to encourage impulse buying as well as "collectibility" (multiple purchases). It has also offered a Pony wardrobe so zanily tuned in to fashion and lifestyle trends that even Barbie would approve. For example, the company's 1985 line of Ponywear offered eight Pony outfits suitable for birthday parties, tennis matches, and other special occasions, such as Having a Luau and Strike Up the Band. The

Flashprance set included a flounced minidress, a pink head-band, a lavender purse monogrammed MLP, a scented sticker, and four pink leg warmers to be worn atop four yellow shoes with sculpted bows. All Pony footwear and legwear naturally comes in fours, although Pony hooves evidently vary in size. The Flashprance shoes, explains the label, "will not fit Medley, Firefly, Bubbles, Seashell or Starshine."

Hasbro had begun to prove itself with G.I. Joe in 1982 and impressed the industry with My Little Pony in 1983, but it was the Battle of the Robots in 1984 that clinched its reputation as a power marketer. Transformable robots had been popular in Japan for several years when Bandai America, the American subsidiary of one of Japan's largest toy companies, showed its Machine Men line prior to the 1983 Toy Fair. Intricately con-structed vehicles or weapons made of plastic and metal, the toys could be converted into robots by twisting and folding their various parts. American buyers liked the product, but they withdrew their orders when Bandai, which had sustained severe losses on its electronics products in 1982, eliminated Bandai America's television advertising budget. Without television ad-vertising, the buyers would take only forty thousand units.

Bandai America's vice president of sales and marketing, Jerry Cleary, left the company when it stopped promoting on televi-sion. While looking for another job, he tried to sell a ride-on toy to the Tonka Corporation for an independent inventor. Tonka turned down the product but hired Cleary. As soon as he joined Tonka, Cleary, who thought the robots were an outstanding product, convinced his associates to look at them. They liked the line, too, and took the license.

In 1983 Tonka was a midwestern manufacturer of toy vehicles. Its Tonka trucks accounted for more than 80 percent of the company's $88 million volume, but chairman Stephen Shank was trying to diversify and the robots looked promising. Tonka called its version GoBots and introduced the line in January 1984. Demand grew so rapidly that some of Tonka's customers were calling to ask why Tonka would advertise before they had shipped enough merchandise. Tonka had not advertised. The product was just hot.

In May, Hasbro introduced Transformers, a similar product it had licensed from one of Bandai's Japanese competitors, Takara, and generated $93 million in the first year. Although Transformers appeared five months after GoBots, Hasbro came from behind and outsold GoBots almost two to one. In 1985 Transformers pulled ahead even further, with sales of $330 million to GoBots' $132 million. That year the category was so popular that a third line of transformable robots called Voltron, also licensed from Bandai, generated $125 million for Matchbox, LJN, and Panosh Place, which sold various parts of the line. In 1986 Hasbro sold $214 million in Transformers, while GoBots and Voltron were dead. Although sales have steadily declined, Hasbro is still turning out Transformers and, even at lower volumes, still making money on them.

Tonka's executives conducted innumerable postmortems, and each of them emphasizes a different lesson from the experience. Jerry Cleary, now president of Tonka Toys, notes that Hasbro's line was better executed, better merchandised, and first on TV, but he also considers Tonka's relative lack of sales experience with promotional toys an important factor. Selling promotional toys requires a different and much more aggressive approach than the Tonka salesforce had needed to sell its trucks.

Pat Feely, who preceded Cleary as Tonka's president, came from a marketing background and saw the defeat in marketing terms. He decided that Hasbro had won because it had taken the right risks and dared to break the rules. Hasbro offered unusually expensive products, and it began its television exposure with a weekly program. "We didn't believe the business was in the high end of the line," explains Feely. "Once the robots cost more than twenty dollars, they became very complicated, but we thought there would be too much price resistance at thirty or forty dollars for these very complicated robots. That was a bad call. Kids wanted them more complicated, and kids don't care about price. When we started researching to find out what was happening, the kids would say, 'I like Transformers better because they're more complicated.' And we thought, Sure they're more complicated—they cost five times as much. The miniature GoBots were much better than the smallest Transformers, but the higher-end products were what the kids asked for. We just never expected parents to give in to them. But parents did buy them, and not only for Christmas. That's how we lost the edge in terms of image of the product with the kids."

Like Cleary, Feely also believes that Hasbro's early television exposure had been crucial. "Hasbro's series was available around the same time as ours, but we both only had a limited number of episodes. We waited until we had enough to air on a daily basis, while Hasbro went on weekly, on Sunday mornings. We had been told it couldn't be done—that no one had done that. We had done two miniseries, and GoBots picked up dramatically—it's one of the best examples of television helping to make a toy successful—but Hasbro was on the air alone for nine months once a week, and because the kids were so interested in the product they watched it religiously."

Stephen Shank came away from the experience reinforced in his conviction that size is important, particularly as the industry consolidates. He was even more determined than before to grow and diversify. "We had much more limited internal product-development resources than Hasbro, and when they saw GoBots explode in the first half of 1984, they just took out their wallets and went for it," he opines. "They simply out-resourced us. They built four or five sets of tools and managed higher inventories, while we took the risks appropriate for our circumstances. GoBots versus Transformers was really about resources and scale. We don't think, all things being equal, a $100 million company taking on a billion dollar company is in a winnable fight.

"Scale is really important in this business. Each one of the product segments tends to be cyclical in itself, so we have to be in all sorts of different categories to ride the ups and downs. You also have to launch a lot of new products for a reasonable success ratio, and that takes a lot of resources."

Stephen Hassenfeld had been saying for years that he wanted balance, diversity, and size. In 1984, at the height of the megahits explosion, he put his promotional money where his corporate mouth was and bought what he had said he wanted all along: staples. Hassenfeld liked to refer to Milton Bradley as the jewel in his crown, and he was right, although many in the toy industry did not see it that way at the time. When he spent $380 million for a game-and-preschool company, they thought he was crazy. If just two of Hasbro's product lines, G.I. Joe and Transformers, could generate $245 million in one year, why pay so much for a bunch of little games that sold only 100,000 units a year? It was not until the megahits became scarcer and scarcer that Hassenfeld's detractors recognized the wisdom of owning a "balanced portfolio," or a collection of staples.

When the news about Hasbro's purchase became public, there was little joy in Springfield, Massachusetts. The fourth-largest company in the toy industry, Milton Bradley had a proud history and strong ties to the community. Employees were stunned at the idea of becoming a subsidiary, or worse. Unlike other toy companies, many of whose products are manufactured overseas, Milton Bradley made 95 percent of its products at its own plant, and although it was publicly held, it had a family-company atmosphere. It employed 1,500 people in Springfield, and everyone from the president down to the workers cutting puzzles in the factory regarded the approach of Hasbro with consternation.

Milton Bradley was by far the senior of the two companies. It had been run by professional managers before Hillel, Henry, and Herman even came to the United States, and its executives had been acquiring subsidiaries all over the country, building a large and effective international operation, and talking about the value of staples for years. The Shea family, which by now owned 10 percent of the stock, had led the company since 1941, when James Shea, Sr., was hired to rescue the failing operation. In 1968 his son, James, Jr., had succeeded him. Both were proud, crusty characters who cherished the company's New England roots, and James Shea, Sr., even published a biography of the founder, called *It's All in the Game.*

When Hasbro bought the company in 1984, Milton Bradley was recovering from its first loss in thirty-five years. Over the objections of his executives and at the worst possible time, Shea had gone into the video game market. In August 1982 Shea had bought General Consumer Electronics, a manufacturer and distributor of a video game system called Vectrex. In 1983 the company wrote it off for $30 million. By 1984 Milton Bradley was restored to profitability, but it never had a chance to enjoy it; 1983 was its last year of independence.

The company was over one hundred years old. In 1860 a Springfield, Massachusetts, lithographer named Milton Bradley put aside a board game he had invented in order to print and sell a portrait of a midwestern politician who, he had been assured, was the coming man. His adviser was correct, and Bradley sold thousands of copies of his picture of Abraham Lincoln. Soon after Lincoln became president, however, the picture's sales ceased, and customers even came to Bradley's door to demand their money back: Abraham Lincoln had grown a beard.

After he threw out stacks of obsolete lithographs, Bradley returned to selling his game, the Checkered Game of Life. In the style of nineteenth-century games, he had injected it with a healthy dose of moral instruction; players who landed on the Gambling square went to Ruin, Intemperance led to Poverty, Government Contract to Wealth (a still-timely sequence), and the ultimate goal was Happy Old Age. Bradley sold forty thousand copies the first year.

Over the years he developed many games and soon branched out into other products. After hearing a lecture in 1868 about the kindergarten movement, he began to manufacture the blocks, paints, beads, and weaving sets the schools needed, even though he knew they would not be profitable for several years. Bradley also continued inventing. In 1881, in response to a request from a printer friend, he designed the tabletop paper cutter still used in offices and schools today.

Another major American toy company began in Massachusetts in the nineteenth century. In 1883 a sixteen-year-old Salem, Massachusetts, student brought a new game called Banking to his informal games club. George Parker and his friends scorned the moralistic board games of the day and played only those whose sole purpose was entertainment. Banking was a card game that allowed players to borrow from the bank at 100 percent interest and make profits through speculation. George's friends liked it so much that they suggested he try to make real money by selling the idea to a games company.

He took it to two Boston book publishers, who turned it down, but George decided to publish it himself, spending forty dollars to manufacture five hundred copies and ten dollars to market them. When he sold out by Christmas and realized a one-hundred-dollar profit, he left school to go into business full-time. Five years later his older brothers joined him, and within ten years Parker Brothers had published nearly three hundred games. They manufactured all kinds of game equipment as well, including tennis racquets, puzzles, blocks, and tiddledy-winks.

Parker Brothers did not invent the premier American board game. Monopoly was brought to the company during the Depression by an unemployed Philadelphia engineer named Charles Darrow. The Parker Brothers executive who originally rejected it exaggerated and told Darrow it contained fifty-two fundamental errors in game design. In fact it had about five. Darrow published it himself in 1933 and sold all five hundred copies (the same number as Banking). When the Philadelphia department store John Wanamaker gave Darrow a substantial reorder, Parker Brothers reversed its decision. It bought the rights to the game in 1935, just in time to rescue the firm, which was about to give up on games and turn to printing. Today the company has sold over 100 million Monopoly sets, and it remains the all-time bestseller of board games.

Darrow did not invent Monopoly either. When he took it to Parker Brothers, the game had been evolving for thirty years. In 1988 the spiritual heir of George Parker, Parker Brothers' research and development chief Philip Orbanes, published *The Monopoly Companion*, revealing the true story of Monopoly's origins. Orbanes, who has been in the game business since he was a teenager, spent years tracing the game's evolution and found that the earliest version was The Landlord's Game, patented in 1904 by a woman named Elizabeth Magie. She produced and sold some copies, and versions of the game became popular among college students. In the early 1920s, it became known as Monopoly, and by the time Darrow played the game in 1933, it was close to the form he submitted to Parker Brothers.

The game business has always been somewhat different from

the toy business. Game people traditionally consider themselves more akin to publishers than to toy people, and toy people have turned up their noses at game companies' low sales, calling the products "tortured cardboard." Game people endured the taunts all the way to the bank, because games can be extremely profitable. Although they are subject to fads just as toys are, the popular games have much longer lives and sell at fairly predictable levels. When Hasbro bought Milton Bradley in 1984, the game company had thirteen games in its product line that it had sold for more than ten years, and those games accounted for 35 percent of its domestic sales. That longevity would be an unaccustomed luxury for most toy companies. Several of the games were much older than ten: The Game of Life was the modern version of Milton Bradley's 1860 game, and Go to the Head of the Class, which was invented by two department store employees, had been introduced in 1938.

One of the company's biggest assets was a little newer. Twister, which the company had introduced in 1966, had been a huge hit for years. Milton Bradley had begun to promote the game by giving it to vacationing college students on the beach in Fort Lauderdale, Florida, and it was well received. But it was Johnny Carson who turned it into a sensation. With no prompting from the company, he played Twister on "The Tonight Show" twice, the second time with Eva Gabor, and Milton Bradley sold more than a million units in the game's first year. Twister survived the electronics era and still remains one of the company's most popular products.

Games have changed over the years, largely because of the accelerated pace of contemporary life. Today games are designed to be quickly understandable because players generally do not want to spend time learning elaborate rules, and they can usually be played in a half hour rather than a leisurely hour. Even with faster-paced products, the game business used to be a relatively tranquil spot in Toyland. Then in 1984 a product hit the market that changed it irrevocably. Trivial Pursuit swept the country, selling in larger quantities than anyone in the game—or toy—business had ever believed possible.

Two Canadian newspapermen, Chris Haney and Scott Abbott, conceived of the game one Saturday afternoon in 1979 while playing Scrabble at Haney's kitchen table. The two enlisted Haney's brother John who was, they agreed, a more serious person, and Ed Werner, who as a lawyer could provide free legal advice. They called their company Horn Abbot Ltd. (Chris Haney's nickname was Horn, and they dropped the second *t* from Abbott's name so that they could use a horny abbot as a logo.) They targeted the baby-boom generation as they created the questions, manufactured 1,100 games at a cost of $60.00 apiece, and sold them for $16.00 wholesale ($29.95 retail). They were willing to take the loss in order to gain credibility, and then credit, and were bitterly disappointed when they sold out but could not obtain funding to manufacture more.

They took their creation to Toy Fair 1982, but both Milton Bradley and Parker Brothers rejected it. Finally they licensed it to another very old game company, Selchow & Righter, which sold Scrabble and Parcheesi and, back in 1889, Pigs in Clover. The family-owned company's sales in 1982 were about $20 million. In 1984 Selchow & Righter sold $350 million worth of Trivial Pursuit, wholesale.

The industry was stunned. Recalls Milton Bradley's president, George Ditomassi, "We would have told you there was no market for that kind of product in that magnitude. . . . It broke all the rules. It had to, to get the kind of numbers it did. Games are primarily played by people twelve years and under, but Trivial Pursuit certainly proved there was one hell of a market for people over twelve, given the right kind of games."

Trivial Pursuit was a megahit, and as usual all members of the industry tried to find the secret of its success. "We did a lot of research, but it was a phenomenon," recalls Ditomassi. "There is no way to explain phenomena in our industry, and there's no way to replicate them. But we all try—constantly."

Even without a Trivial Pursuit, Milton Bradley soon proved its value to Hasbro. By 1988 the game division's domestic volume alone accounted for 20 percent of the company's sales, and even more of the profits.

8

MARCH–AUGUST 1986
Why Toymen Spy On Innocent Children

THEY HAD DONE IT. DICK LIKED THE IDEA.

After the rest of the audience finished congratulating them, Jim, Mike, Woody, Warren, and Lee began to breathe normally again. That was when Dick asked the only question they had never anticipated. "That was great, guys," he said again. "But what's the next step?"

None of them had a clue.

Fortunately, Dick had a few ideas. The next step, as he saw it, was to figure out how to dip a corporate toe into the waters without committing their whole body of capital. New products are more fun, but they consume more money, more time, and more attention. The team also knew that falling in love with one's product is one of the surest routes to disaster. A company that loves its product too much may lose all judgment about appropriate levels of expenditure. Everyone in the meeting was well aware that with Dino-Riders the phrase "in love with the product" was already a serious understatement, so they honestly welcomed the discipline of a conservative approach—just so they could try.

127

Over the next half hour they decided to develop the product line in stages, each with its own budget. At the end of each stage, they would evaluate the results. "We won't go to the next stage unless everyone is enthusiastic about the last," Dick ruled. (Grey recounts this decision with a straight face, giving no indication whether he knows Tyco's generally accepted definition of "everyone.")

The first stage would be market research. They would design and sculpt models of six dinosaurs and test them on small groups of children. They budgeted about $150,000: $120,000 for the models and $25,000 for the tests. Because security was so important, they gave the project a code name, B.C. All written or verbal communications were to use B.C.; the word *Dino-Riders* was forbidden.

A few weeks after the meeting, Woody and Mike Hirtle sent Dick a memo formally recommending the development and testing of the Dino-Riders concept. All targets and costs were based on a projected $27 million in sales for the first year. This figure had been imposed from above.

Woody had originally set first-year sales at $60 million. Dick had laughed and sent him out of his office, saying, "Woody, get realistic." Woody came back about two weeks later with a new plan: estimated sales, $40 million.

Dick glanced at it and looked up at Woody. "Let me tell you how it's going to be: $19 million. I want you to cut this number to $19 million."

Woody was disgusted. That might be a good number for a Tyco product line, but as far as he was concerned, in a billion-dollar category $19–20 million was a nonevent. "Some of the lines that never even happened shipped $20 million," he muttered to himself. "You could sell $20 million at flea markets." In the end, Woody could not bring himself to write a $20 million plan, so they compromised. The memo Dick finally accepted estimated first-year sales at $27,791,000. Six months later, when Woody had to delegate primary responsibility for Dino-Riders to someone else, the first thing the new marketing director did was calculate his own sales estimate. He came up with $60 million.

The next few months were a blur to the product-development department, particularly Lee Volpe. The timetable on Woody's memo worked backward from a shipping date of December 15, 1987, but the members of the design department conveniently forgot that and began operating at triple speed. They assumed that they would really introduce the line at the February 1987 Toy Fair and begin shipping the first products that April. Weren't they the ones who had brought off Cliff Hangers in nine days? They prided themselves on working quickly and efficiently.

Lee had so many outside designers working on the project that he was never in the office. "I don't want them to lose a day coming here, so I'll go to them," he would explain to Mike as he bustled out of the office, his Darth Vader helmet tucked under his arm. Mike would try to catch him, saying, "But . . . what about . . . and have you done . . ." but Lee was always too quick for him.

Product development had so many new products in progress for the following year that Lee farmed out practically the entire Dino-Riders project. Warren was crushed when he was sent back to vehicles. Jack got in a little more weapons design but had to spend most of his time on other Tyco projects. Mike had to oversee the entire department. Only Lee was having a wonderful time, living mostly in 65 million B.C.

Although they were not working directly on the project, every member of marketing and product development was obsessed with it, and they all worried constantly about the competition. Parallel development is inevitable in any fashion-oriented industry, and dinosaurs already seemed to be popping up everywhere. They were not being paranoid; even the *New York Times* ran an article on the growing popularity of dinosaur products that year.

To add to their worries, Dick began toying with the idea of farming out the entire project. One day he told Jim that he thought the project might be too big for Tyco. He loved the concept, but perhaps they should let someone more experienced develop it—like Marvin Glass & Associates, the largest toy-invention firm in the industry. "Maybe they'll do it for a reduced royalty fee, say 3 percent, since Tyco has already come up with the concept," he speculated.

This idea was about as welcome as a bomb threat and threw everyone into a similar panic. Mike spent several hours making charts that allocated the entire product-development department's time, to prove that they could handle Dino-Riders. Jim and Woody walked around wringing their hands and saying, "Not our baby . . . we're not going to give up our baby." More constructively, Jim continued to insist that Tyco's team would do a better job than anyone from the outside, and eventually Dick abandoned the idea. Everyone sighed with relief and went back to worrying about the competition.

The product-development people pushed themselves and their vendors so hard to produce samples in time for market testing in August that later it seemed like a departmental dream, albeit a dream in fast motion. As he wove his motorcycle in and out of traffic, accumulating a hefty stack of speeding tickets, Lee Volpe dreamily refined his ideas for the Dino-Riders fantasy.

He imagined the Sauresians to be a noble race, superior to humans. Highly intelligent, brave, and at the same time more sensitive than people, they were heroic, elfin aliens. They would have big, soulful eyes like those of the sad-eyed children painted by the artist Margaret Keane in the 1960s. They would respect the organic, the natural, the light, while their enemies would favor mechanistic, angular heaviness. When drawings of Lee's Sauresian prototype began to circulate, his coworkers were less reverent. They pronounced Lee's heroic elf a cross between Michael Jackson and King Tut, and they christened him Michael Tut. The name stuck and became their shorthand for the generic Sauresian.

Meanwhile, Tyco's advertising vice president, Bob Lurie, began arranging for market testing. In April he asked the top people from the company's advertising agency, Bozell, Jacobs, Kenyon & Eckhardt in Los Angeles, to come to New Jersey to hear about a new product idea. Only the Tyco account supervisor, the agency's creative director, and the agency chairman, Cy Schneider (the same Cy Schneider who had spent twenty-six years working with Mattel), were allowed to come, and even to them Bob doled out information parsimoniously, on what he considered a need-to-know basis. He, Woody, and Jim practically insulted their visitors, reminding them several times that the project was always to be called, orally or in writing, by its code name, B.C.

Plenty of products are put on the market without research, but market testing is used constantly in the toy business. The earliest form—kitchen research, or taking a product home to one's children—is still employed and, even in an era of regression analysis, can prove surprisingly informative, especially about questions of product design. One child, playing with a toy, may demonstrate instantly to a designer or engineer that a switch is difficult to push, or is in the wrong place, or requires a combination of strength and dexterity too hard to manage.

The appeal of a product is better tested on samples larger than one, but toy people would never give up kitchen research even if they knew it was totally useless. Toy executives are among the few white-collar workers whose children can understand what they do for a living, so kitchen research gives them the opportunity to show off.

Toy companies vary in the degree to which they rely on real research. Most subscribe to a quantitative research service that has become a virtual bible, the TRSTS (pronounced "trysts") reports (Toy Retail Sales Tracking Service), compiled by The NPD Group, a large Long Island market-research operation. Instigated in 1983 at the urging of the TMA, the TRSTS yield retail-sales information on thousands of specific items. Companies can subscribe to the reports in several degrees of detail to decipher trends, track the products' performance, and monitor their competition. Many also subscribe to other services, including those that measure the appeal of popular or recognizable characters, television shows, and other licensable properties.

For Dino-Riders, Tyco wanted qualitative market research—testing products and concepts on small focus groups of children. Under the supervision of a trained moderator, the children would be shown products (no touching the $120,000 worth of prototypes) and told about the concept of Dino-Riders. Their reactions would be observed through a one-way mirror, recorded, in some cases videotaped, and later analyzed.

Mattel was first in the industry to use market research on a systematic basis (as early as 1959), but its operation really expanded in 1963. The company hired a man named Victor Cole, who had conducted research for Gillette Corporation, one of the most sophisticated marketing companies in the country. At Mattel, Cole built a group of three clerical workers into a department of sixty researchers: thirty processing and analyzing numbers and another thirty in the field gathering sales information. He designed many of the reports and systems later copied by the rest of the industry, and his people generated many of "the numbers" that became so crucial to Mattel in weighing its hundreds of competing products. He also used qualitative testing extensively, first on product design and appeal and later on commercials. Several of the testing procedures commonly used today evolved from Cole's work at Mattel.

Most companies use outside testing firms for their research, but Mattel and Fisher-Price have maintained in-house testing facilities for years, Little Tikes runs its own nursery school, and Kenner has a special studio for taping tests on its premises. Companies may test complete products, such as Dino-Riders, or just one aspect of a product, such as color. Even in testing color, they ask different questions at different times—which color looks best to children (green is generally considered a loser) or should the product be made in realistic or fantasy colors (should the bear be brown or pink).

Toy companies often use testing to compare the importance to children of different product features. If children are less interested in certain features than in others, the less interesting features can be eliminated to lower the cost of the item. When Mattel tested a line of action figures for girls based on He-Man's sister, She-Ra, Princess of Power, She-Ra's Crystal Castle originally included a special bird's-beak entrance. The beak would swoop down and pick up the figures to bring them into the castle. Not only were the girls uninterested in the mechanical feature, but they (as well as their mothers) preferred a softer, less action-oriented product. Mattel substituted a traditional castle door.

Different models of the same product can also be pitted against each other. Barbie doll designers used to test different wedding dress designs, and among themselves they called the choices "gaudy," "gaudier," and "gaudiest." It did not take long to teach Mattel that little girls were going to prefer "gaudiest" every time.

Even its most enthusiastic adherents are quick to note the limitations of market research. Qualitative testing can be used to adjust a product or choose a color, but it is not a reliable predictor of hits and flops. Tests are generally better at predicting failure than success, so they are often used to reject products. Consequently, critics contend that testing is used as a substitute for judgment and real decision making—a sort of toy industry version of the "no one ever got fired for buying IBM" form of risk avoidance.

Even a test's ability to predict failure is limited. If a toy does poorly in testing, that proves only that the specific toy, in the specific format, color, and form used in the test, did poorly. It does not tell the tester that if the color were changed (or the head, or the weight, or any one of a thousand variables, including the choice of target audience), the product could be a real winner. Everyone in the industry knows that Hasbro had the forerunner of Cabbage Patch Kids tested and that it tested poorly. Hasbro tested on children, however, and after the dolls' success Hasbro's vice president for girls' toys concluded that Hasbro should have tested them on adults.

Even if Cabbage Patch Kids had tested well, its maker would have had no clue about how many to make. A test that correctly predicts a winner cannot really suggest the dimensions of a hit. That is because the enormous hits just happen; fads and crazes are phenomena that feed on their own momentum. A positive test may confirm a product's appeal, but it cannot forecast mob psychology.

For Tyco's tests, Bozell, Jacobs' research director hired a Connecticut testing firm to run eighteen focus groups, nine in Connecticut and nine in Los Angeles, on four- to ten-year-old boys, the primary target market. The groups would be used to test both the concept of Dino-Riders (could the boys understand the background story, and did they like it) and the appeal and features of the toys themselves.

The night before the tests was a sleepless one for Woody and Lee. They loved their product, and they believed that everyone who had heard about it, from Dick to the outside designers to the agency people, was as entranced as they were. Even so, they were realistic enough to understand that they had lost perspective. "You see a lot of product out there, and some of it is so bad you just can't believe anyone would think it could sell," Woody would say, to general agreement.

"But someone did," someone would reply, finishing Woody's thought. "And what if this is a loser, too, and we just can't see it?" They kept waiting for their first negative response. The very worst source it could come from would be the kids, so August 18 would be the day of reckoning. They dreaded it.

Woody got up at 2:30 that morning to drive to Connecticut. The drive from his home in Indian Mills, New Jersey, to Darien usually takes about three-and-a-half hours, but Woody did not want to take a chance on being late. The tests were not scheduled to begin until 11:00, but the weather report had forecast heavy rains. Since his car lacked windshield wipers, he figured that he should allow himself extra time in case a storm came up and he had to stop by the side of the road and sit it out.

Woody dearly loved his 1969 Porsche 911. He had bought it to celebrate when he took the job with Tyco. The car had a great engine and a terrific body. Unfortunately, everything else seemed to need replacing; repairing one thing just triggered the next problem. The broken Porsche part that week was the windshield wipers, which was why Woody was driving up the New Jersey Turnpike at 3:00 in the morning.

To no one's surprise but Woody's, the weather report was wrong, and Woody found himself in Darien a little over two hours later. There is not much action in Darien at 5:00 in the morning; he briefly considered sleeping in his car for four or five hours, until someone showed up at the testing site. He found that prospect unappealing, so he drove to the hotel where he was scheduled to stay the coming evening and strolled nonchalantly up to the front desk. "I know I'm a little early for my reservation," he told the sleepy-eyed clerk, "but if my room is ready, could I check in and use it?" Woody's arrival was probably the most interesting event of the night clerk's evening, and he was glad to oblige. Woody went to his room and fell sound asleep at last.

Later that morning he arrived at the testing offices refreshed and rested. There he encountered Lee Volpe dragging two specially made carrying cases containing $120,000 worth of samples. The two set up the products and retired to preview the videotape the moderator would use to introduce the Dino-Riders concept. No one at Tyco had seen the tape. Bozell, Jacobs had used a freelancer who had fallen so far behind schedule that the agency people had carried it with them when they came in from California the day before.

As the tape began to roll, Woody began to steam. By the time it ended, he was shouting at everyone in sight. The videotape was terrible. The narrator was drawling, the illustrations were unattractive, and the total effect was boring. Woody ranted and raved for about ten minutes, but a cartoon bubble over his head would have summed up his thoughts in one sentence: I'm looking at the biggest opportunity of my career, and you guys are messing it up with this goddamn crappy tape!

Finally he settled down, mollified because everyone clearly agreed with him that the tape was bad. They watched it again and decided there was some salvageable footage—about thirty seconds' worth. Woody decided to rewrite the background story and let the moderator read it to the children. When she reached the middle of the story, she would turn on the television and run the only part of the video Woody considered worth showing, even to a group of little boys.

They began writing and rehearsing at 10:00, and when the first group showed up at 11:00, they were ready. By then Woody was so mellow that he even agreed to help the agency hide the tape from the Tyco home office. They all assumed that if anyone senior to Woody saw how badly Bozell, Jacobs had screwed up the assignment, the agency would be fired.

The Tyco group had a simple, if inelegant, criterion for success in the Dino-Riders tests. They told their agency that they

wanted the kids to be so excited by the product that they wet
their pants. Tyco does not require a wet-their-pants level of
enthusiasm on all its products, but since Dino-Riders would
require an investment far larger than anything the company
had ever done, its prospects needed to be outstanding.

At half the sessions the boys would be exposed to the story,
the characters, and the concept first, so that they could respond
to them before seeing the products. In the other sessions the boys
would see and discuss the toys first and hear the story after that.
This procedure, called the discrepancy method, is used to test
the strength of the two separate elements. If the story is stronger
than the product, or if the product is exciting but the story line
dull, the tests theoretically isolate the weaknesses. In practice,
action-figure products generally cannot stand on their own
without at least some background story, so the distinction was
a little blurred.

At 11:30 the first group of four- and five-year-old boys trooped
in. After finding out their names and ages and talking with
them about what action figures they liked, the moderator read
them Woody's summary. Woody was not the only one who could
have written it. Everyone at Tyco and Bozell, Jacobs who had
gotten near the project had wanted to help craft the original
background story. They loved discussing Michael Tut with Lee
and dreaming up names for the nefarious villains, the evil
Rulons.

One of their plot problems had been logistical. None of them
could figure out a believable way to move the Sauresians back
through time and space. They tried an intergalactic war with
someone hitting the wrong button; a special device that could
navigate time as well as space; even a time/space warp that
pulled the bad characters in with the good. Finally they gave up
and decided that they didn't have enough time for such elaborate
explanations and that "The visitors crashed to earth" would
have to suffice. To their surprise, it did.

The narrator read Woody's version, and then she turned on
the television set. The boys heard music, mood-setting sound
effects, and a narrator describing and naming the different
kinds of dinosaurs the Sauresians encountered when they

landed on earth. The *Tyrannosaurus rex* was Tyrant, and the Rulon leaders were Kermit, Antman, and Sharkey. Tyco had named the chief villain Kermit because he looked like a frog.

After the brief television exposure, the moderator began asking the boys questions about what they had just heard and seen, but in the middle of the discussion she suddenly heard a knock at the door.

"Come in," she called, the first of many times, and just like television's Mr. Rogers, in strolled Lee Volpe. He was introduced to the children as the person who had made the toys they were going to be shown. Through all eighteen sessions Lee never tired of demonstrating all the dinosaurs, every little weapon, each noble Sauresian, and every evil Rulon. As he worked each mechanism, he listened intently to the boys, and even though many of the sessions were taped, he also kept notes. Tyco did not use tests frequently, so he wanted to extract all the information he could.

The research firm considered the tests a resounding success in terms of both the boys' responses and the amount of usable feedback. The tests confirmed that the boys were strongly interested in dinosaurs; knew many of the names, shapes, and sizes; and took quite easily to the idea of utilizing different species as different vehicles. Without articulating it, the boys also shared a common vision of what action-figure lines entail (good guys, bad guys, battles, weapons) and made suggestions about how to improve the line.

Besides comments such as "awesome," "rad," and "I'm going to get one as soon as it comes out," a number of the boys' specific ideas were useful enough for Jim, Woody, and Lee to take seriously. The boys suggested that both the Sauresians and the Rulons fit on all the dinosaur seats, so that the dinosaurs could be used by both sides. Several mentioned the importance of a television program. "Any company should do a year's cartoon to educate people about the product," explained Matthew, eight.

Many of the suggestions improved the opportunities for combat, the central activity of any action-figure line. The boys requested a headquarters for each side, special leaders for each

group, and, and, most important, more weapons. Some wanted the
weapons to shoot actual projectiles.

Others had more fundamental concerns. One advised Lee
emphatically, "Don't use girls!"

The boys also liked the concept and the story. They liked the
name Rulons, which had come from product development's
earliest brainstorms, but Sauresians was difficult to remember.
When the moderator in California took out a dollar and offered
it to anyone who could remember the name, no one could—
although one little boy offered reassurance: "As soon as it gets
on the market, people will remember." Another came up with
a reason for the name's lack of appeal: "It's hard to say, especially with two teeth out."

The name Dino-Riders was also tested against the project's
code name, B.C., because Dick Grey had begun to think B.C.
might be better. Everyone else at Tyco and Bozell, Jacobs hated
it, and much to their relief Dino-Riders won in every test. The
moderators found that some of the boys were already familiar
with the caveman comic strip "B.C.," and a few others knew
that B.C. could mean Before Christ. But they liked Dino-Riders
better "because that's what they do."

Some of the responses were too enthusiastic for comfort. The
largest, meanest, best-known dinosaur, the *Tyrannosaurus rex*,
always attracted the most interest. The boys had been forbidden
to touch the models, but one just could not resist temptation.
Woody, who sat behind the one-way glass for all eighteen sessions, watched as one little boy eased away from the group and
edged silently toward Tyrant.

Lee droned on, happily oblivious to the menace creeping
toward his thirty-thousand-dollar model, and Woody began to
squirm. If he called out, he would ruin the test. But wasn't
ruining one session a small price to pay for saving the centerpiece of the line? Without the *T-rex* the rest of the sessions would
be ruined. Woody was getting desperate when he was seized
with a sudden inspiration: mental telepathy! He concentrated
intently. Look to your right, Lee, he signaled over and over.

It seemed to Woody that he transmitted for somewhere between five minutes and five years. In reality it was probably only five seconds, but he made contact. Lee received the message, took in the situation, and casually snapped, "Get back here, Jason."

It was all over. Tyrant was saved from a fate worse than a Rulon Brain Box, and Woody began to breathe again. Michael Tut could not have done it better.

9

To Market, to License, to Sell a Hot Toy

Market research is a daily event in Toyland; Fisher-Price and Mattel in particular are sometimes accused of researching products to death. Toy companies need all the help they can get because of the short life span of many of their products and the self-liquidating nature of most toy purchases. Satisfied toothpaste customers become repeat customers, but no matter how much fun families find their Monopoly game, they are not going to go out and buy another. It does not get used up.

In other industries, makers of durable goods are able to count on customer satisfaction to sell other products, trading on the strength of their good name. A consumer who has a good experience with a Sony TV set will look favorably on other Sony products. Selling to children, toy companies cannot trade on brand loyalty. Children could not care less what corporation made the last doll they received (and probably do not know what a corporation is, anyway); the fact that Parker Brothers made Monopoly will not steer even older children toward other Parker Brothers games.

In the preschool market, toy companies can inspire brand

loyalty and enjoy the repeat business it generates because they sell to adults, not children. Fisher-Price, Playskool, and Little Tikes design products that appeal to adults (although children are the users, they are not the choosers), deliver high quality, and then reap the benefit of a good reputation: a stable, healthy sales pattern. That is why so many other companies are trying so hard to get into the preschool market.

Even though some products have lasted so long that they are household names, the companies that make them are largely unknown to adults as well as to children. Barbie, Hula Hoops, Raggedy Ann, Silly Putty, Slinky, Monopoly, Cabbage Patch Kids, and G.I. Joe are familiar to almost everyone, but the name Hasbro rings few bells. Even the engaging company name Wham-O (whose owner produced Hula Hoops and Frisbees, two of the biggest hits in toy history) draws blank stares.

Toymakers are an enterprising breed, however. Faced with a high ratio of product failures, short product life spans, and no brand loyalty from their target market, they still manage to push billions of dollars' worth of toys into the hands of children who had no idea they wanted them.

The key is marketing. Louis Marx led the industry by being the low-cost producer. He delivered wonderful products more cheaply than anyone else. The Handlers overtook him when they turned to television and reached a much bigger audience. Even as they increased in marketing sophistication, at Mattel product was still king (or queen). Then, throughout the late 1970s and early 1980s, the large companies absorbed a growing number of professional managers who were outsiders, not native toy people, and they began to apply as many of the techniques of the consumer-products companies as they could.

One of the earliest innovations, aimed directly at the self-liquidating–purchase problem, preceded the employment of the outside professionals. Gillette had made the razor/razor blade strategy famous, and the Handlers applied it directly to their Barbie doll. Once Gillette customers bought a Gillette razor, they might never buy another one, but they would have to keep buying razor blades for the rest of their lives. A little girl of the 1960s may have had only one Barbie doll, but by creating a constant stream of new clothes and accessories Mattel's designers could make Barbie's wardrobe seem permanently incomplete.

Toy companies also began to extend their products into product lines wherever possible. Barbie and G.I. Joe are the best early examples. Barbie expanded from one friend (Midge), one escort (Ken), and one little sister (Skipper) to several themed Barbies a year, a car, a house, and a selection of furniture. (Mattel people joke that a dressing table with a mirror is always Barbie's most important piece of furniture.) Expanding a product into a product line simultaneously addressed two of the toy companies' major problems. Product lines gave them the opportunity to generate multiple purchases and at the same time enabled them to use their strongest products to create brands that would appeal to children. Children would not be interested in a toy because Mattel or Hasbro had made it, but they might want it because it was related to Barbie or G.I. Joe.

They also built brands through licensing. Licensing—paying for the use of a name, an endorsement, a logo, a look, a product, or a concept—is neither new nor unique to toys. Walt Disney began licensing his characters in 1929, and the popularity of merchandise based on Mickey Mouse saved several companies during the Depression—including Lionel, which offered a Mickey and Minnie handcar in 1935. One of the industry's most historically prominent members, Ideal, traces its turn-of-the-century origins to a toy associated with a celebrity. Ideal continued that tradition through the years, and its experiences illustrate both the pleasures and the pitfalls of hitching corporate wagons to stars.

The toy bear, from Pooh to Paddington, has been among the most perennially appealing of toys. Although its origin is subject to competing claims—the German company Steiff is among them—the term *teddy bear* is usually attributed to Morris Michtom, the owner of a Brooklyn candy store. President Theodore Roosevelt went to Mississippi in 1902 to settle a border dispute, and when he took time off to go hunting, he refused to shoot a bear cub. The incident attracted national attention after Clifford Berryman dramatized it in a cartoon that was picked up by newspapers around the country. According to the legend, Michtom wrote the president asking if he could make a stuffed bear cub and sell it as "Teddy's bear." Roosevelt supposedly answered that he did not think his name was worth much, but Michtom was welcome to it.

Manufactured by Ideal, Steiff, and anyone else who could sew them fast enough, Roosevelt's bears, as they were sometimes called, became the rage for many years. In 1907 alone Steiff sold almost a million. Various manufacturers offered bears their own sweaters, overalls, and baseball, tennis, or bathing suits, as well as miniature motor hats with goggles. Bears needed lots of clothes because they went everywhere. "Habitues of Central Park . . . were confronted by the sight of a pretty young woman dressed in the height of fashion and speeding along with the utmost unconcern," *Playthings* reported in November 1906. "She was driving her Columbia electric victoria and by her side was not a girl companion, nor a footman, nor even the accustomed pet bull terrier, but a small Teddy bear who sat up in solemn state."

The usual imitators were at work, even in those days. In 1909 the teddy bear was declared passé by an observer who announced that Billy Possum was to be the next rage. (Billy was named for President-elect William Taft, who had enthusiastically eaten roast possum on a visit to Atlanta.) The stuffed possum failed to generate the same excitement, however, and the hapless manufacturers who had rushed to meet the expected demand for possums were doomed to disappointment. The reports of teddy's death turned out to be premature. Some eighty years later, they still are.

To celebrate its fiftieth anniversary as a toy company in 1957, Ideal chose not to reproduce the teddy bear, because its executives considered it "too stylized." Instead they reissued the best-selling doll in the company's history, a doll that had helped it weather the Depression: the Shirley Temple doll. During the six years 1934–1939 Ideal sold more than one and a half million dolls at $6 and $12 retail. Even though children in 1957 did not know who Shirley Temple was, the dolls were a huge success.

Ideal had its share of disasters. When it licensed the right to make a line of motorcycle toys based on Evel Knievel, "daredevil . . . showman . . . egomaniac . . . con-artist," it found itself with the hottest license in its history. In their fourth year, 1976, Evel Knievel toys were still popular enough to account for 18 percent of Ideal's $137.6 million in sales. Unfortunately, the following September Knievel hit his former press agent over the head with a baseball bat outside the Twentieth Century Fox studios. The agent suffered compound fractures, and Knievel was sentenced to six months in jail. He said he wasn't sorry he had done it, though, because the agent had written a book about the Knievel family that Evel considered to be full of lies. Ideal, which had been prepared for some sales decline in the product line's fifth year, was disappointed but not surprised when the demand for Evel Knievel toys disappeared overnight.

The Evel Knievel episode put Ideal in the red for 1977, but the products had given the company four good years first. Twenty years earlier, Ideal, which has always been known for its dolls—including Bibsy, a doll that really drooled; Patti Playpal, a thirty-five-inch doll that could wear real three-year-olds' clothes; and Toni dolls with permanent-wave kits—had produced one of the most famous failures in the history of the toy industry.

In 1957 Ideal's president, Ben Michtom, the son of the founder, went on a European tour. While he was in Italy, he met the pope and was so impressed by the experience that he decided Ideal ought to produce a Baby Jesus doll. Michtom, who was Jewish, was convinced that Christian children and their parents would love to have a doll based on the infant Christ. He talked to a number of religious leaders and even secured the pontiff's blessing for the idea.

He returned to the company's Queens, New York, offices fired with enthusiasm, but the response from his co-managers was considerably less than he had expected. Most of them thought it was a terrible business idea and in questionable taste at best. The doll became a political issue around the company, dividing it into pro- and anti-Baby Jesus doll factions. Finally Michtom checked with some local religious leaders, who suggested that instead of calling it Baby Jesus, Ideal modify the name somehow. In 1958 Ideal brought the world The Most Wonderful Story. The nine-inch infant "Christ Child" doll was imaginatively packaged in what appeared to be a large book. When opened, the book exposed "cardboard color figures of the Blessed Virgin and St. Joseph" with the Jesus doll lying between them in a crib of straw.

The buyers accorded it a mixed reception, but Ideal was one of the industry's leading companies, and it was promoting the doll as an important product, so they all bought it. Ideal shipped it to the stores and waited, but customers never came. Thousands and thousands of The Most Wonderful Story sat on the shelves across the country. One store invested in a huge newspaper advertisement announcing and sold six.

Adults were not at all enraptured. They were horrified at the idea of children undressing a doll based on Jesus—and taking it into the bathtub, dragging it around, and subjecting it to all the normal indignities beloved dolls endure. The retailers were just as uncomfortable. "How do you mark down Jesus Christ?" they asked Michtom indignantly.

On those rare occasions when everyone agrees that a product is such a mistake that it cannot be sold at any price, the manufacturers override their "no-returns" policy and take it back. They would lose too much goodwill if they did not. As the junior man in the management hierarchy, Michtom's young relative Lionel Weintraub (who survived the ordeal to become president of the company) was given the delicate task of doll disposal. The story of the Jesus dolls has as many endings in Toyland as there are raconteurs. The most outrageous is that Ideal broke the dolls into pieces and shipped them to underdeveloped countries for sale as relics. The truth, according to the man who did the actual deed: "Every worker in the company's factory was given one for Christmas and the rest were destroyed." Sometimes the best place for an ill-conceived product is a landfill.

Even when licensed characters are popular and the toys are in demand, they do not always generate reliable royalties for their licensers. Nimble producers jump in fast with counterfeit or unlicensed merchandise while there are shortages and slip out again ahead of the infringement suits. In the mid-1950s Walt Disney's *Davy Crockett* adventures created such a gold rush of business in western-style items that, in the words of one observer, "Any cat fool enough to wander across the street had three things to worry about—dogs, cars, and coonskin-cap manufacturers." One manufacturer even took the stuffing out of his toy bears, laid them out on the floor, and put a sign over them that read, "The Bear that Davy Crockett Shot."

Licensing in the world of toys increased in importance throughout the 1960s and 1970s, with character licensing predominating. The 1960s fads included the Beatles in 1963 and Batman in 1966, due to the popularity of ABC's TV show (a good example of the industry's cyclicity—the 1989 movie made Batman the hottest licensed character of the year). In the late 1970s personality fashion dolls were extremely popular, and it became something of a status symbol to be reproduced in miniature. Farrah Fawcett-Majors, Sonny and Cher, and Brooke Shields were among those so honored, a distinction that sometimes carried considerable rewards. Mego eventually paid Cher $1 million in royalties.

During the same period Cincinnati's Kenner Products Corporation produced Star Wars toys and Strawberry Shortcake, a pair of license-based product lines so successful that they revolutionized the way the toy industry approached licensing. By the early 1980s licensing would evolve from a marketing tool into a marketing crutch as toy companies relied on licenses instead of product development and innovation. In 1985 the Licensing Industry Merchandisers' Association estimated that nearly two-thirds of the toys sold were licensed products. A hot license backed by elaborate marketing became the way to make big money. Brand creation substituted for genuine play value.

Kenner, known for its Play-Doh and Easy-Bake Ovens, did not rely solely on licensed products. One of its biggest failures came from a licensed product, while one of its internally developed products provided it with one of its most famous (or infamous) successes. The idea of basing a doll on a Boy Scout was brought to Kenner from outside. The Kenner people were enthusiastic about the idea and created a major toy line around the concept, offering thirty different items, or SKUs (stock-keeping units). Sales never took off, and Kenner later concluded that Steve Scout was just too square and too close to life; he should have been larger than life.

Kenner did not make that mistake with its Baby Alive doll. In 1972 Kenner's president, Bernard Loomis, and executive vice president, Joseph Mendelsohn, took two products they considered exciting but potentially controversial to Minneapolis to show their corporate parent. At that time Kenner was owned by General Mills. Mendelsohn demonstrated the first product for the chairman and president of the conglomerate: a pregnant mother doll. The mother came with a removable baby doll. Worried about their corporate image, General Mills' chairman and president were unenthusiastic.

The other doll had been invented at Kenner. Dolls that could drink and wet had been around for years, but Baby Alive was more advanced: she could eat "solids." When someone held a spoon or bottle up to her mouth, she masticated. Then, after a suitable interval, she defecated. The cereal executives were horrified, yet fascinated. Once Loomis forgot to put a disposable diaper on the doll before feeding it, and it extruded poo-poo gel all over his arm. "Who in the world would ever want such a messy thing?" asked his disgusted boss. As it turned out, there were vast hordes of children eager to own a defecating dolly. Baby Alive was the number-one-selling doll in 1973, and Kenner went on to sell three million of them. Extra "cherry, banana, and lime" food packets were available for extra feedings (and to answer the obvious question, yes, what went in red, yellow, or green came out red, yellow, or green).

Kenner president Bernie Loomis was becoming one of the giants of Toyland, his reputation secured by the successes he enjoyed at Kenner. Known throughout the industry, he has been described as brilliant, astute, creative, a marketing genius, "a legend in his own mind," tough and demanding on subordinates, long-winded. A white-haired, jowly man, he had come to Kenner from Mattel, where he had spent eleven years ("ten great years out of eleven") rising through the ranks of sales management to become vice president of Mattel's wheels division.

When Mattel became entangled in legal problems in the early 1970s, Loomis decided to leave Mattel, get a Ph.D., and teach business at UCLA. General Mills approached him to run its entire toy group (which included Kenner, Parker Brothers, Lionel Trains, and some other small toy companies the conglomerate had acquired), but Loomis refused. He did not want an administrative job: he was a hands-on toyman. Eventually General Mills came back and offered him the job of Kenner's president, which was what both he and General Mills had really wanted for him in the first place.

Kenner tasted its first big (over $50 million) television-promoted success with an action-figure line based on the television program "The Six Million Dollar Man," whose pilot program the company's design director had spotted when he awoke from a doze in front of the television set one evening. His enthusiasm was confirmed when a marketing director heard a little boy in a focus group for Kenner's Boy Scout doll say, "I don't want to be Steve Scout, I want to be Steve Austin." Kenner took the hint, captured the license, and later followed up with the Bionic Woman doll. Action figures for girls are never as popular as those for boys, but, aided by her accessories (Kenner's designers gave her a Bionic Beauty Salon and a Bionic Sports Car), she returned a nice, if not bionic, profit.

It was another action-figure line from Kenner that stimulated the entire action-figure category into becoming the dominant boys' toy category for the next several years. Action figures' only real competition has been electronic games.

Kenner did not seize on *Star Wars* immediately. Twentieth Century Fox had sent a rough version of the story to several toy companies to drum up interest, but, like Mattel and others, Kenner had already decided not to pursue it. Space was considered dead at that point; the successful action figures were land based. Also, movies were considered risky licensing prospects, since they tend to be short-lived properties. Even products based on the blockbuster *E.T.* failed to translate into widely successful toy sales. Television, which presents the same characters week after week, is considered a more reliable source of licensable properties for children's merchandise. Furthermore, Kenner already had more than enough projects.

Several people became extremely excited about the concept of *Star Wars*, however. Two of the designers, science-fiction buffs, were familiar with the work of George Lucas, who was then relatively unknown, and they worked up so much enthusiasm about the idea that they convinced the vice president of product planning to approach Loomis. Dave Okada, who was one of the designers, remembers their exhilaration when Loomis agreed to bid. "Bernie Loomis was the type of boss who, once he was comfortable with a subordinate, would give him a lot of rope. We were a bunch of Young Turks in our early thirties, and he allowed us to race ahead with time, energy, and money. We were racing back and forth to the West Coast to talk to Alan Ladd, Jr., Dennis Stanfill, George Lucas at his ranch, working so hard and crazy on the little guys, just trying to get the characters and vehicles ready fast enough and good enough."

Once Loomis committed, he took no half measures. Kenner tied up all toy and game rights to the property, except for one item already licensed to Damon, a hobby company. News about the deal began to leak out almost immediately. Loomis's daughter Merry was leafing through *Time* magazine in the reading room of a kibbutz in Israel when she saw a story noting mysteriously that a major toy executive had licensed the rights to the characters of the hit movie *Star Wars*. I sure hope it's Daddy, she thought to herself, otherwise he'll be unbearable to live with.

Merry Loomis was not the only one to learn about the deal from the press. The *New York Times* ran an item saying that the world's largest toy company was going to make a line of toys based on *Star Wars*, and, after its stock jumped four points, the world's largest independent toy company, Mattel, issued a denial. Then the Securities and Exchange Commission contacted General Mills, whose toy companies' combined sales exceeded Mattel's, to see if it had bought those rights. If so, the SEC wanted it to announce the fact to prevent insider trading on the basis of that information.

General Mills' chairman had no idea. When he asked, Loomis was happy to report that he had. With a whimsicality unusual in a conglomerate, General Mills then told the press that Kenner had not acquired the national rights. It had not even bought the international rights. It had bought the galactic rights to *Star Wars*—at a minimum rate of $500,000 a year. Since Kenner eventually sold more than 300 million *Star Wars* toys, it had been astute to lock up the galaxy.

During one of the early meetings on the Star Wars products, Loomis and Okada casually made a decision that affected the action-figure category for years to come. Okada asked Loomis what size he thought the figures should be, and Loomis noted that they should be smaller than other action figures because they wanted to sell a lot of vehicles and accessories, and if they made the vehicles too big they would have to price them too high to sell big volumes. "Luke Skywalker should be this big," pronounced Loomis, crooking his large thumb and index finger into a backward *C*. Since he was a designer, Okada always had a measuring tool with him, and he measured Loomis's finger spread. It came out to three-and-three-quarters inches.

The next day Okada walked into Loomis's office and set a group of figures onto his desk like a police lineup. Starting with Luke Skywalker at three-and-three-quarters inches, he had made the malevolent Darth Vader larger and the endearing robot R2-D2 smaller. The line set a new scale for action-figure toys, one that became standard for many years because it enabled manufacturers to offer major accessories such as vehicles and headquarters in smaller and more affordable sizes.

None of the merchandise could be ready by Christmas 1977, but the movie was so popular that Kenner was loath to miss the major buying season. The company startled the industry, and its customers, by offering to sell "early-bird certificates"—IOUs promising to deliver the purchased item as soon as it was ready. Some merchants scorned the certificates, but those who took them quickly sold out. Kenner's competitors leapt into the breach with any substitute they could manage, to try to skim off some of the demand. Ideal Toys offered customers Space Warriors and the Star Team. Kenner later sued, and it won by convincing the judge to watch the movie and see for himself how imitative Ideal's products were. The judge did not want to watch the movie, but Kenner's lawyers kept insisting it was important. Once he finally saw it, the judge decided that he had to view it several times just to be sure. He also found that he needed to bring his grandchildren along to help him.

A couple of years later Loomis and Kenner tried another innovative strategy that turned out to be so successful that it came to dominate the toy industry's marketing in the 1980s.

The American Greetings Corporation had been involved with character licensing before, but licensing had never been a big part of its operations. Second in size to Hallmark, the greeting card company had started licensing by accident, with its Hollie Hobbie character. It had been selling cards and giftware based on the little girl in a poke bonnet ever since 1967, when a young woman actually named Hollie Hobbie had sent in some samples of her work. In 1971 the company included a rag doll in an ad for its Hollie Hobbie merchandise and received so many inquiries about licensing the character that it began a modest licensing operation. It allowed Knickerbocker Toys, which manufactured Raggedy Ann and Andy, to make a Hollie Hobbie rag doll. The income stream was so steady and so profitable that the company began to seek licensees actively. By 1977 it had forty.

Sensing a new business opportunity, American Greetings' president put Jack Chojnacki in charge of licensing and marketing and Ralph Shaffer over the creative process. Chojnacki, a

friendly man who likes ties adorned with ducks, possesses the
most difficult name in the toy business; its pronunciation, hoy-
nat'-ski, is so unrelated to its spelling that he has the phonetic
spelling printed on his stationery and business cards. Chojnacki
and Shaffer decided to take some of their ideas for greeting cards
around to two or three manufacturers that had licensed the
Hollie Hobbie character, to see if they were interested in getting
in on the ground floor and launching their products at the same
time American Greetings brought out the card series.

About that time, 1978, they first met Bernie Loomis. Loomis,
who had just been promoted to head General Mills's entire toy
group, had gone to American Greetings to talk about Hollie
Hobbie tea sets, which were licensed by an English company
General Mills had just acquired. After the discussions, Chojnacki and Shaffer showed him the portfolio of concepts they
were exploring as licensing properties.

Leafing through it, Loomis stopped at the picture of a little
girl wearing a red dress, white pinafore, green-and-white-
striped stockings, and strawberry-patterned bonnet. This character, which American Greetings was planning to launch in
1979, had evolved because the company's market-research department had found that strawberries sold well on cards and gift
wrap. One of the art directors had taken a popular figure from
previous cards, a little girl with an orange hat, and had
"strawberrified" her. According to Toyland legend, Loomis
looked up from the drawings and announced, "We're going to
make history."

American Greetings delayed the introduction of Strawberry
Shortcake greeting cards for a year and teamed up with Kenner
to create a major line of toys and an aggressive licensing campaign based on a brand-new character. Up to that point, a
licensable property was a property so successful in one medium—movie, television, or comic-strip, for example—that it
could be used to presell other products by trading on its recog-
nizability. With Strawberry Shortcake, American Greetings and
Kenner took a character without a past and created a personality
expressly for licensing and using as a brand.

They launched it to the trade by saying Hollie Hobbie had

merged with Star Wars to create Strawberry Shortcake. In the first year (1980), backed by $4 million in advertising and a television special, forty-eight companies brought Strawberry Shortcake products into the market and generated about $100 million worth of clothes, toys, housewares, sheets, and towels—some of which were even strawberry scented.

In 1981 sixty-three companies manufactured Strawberry Shortcake merchandise. The character was supported by a $7 million advertising campaign, another television special, personal appearances on the National Easter Seal Society telethon and in stores (American Greetings loaned them costumes), feature stories in the *New York Times* and the *Wall Street Journal*, point-of-purchase advertising, special boutiques in stores, and her "berry" own float in the Macy's Thanksgiving Day parade. Result: $500 million in retail sales for the year.

By 1982 American Greetings, which had formed a separate licensing group, Those Characters From Cleveland (TCFC), began issuing the kinds of manuals and suggestions now standard in the licensing business. TCFC, for example, offered retailers Strawberry Shortcake's "Baker's Dozen," thirteen ideas for in-store promotions, including coloring or look-alike contests, fashions shows, and "sweetstakes." More than 56 million Strawberry Shortcake toys were sold altogether.

Toy companies with strong products began licensing them out to hundreds of other manufacturers. Barbie, G.I. Joe, and Hot Wheels stared out of every imaginable kind of merchandise. (One of Mattel's favorite experiences was licensing the Hot Wheels brand to a pediatric-wheelchair company.) Licensing companies were promoting their characters as spokespersons for national charities and other public-service campaigns; even the White House allowed a large number of the characters to participate in its annual Easter Egg Roll.

While American Greetings created TCFC, Bernie Loomis formed the Marketing and Design Group (MAD) to create toys and licensable properties for the General Mills toy companies and others. Loomis had not liked running General Mills' entire toy group, and all parties agreed he was better with products than administration, so General Mills allowed him to branch out. The first time MAD teamed up with TCFC, they created Care Bears, small bears with patented tummy designs (a heart for love, sunshine for happiness)—which became another huge hit.

Two hits in a row is usually the limit in the toy business, and after Care Bears TCFC began to have a few flops—such as the unmemorable Herself the Elf. Loomis left General Mills to go into a joint venture with Hasbro that he called Great Licensing And Design (GLAD). After that he disbanded GLAD and began consulting for a number of toy companies under his own name.

TCFC has remained one of the most successful companies in the business at inventing licensable characters. In the past few years it has sold Lady Lovelylocks miniature dolls and Popples transformable plush toys to Mattel, Nosy Bears to Hasbro, Special Blessings praying dolls to Kenner, and Ring Raiders to Matchbox Toys.

Strawberry Shortcake was the face that launched a thousand properties. Ever since her success, companies have been trying to develop original properties to sell as toys and generate licensing royalties at the same time. As usual, it is not as easy as it looks, and there have been hundreds of failures. But even when it has not created an original character, nowadays any company serious about a promotional line of action figures, small dolls, or even vehicles tries to set up a licensing program—pajamas, lunch boxes, sheets—to maximize its product's exposure.

In 1989 Mattel accorded Strawberry Shortcake the sincerest form of flattery when it appeared at Toy Fair with a line of miniature dolls based around a character called Cherry Merry Muffin and backed by an ambitious licensing plan. Although Cherry's scent was changed, her lineage was clear—all the way back to her "berry pink" ancestor.

A good licensing program can never ensure a hit toy, however. It can only increase the return on a good property.

What makes a property catch on remains a mystery. A good property is a phenomenon without explanation.

10

OF CABBAGES AND KINGS

BY THE END OF 1983 THE UNITED STATES of America was in the middle of an epidemic. The disease was Cabbage Patch Kid Mania, and the symptom was an insatiable desire to obtain at least one Cabbage Patch Kid doll, presumably for a child. At a Zayre store in Wilkes-Barre, Pennsylvania, a woman's leg was broken when a crowd grew tired after waiting eight hours for the dolls and erupted into a riot. The store manager protected himself with a baseball bat. In a New Jersey Child World store a pregnant woman was reportedly knocked to the ground by a crowd of people running for the dolls. A Kansas City postman who couldn't get one for his daughter locally flew to London to buy one.

In November a pair of disc jockeys on KWTI-FM radio station in Milwaukee, Wisconsin, joked that a B-29 bomber was going to fly over the local stadium and drop two thousand Cabbage Patch Kids to anyone bringing a catcher's mitt and a credit card. They were as stunned as anyone else when more than a dozen people braved thirty-seven-mile-an-hour winds and subzero temperatures in the forlorn belief that the impossible-to-obtain dolls were actually going to fall out of the sky into their outstretched mitts.

Whether the mass hysteria stemmed from children's wishes or from adults' competitive instincts, the rage lasted for several years and made millions of dollars for the inventor, the manufacturer, the licensing agent, and even the outside designers. While it raged, it virtually eradicated the rest of the baby-doll market. Sales of other large dolls did not start to make a comeback until Cabbage Patch Kids had been on the market several years.

Today the converted red-brick schoolhouse that was Coleco's headquarters during that extraordinary period has been sold to the Ames Corporation. The West Hartford, Connecticut, building was just one of the casualties of the bust that followed the boom.

Across Long Island Sound, a wood-and-glass house belonging to Artie and Judy Albert perches on a knoll overlooking the water. Calder sculptures and an artificial pond adorn the grounds, and inside, rich-hued rooms and Memphis-style furniture reflect the artist's eye.

Eight hundred miles to the south, a quartet of paintings greets visitors to the sleek reception rooms of an Atlanta, Georgia, marketing and licensing firm. Clearly the work of the pop-art king, the paintings' message is obvious. Andy Warhol decreed that Cabbage Patch Kids, like Marilyn Monroe and Campbell's Soup cans, were important icons of American culture.

It is no secret that Schlaifer Nance & Company owes its elegant, expensive decor to that very icon, so the Warhol art sends another message, this one subtler: we know the dolls made us what we are, but don't confuse us with the product. Cabbage Patch Kids are Middle America, but we're not.

Middle America lies one hundred miles to the north, in the foothills of the Appalachian Mountains. Right in the middle of Cleveland, Georgia, population 5,100, sits a pair of white frame houses, circa 1919. Bright pink shutters frame their windows, and a profusion of flowers and cabbage plants erupts in front, in back, and all around. Visitors, whose ages appear to range from three minutes to one hundred years, enter and leave the buildings in a steady stream all day, every day—at the rate of about a million a year.

One of the buildings is BabyLand General Hospital, as professional an operation as Coleco or Schlaifer Nance. Its interior is just as carefully calculated as the decor at Schlaifer Nance, although here the signals are even more complex. The apparent folksiness of BabyLand General should never be mistaken for naïveté. This, too, is a sophisticated operation.

Cabbage Patch Kid dolls generated $600 million in wholesale revenues for Coleco in 1985—and $540 million the year before. Add in the other licensed products, and the totals edge up to about a billion dollars a year, wholesale. Part of every dollar went back to Cleveland, Georgia.

Xavier Roberts is the father of the Cabbage Patch Kids. The story of Roberts's own life sounds like something he might have invented. The youngest of six children in a poor mountain family, Roberts lost his father in a car accident when he was only six. His mother, Eula, supported the family by working in a factory and sewing quilts at night. As he grew older, Xavier, artistic like his mother, made and sold crafts and quilts. His high school senior class voted him "Most Talented."

With the help of a grant, Roberts managed to enter Truett McConnell College, also in Cleveland, where he majored in art. He and Debbie Morehead, a painter friend, began traveling to craft shows and flea markets on the weekends, showing his pottery, her paintings, Eula Roberts's quilts, wooden toys, and other handmade items they thought they could sell. During the week Roberts managed the craft shop at the area's Unicoi State Park, and at the flea markets he sometimes met artists whose work he would take to sell in the shop.

At this point in the story, the official *Legend of the Cabbage Patch Kids* explains that in 1976 Roberts was doing research in the school library when he learned about an old German folk art called needle molding. He supposedly began experimenting with the medium, now known as soft sculpture, and went on to create the Little People, the Cabbage Patch Kids' predecessors.

In fact, Roberts did create the Little People, but it was after he had seen some soft-sculpture dolls by a Kentucky artist named

Martha Nelson at one of the shows he had entered. Soft sculpture had been around for years, but Nelson's dolls had a great deal of personality, and Roberts offered to sell them in the Unicoi shop. Nelson agreed, but the two quarreled, and she took them out of the shop. Roberts soon began showing his own creations. In 1980, after BabyLand General began making millions of dollars and receiving national publicity but before the dolls were a national craze, the artist (now named Martha Nelson Thomas) sued Roberts for stealing her idea. The judge in the case ruled that Roberts had indeed used elements of her design, but since she had not copyrighted the design, there had been no infringement. Roberts paid her a settlement, but the story of German needle molding became the party line.

The source of the inspiration is not really important. Xavier Roberts is the true creator of the Kids because he is the one who brought them to life. A slight, handsome, bearded man with boyish charm, Roberts is shrewd, calculating, and worldly—and at the same time naive, innocent, and extremely hardworking. A multimillionaire, he still dreams of becoming the next Walt Disney.

Roberts always saw the dolls as sculptural caricatures of children, and once he began to exhibit them, the dolls soon eclipsed the other craft-show merchandise he and Morehead offered. "Our work was great until the babies came along," he recalls. "But there were lots of painters and lots of potters, and the babies were fresh. So we put our other things on the back burner." He treated the dolls as real people, calling them babies, displaying them in cribs in realistic poses, and never branding them with a price tag "because I thought that was terrible" to do to a human being. (It also allowed him to charge whatever he thought the market would bear.) "This is Lorna May," he would say, holding the doll gently. "She's been a little cranky because she had to eat her peanut butter sandwich without jelly today, and she hates peanut butter without jelly."

Roberts's combination of creativity and salesmanship enabled him to add to the concept as he went along, and that is how Cabbage Patch Kids evolved: a product of serendipity, opportunism, and logic. Logic dictated that since the dolls were supposed to be alive, he would call them babies instead of dolls. To this day, *doll* is still the *d* word in Cleveland, Georgia.

The adoption gimmick came about by accident, but Roberts was astute enough to capitalize on it. "Everyone was always saying, 'how much are they, how much are they,' " he recounts with an irritation that is difficult to understand, since he chose to sell a product but refused to give it a price tag. One day Roberts had a headache, and when a customer ventured to ask a doll's price, he snapped, "They're not for sale." He recovered himself and thought fast. "They are up for adoption," he explained, and an important part of the fantasy was launched.

The adoption process, which required purchasers to raise their right hand and repeat an Oath of Adoption Roberts had written, made the dolls even more popular. But the dolls' success turned the operation that had begun as a handicraft into a treadmill. "It was no longer art," says Roberts. "It was paying the bills. The fun had gone. We'd go to a show and do real good. Then we'd take all that money and buy more art supplies. We'd work real hard all week—Debbie, my mother, and I were all sewing—and they were also going to yard sales to get clothes for the dolls (I'm saying dolls because that's what you'd say). But the more we sold, the more pressure we had to get clothes. Then we'd drive to the shows on the weekends and have to smile at all these people and act like we were the happiest people in the world."

They were exhausted, but the dolls were receiving publicity and recognition. In October 1977 at a Kissimmee, Florida, craft show, they won awards in two categories, both accompanied by welcome cash prizes. Dexter, a bald Little Person, won first prize in the sculpture division. The selection was angrily contested by other artists, who derided Dexter, calling him a "rag doll" and, worse, a "stuffed sack." Dexter, needless to say, had the last laugh and today resides in Cleveland, where he occupies a place of honor, his very own glass case.

Debbie Morehead dropped out about this time, but Roberts carried on. "It was a very depressed time of my life. I was going to quit—we were so tired. I only kept going because I always saw grandeur the next week." In 1978 he attended a six-show circuit of Florida art shows. He and a friend packed the dolls into his used Jaguar ("Instead of buying a car that was functional, I bought one that was beautiful"), and everything began to go wrong.

The car broke down, and they had to waste time and money getting it towed. Then they had to rent another car, repack, and hurry down to make the first show. They needn't have bothered. "The first show was a complete bomb. The second show was awful. We were getting third-degree burns, just sitting there with no business."

Finally, their luck turned. "At the last minute this lady walked up and bought five quilts and adopted four dolls. And paid cash. I've never forgotten her name. She was a Mrs. Losenta from Chicago—she owned a macaroni factory, I think. She was old and sent her car around to pick everything up. The car was a Rolls-Royce. She took us out to dinner and even let me drive the car. It really gave me a taste. I thought, I want one of those—and today I have one [and a few other luxury cars, besides]. She was a very nice lady. I probably would have given up if she hadn't come around that day.

"When I came back from that trip I decided I was going to do one of two things: I was either going to quit or form a company. I knew the idea was great. People always went crazy over [the dolls]. You'd see them at a show. They'd say, I'd never want that, I never would. Then they'd see it again. Then they'd hold it and look at it. Then they'd start listening up and begin to say, I have to have one. And of course, the price was going up. The week before it had been thirty-five dollars, and now it was forty dollars. So I'd say, you'd better get one right now, next week it's going to be fifty dollars. Even from the beginning they were collectors' items, but I was out there hawking them, bringing them to life. That's really been the key."

Roberts is right. The fantasy was what made the dolls special. When the purchasers, most of them adults, participated in the fantasy, the experience transcended a simple purchase and the doll became more than a doll. Adults would take their dolls to restaurants, fuss over them in public, buy them things. Strangers would come up and ask about them.

In July 1978 Roberts and five friends formed Original Appalachian Artworks (OAA). Each brought unique talents or assets. Roberts's high school friend Paula, later OAA's president, kept her job as a waitress, which eased the economic situation. His college friend Linda could write, so she wrote everything from letters to advertisements. Roberts had worked with Sharon at the Unicoi shop, and he knew she was a good organizer. Carol owned a sewing machine, and her husband, Terry, was strong and willing. Each of them other than Roberts held 5 percent of the company; today they are all out.

Roberts describes all their decisions as simple logic. "None of it was a stroke of genius," he explains. "It was just a lot of common sense. We called ourselves Original Appalachian Artworks because that was what we were selling. They were supposed to be real, so we called them babies. Babies are born in a hospital, so we put them in a hospital." They planned to call their shop BabyLand General Hospital, even before they found a building.

Sharon's ex-husband's mother was the daughter of the late L. G. Neal, the Cleveland doctor who had delivered most of the babies in the county. Sharon and she were still on good terms, and Dr. Neal's house and clinic had been vacant for nine years, so she let the group use the buildings as a headquarters in exchange for renovations. They restored the buildings themselves and furnished them with used hospital equipment and baby furniture they found at yard sales. Since their energy exceeded their funds, they financed OAA's capital investments with Roberts's VISA card until VISA cut him off for nonpayment.

BabyLand General was an immediate success. The employees dressed like doctors and nurses and staged deliveries from the cabbage patch. Wearing surgical gowns and masks, they would inject a cloth cabbage with imagicillin, cut the stem with an easyotomy, spank the newborn Little Person, wrap it in a receiving blanket, and solicit names from the audience.

Roberts had never loved selling his sculptures to children, and most of the BabyLand "parents" were women. OAA promoted the dolls as collectibles, stressing their value as investments whose value would increase. Over the years many customers have bought large numbers of the dolls. Some have made special clothes for their Little People, even sewing outfits that match their own or their children's. Others hold parties for them or take them on regular outings. Many, encouraged by OAA's estimates of their rising value, simply enjoy calculating the supposed increases in the worth of their assets.

Roberts abandoned art shows and took the dolls to gift shows, where he hoped to attract orders from large retailers. Even if he had landed an order, he would not have been able to fill it because OAA lacked the facilities for mass production. That never worried Roberts. He always believed in himself.

Although OAA failed to get national distribution, the dolls attracted national publicity, which ultimately proved more valuable. Reporters covering the gift shows for the local newspapers and television stations always featured them, because they were interesting and different, and soon BabyLand General began to attract attention from the national media.

The coverage did not appear by accident. OAA quickly learned how to throw a media event. The group staged a delivery of the first and only BabyLand quintuplets (adopted as an investment by a Georgia couple for five thousand dollars); a Great Egg Hunt, which included a golden egg, an Easter parade, baby chicks, ducks, and rabbits; and a Christmas Extravaganza featuring the World's Largest Christmas Stocking, thirty-six feet long and twenty-four feet wide.

Both *Newsweek* and *Time* ran stories about the dolls (*Time* called them "bundles of polyester joy"), and Amy Carter was frequently photographed with her Little Person. Their biggest publicity break came when they were featured on a nationally syndicated program called "Real People," which specialized in bizarre subjects.

By that time Roberts was making so much money he began building a dream house, a fantastic creation he had designed with his brother. The walls are rows of wood-framed windows that open onto breathtaking views of the surrounding mountains. The roof is a mass of gables. Three stories of rooms surround an indoor swimming pool that could be entered by sliding down a three-story slide. Unfortunately, the lush plants all over the house were the only ones to enjoy the pool; the walls and ceilings began to crack and peel from the humidity produced by the pool, and Roberts finally had to drain it.

Today the house, evidence of what Roberts calls his "visions of grandeur," has been turned into OAA headquarters, and the rooms are stuffed with desks, drawing boards, telephones, filing cabinets, computer terminals, and every other kind of office paraphernalia. Roberts and his fleet of cars reside at a more modest residence, and he has transferred his visions of grandeur to his Villagio di Montagna, a luxury resort complex he hopes will attract affluent travelers to the area.

A year after BabyLand General appeared on "Real People," sales began to slide for the first time. Roberts had to lay off a number of employees in 1981, but he did not relinquish his dream of selling his "babies" nationwide.

Soon afterward, Roger Schlaifer showed up in Cleveland. Smooth, polished Roger Schlaifer was never the city slicker out to trick the simple country boy. He was too smart to underestimate Roberts. Believing that he could offer Roberts a valuable channel into the world of mass marketing, Schlaifer wanted to help OAA with its marketing, develop a large-scale licensing plan, and take over as OAA's advertising agency. With his wife, Susanne Nance, he ran an advertising and concept-development company that had worked on a range of diverse products from IBM and Coca-Cola to Hot Rollers, roller skates that looked like jogging shoes with wheels.

Schlaifer had become intrigued by the Little People when he had seen his six-year-old daughter, Jessica, develop an immediate and overpowering attachment to Lavinia Merle, a Little Person that arrived on Christmas 1980. Fascinated by the strength of the fantasy, he began to imagine the product as a property for a national licensing program.

Roberts liked Schlaifer's ideas, and they signed a contract making Schlaifer Nance the product's licensing and marketing agent, although not its advertising agency. OAA also retained the right to make its own handmade dolls even if Schlaifer Nance licensed the toy rights to another company.

The first thing Schlaifer Nance and Roberts changed was the name of the product. Fisher-Price had been producing thumb-sized plastic-peg figures called Little People for years, so the name Little People was already taken and well established in the toy category. Schlaifer liked the idea of making them "kids." Both he and Roberts hoped to make the property appeal to boys as well as girls, and to do that Schlaifer considered it essential to position the dolls as children rather than babies. "What red-blooded American boy is going to walk around with a baby?" he asked. He also thought "kids" added a sense of rough-and-tumble naughtiness. OAA had already established the cabbage patch as the dolls' birthplace, so the name Cabbage Patch Kids evolved naturally.

Schlaifer intended to use the dolls' country flavor to establish Cabbage Patch Kids as an updated American brand—a sort of Laura Ashley look for children. His wife wrote a new background story for the Kids and created a number of new characters, because Schlaifer hoped to expand into television, books, and movies.

Schlaifer's licensing priorities were toys, apparel, and bedding. Toys were the most important, and he approached the major toy manufacturers by sending each of them a doll by courier service. Accompanying each doll was a handwritten note to the chief executive officer from the doll introducing itself, describing the concept of Cabbage Patch Kids, and explaining that she was looking for a licensee.

The doll that eventually became the biggest new doll product in Toyland history was turned down by everyone. Mattel, Kenner, and Fisher-Price all said no. Hasbro at least market-tested the doll, but the Kids performed poorly. The most encouraging response came from Tomy America, the American subsidiary of a giant Japanese toy company. At the time Tomy was headed by Bill Carlson, whose sensible midwestern demeanor must mask a bizarre sense of humor and an unusual style of leadership: as president of Playmates Toys, he brought the world Teenage Mutant Ninja Turtles, and he first learned of his company's interest in Cabbage Patch Kids when he walked into the office of his marketing vice president Bill Reiter and found a Little Person tied to a chair.

A few days earlier, Schlaifer Nance had received a note on Tomy stationery. Constructed of words pasted together, it warned, "We have Pauline Zandra and we are holding her for ransom and it will take a royalty-free license to save this special child. Please act fast. We mean business." It was signed "Bill Reiter's Gang."

What Carlson saw was the photography session for the next step. The extortionists followed up with a Polaroid picture of Pauline Zandra gagged and tied to a chair with a knife held to her throat. "Help! Do Not Delay!" urged the note, typewritten and unsigned this time. "Time is running out for little Pauline."

Schlaifer was pleased to hear from Pauline Zandra's captors because he considered Tomy one of the top toy companies in the country. After the second note, however, the gang's urgency seemed to dissipate. Although Schlaifer responded, he heard nothing more from Tomy America. Meanwhile, a company that he had not even approached about manufacturing the doll became interested. Coleco, which was dominated by electronic products, had never produced any kind of doll. Schlaifer had been negotiating with the company to license the Cabbage Patch Kids brand for a ride-on toy, but when Coleco's president, Arnold Greenberg, heard about Schlaifer's problems licensing the dolls, he suggested Coleco.

Coleco was interested specifically because the company had no similar product. The company had twice watched the market for its electronic products disappear overnight, leaving it stuck with mountains of expensive inventories, and it was looking now for basic, more traditional products. As Greenberg pointed out, "A doll is about as basic as you can get." Any new product requires a large initial outlay, but the cost of starting up a doll would be minuscule compared with that of starting up an electronic product.

No one at Coleco had any experience with dolls, but they made some good decisions and enjoyed a little luck. Al Kahn, the marketing vice president in charge of the project, was not even experienced at marketing, but he was willing to listen. Dick Schwarzchild, an experienced toy marketer who headed Coleco's advertising agency, suggested that Kahn contact Artie and Judy Albert to design and market new versions of the doll for Coleco. Kahn hired them and then left them alone.

Artie and Judy had both spent over twenty years in the doll business, most of them at Ideal Toys. Judy had been designing dolls and doll clothes for Ideal since 1959, and Artie had run the doll division for many years. The two had left Ideal shortly before it had been taken over by CBS and had been on their own for about a year.

The Alberts flew down to Georgia and talked with Xavier Roberts. They believed in the strength of the concept from the beginning: it would have been surprising if they had not. While visiting BabyLand General, Judy found herself standing next to a middle-aged woman. The woman's husband had one doll, and she held two. As she gently adjusted a necklace on one of her dolls, she turned to Judy. "Some people just buy the babies and then they never pay attention to them," she explained sadly.

Judy designed three versions of the Kids: miniature statues that a company called Panosh Place later licensed; six-and-a-half-inch figurines; and soft versions of the originals. Although she made the soft dolls smaller than Roberts's, she made sure to retain the heft of a real baby. She also duplicated the Little People's chubbiness and the supplicating position of their arms. To her, their homely faces and upstretched arms said, Pick me up, I need you.

Coleco tested all three on Atlanta women and children who already owned at least one of the Little People. At the time OAA's Little People were selling for $80.00 to $100.00—or for even more if they were signed personally by Xavier Roberts. The women at the tests were enthusiastic about the rigid plastic figurines, but when the moderator pulled the cloth away to reveal the soft dolls, they gasped with excitement. They told the moderator they would gladly pay $50.00 for the dolls. Coleco had been planning to sell them for $18.50.

Roberts and his entourage, who now treat him like a rock star, watched the tests and were thrilled by the strength of the women's response. On the way back to Cleveland, however, they admitted to one another that they were beginning to worry that the Coleco product might destroy the demand for their hand-made "babies." Instead, it helped them.

Coleco used tests extensively, first to shape the product and then to plan the marketing campaign. It found that children really liked the dolls' southern-style double names, such as Tyler Bo and Sybil Sadie. The fact that the names were difficult to pronounce was a positive factor; the children liked mastering the complicated names and impressing adults.

Children were also fascinated by the idea of adoption. In his marketing plan Artie had advised Coleco to retain the concept, even though the ceremony could not be duplicated with a store-bought, mass-market doll. Coleco worried that the concept would be controversial but took the risk and used it anyway.

The Alberts believed that the most important element of the fantasy was the unique individuality of each doll. Searching for a process that would enable a manufacturer to make an enormous variety of one product even though the product was mass-produced, Judy worked out a matrix. Coleco used different heads, eye and hair colors, hair and clothing styles, and the presence or absence of freckles to produce about 100,000 different dolls in the first run. Furthermore, each doll was given a different double name.

Even if Coleco manufactured millions, each doll could be a unique individual, just as each human being is. Later on, when Cabbage Patch Kids became a phenomenon instead of just a toy, psychologists and marketing experts speculated on the key to the product's success. There was the dolls' homeliness, which enabled children to identify with them. And the adoption process. And the quality of the product, not to mention the cachet of owning a scarce commodity. But the dolls' individuality tied all those elements together; their uniqueness made them more like people than any other doll ever made before, which gave the whole fantasy a kind of eerie credibility.

To set up production, the Alberts flew to Hong Kong in November 1982 and began scouting for fabrics, buttons, laces, embroidery, and other trimmings to give the dolls just the right country look. Finding fabric patterns in a small-enough scale for doll clothes is often a problem, but they discovered a manufacturer who was willing to knit them some samples they liked in a day.

The Alberts labored over every detail on the Cabbage Patch

Kids because details were important. They had given a Hong Kong manufacturer stencils for the dolls' eyes, but after seeing his interpretation of her instructions, Judy decided to make them herself. Holed up in a factory, she worked twelve hours a day for five days. She was so allergic to the hair used to make the sample dolls that her eyes were teary and red the entire time. The bathroom smelled so bad she could not use it. The neighborhood seemed so dangerous she was afraid to go out by herself. Artie came by once a day and took her to the local McDonald's so that she could eat and use the bathroom.

Meanwhile, back in the United States, OAA, Coleco, and its advertising agency, Richards and Edwards, were arguing over the marketing plan. The copywriter for the commercials was trying to follow the marketing plan, which called for commercials directed at boys as well as girls. Aligned with the agency was Xavier Roberts, who was just as committed to making a toy for both sexes. Opposing them was Coleco, backed by the conventional wisdom that "you don't put boys in doll commercials."

The same argument extended to the packaging. Coleco wanted the dolls in pink boxes because "pink is the color girls like most." Roberts didn't want a box at all because "you don't put people in boxes." Even he had to concede that putting the dolls on the shelves with no boxes was impractical for the mass market, but if they had to be kept clean, he still didn't think they had to be kept in pink boxes.

The result was two victories for nonsexist child rearing. Boys were put into the commercials, and the Alberts and Schlaifer Nance designed cream-colored trapezoidal packaging that ended up pleasing everyone. As it turned out, the commercials were charming but superfluous. Once the dolls hit the stores, they began selling so fast that Coleco spent three years catching up with the demand. It pulled the commercials off the air not long after they began to run.

The February days just before Toy Fair were frantic, as usual. The Alberts did not have enough samples to set up the display until the last minute. Artie spent the Sunday before the fair opened driving all over Long Island buying additional props. By late Sunday night Artie and Judy were still in Coleco's showroom rearranging the scenes and redrawing some of the hand-made boxes. On Monday morning the showroom, transformed into a nursery to display the adoptees, captured the attention of both the trade and the popular press.

Even so, the buyers at Toy Fair were not overly impressed. The most important, Toys "R" Us, was one of the most negative: the chain's merchandise manager, Sy Ziv, renowned for his product sense, hated the Cabbage Patch line. All the major retailers ordered cautiously.

Then both the commercials and a $100,000 public relations campaign headed by a veteran, Richard Weiner, began to attract attention to the dolls. Weiner held June press parties in New York, Boston, and Atlanta and invited retailers, teachers, children, and hundreds of media representatives. Especially targeted were editors preparing the Christmas issues of women's magazines. The highlight of each party was a mass adoption, during which all the children adopted a doll. It was a captivating scene, and the dolls appeared in the publications in the fall.

By that time retail sales were already so strong that Weiner was told to expand the operation. Eventually he had twelve professionals running a $500,000 campaign. Coleco representatives went on a twelve-city tour and gave out a "Cabbage Patch Kids Parenting Guide," written with the help of two child psychologists. Nancy Reagan gave the dolls to Korean children in a Long Island hospital, and Cartier featured them in its windows, offering a free doll with every $100,000 purchase of jewelry.

The dolls were on television constantly. The PR people sent a doll to then-pregnant Jane Pauley, who featured it for five-and-a-half minutes on "The Today Show" in the middle of November. Two weeks later Betty Furness showed the product on the show again and quoted the psychological research on adoption that the PR agency had provided. Johnny Carson mentioned or showed the Kids on "The Tonight Show" almost every night for about two weeks.

The biggest triumph for Weiner was a cover story in the December 12 issue of *Newsweek*. "I couldn't believe it," the PR man recalled later. "I read it with misty eyes. I was in a dream."

As important as the marketing, advertising, and promotional efforts were, the riots made Cabbage Patch Kids. And contrary to what cynics said at the time, Coleco had nothing to do with them.

Artie's original marketing plan forecast $50 million in sales for the first year. Coleco insisted he cut the estimate in half. In 1983 Coleco sold two-and-a-half million dolls—all it could make—for $67 million. The company even shipped some dolls by the planeload to try to satisfy demand, but it never came close. By Christmas the demand was sheer hysteria.

In 1984 Coleco's sales of dolls and accessories, which included new Cabbage Patch twins and imaginary Cabbage Patch Pets called Koosas, reached $540 million. Overall, Cabbage Patch Kids products generated over a billion dollars. Cleveland, Georgia, received over 100,000 visitors and considered adding a third traffic light to its thoroughfares. A New Jersey dentist founded Camp Small Fry where, for $30.00, a Cabbage Patch Kid could go to camp. The Kids appeared in the Macy's Thanksgiving Day parade. Thousands of counterfeit Cabbage Patch Kids were confiscated by U.S. Customs agents; some of them were spotted when they emitted a strange chemical odor and others because they lacked belly buttons. A Cape Coral, Florida, scam took in thousands of dollars with an advertisement that appeared in newspapers across the country reading "Send $34.95 and we will send you a Cabbage Patch." Victims of the scam received a fifty-cent packet of cabbage seeds.

The following year Coleco took in $600 million from Cabbage Patch Kids. Some of them had new silky hair—Cornsilk Kids. Xavier Roberts opened his second retail outlet, BabyLand on Fifth, on New York City's Fifth Avenue. Besides the Cabbage Patch Kids, the store carried Furskins Bears, stuffed bears dressed in country clothes and work boots. Roberts had commissioned Judy Albert to design the bears, and Roger Schlaifer protested that Roberts was cutting him out of Furskins, which he contended were part of the Cabbage Patch family of country characters. In December OAA sued Schlaifer Nance to prevent its licensing agency from receiving any of the Furskins' proceeds, and shortly thereafter Schlaifer Nance countersued.

In 1986 OAA sued Topps Chewing Gum Company to prevent the sale of its Garbage Pail Kids line of bubble-gum cards. Topps, which had sold more than 800 million cards since it had introduced them in 1985, had lined up twenty companies to license its popular parody; the characters had repulsive double names (Acne Amy, Slimy Sam) and bore a deranged but unmistakable resemblance to Coleco's cherubic dolls. Coleco sold $230 million worth of Cabbage Patch Kids, missing its $450 million sales estimate by a factor of 50 percent, and losing $111 million for the year.

In 1987 Coleco introduced Cabbage Patch Splashing Kids, a line of waterproof dolls that children could play with in the bathtub, and Cabbage Patch Kids Talking Kids, which could sense each others' presence electronically and carry on doll-to-doll conversations. It wasn't enough. Coleco sold $126 million worth of Cabbage Patch Kids merchandise and lost $105 million for the year. After losing money for two years, Xavier Roberts closed his New York store. Furskins were not selling very well either. OAA and Topps settled their case with the usual declaration by both parties that they had won. Topps was permitted to continue selling Garbage Pail Kids bubble-gum cards but had to pay OAA an undisclosed sum of money. The Alberts sued Coleco for denying them royalties on the concept of cornsilk hair on the new 1987 Cabbage Patch Kids.

By 1988 Coleco was so overextended that it was barely able to function. The company was laying off employees, selling product lines, and trying to renegotiate terms with its creditors. It brought Cabbage Patch Kids with Growing Hair to Toy Fair 1988, but the saleability of extendable hair was not the issue. The burning question of Toy Fair 1988 was, Were Cabbage Patch Kids going to be able to save Coleco?

It was clear that nothing else could.

11

SEPTEMBER 1986–JANUARY 1987
When Toymen Have Fantasies

No ONE AT TYCO NEEDED TO WAIT for the research report. Everyone who had watched the tests had felt electricity when the boys oohed and aahed and pronounced the products "totally radical."

It was full speed ahead: they had a product line.

Woody's original plan called for shipment starting in December 1987, which would make Dino-Riders a 1988 product, but that schedule had been ignored for months. By the time the test report came back in September, the product-development department had already started on Phase II.

Phase II was pattern making, and its original budget of $145,000 soon expanded by another $30,000. Patterns are derived from the three-dimensional models, and they must be precise because they are the blueprints from which the prototypes are made. Lee had the patternmakers on overtime by August.

In August they also realized that it was already getting late to look into the possibility of a television tie-in, but no one knew quite where to start. At the time a television program was considered essential for an action-figure line—the most successful lines had them—but it was by far the most daunting element of the package. They knew it had to be expensive, although they had no idea exactly how expensive or how to go about making one. They were toy people, not television producers.

In September advertising vice president Bob Lurie thought of Jay Garfinkel, a man with a varied background in television. When Garfinkel had worked for Marvel Entertainment, he and Bob had collaborated on a comic book for Tyco's U.S. 1 Electric Trucking sets. Garfinkel was now in Washington, D.C., putting together an international twenty-four-hour-a-day news network for the United States Information Agency (USIA).

Bob called Garfinkel and told him he had an intriguing project. Garfinkel said he was not interested. He was busy, he was fulfilled, and he didn't need the money. Bob persisted. "Just come for lunch," he urged. "We can meet in Philadelphia." Garfinkel is from Philadelphia, and he liked to get back periodically, so he allowed himself to be talked into a lunch on the waterfront.

Bob brought Woody along, and the three exchanged pleasantries for a few minutes before Bob got down to business. "I'm not going to try to talk you into anything," he began. "I'm just going to say one word." He paused, then dangled the bait. "Dinosaurs."

He knew this man. "I'll do it," Garfinkel replied.

Bob had rightly suspected that he could tap the fascination dinosaurs exert even among adults. "It is the dream of every producer and writer who loves dinosaurs to be able to work on a dinosaur show," Garfinkel later admitted. "That way he can use his ideas, tell his stories, impose his own fantasies on those primordial beings. I knew I would have my pick of writers because so many of them would love the work. Dinosaurs lived. They are not like unicorns or other imaginary creatures. To be able to tell your own story of what really happened to these creatures who really lived is a science-fiction writer's dream."

Bob needed facts first, not fantasy. "Educate us," he told Garfinkel. Tyco needed the costs and benefits of television programming, and fast.

Garfinkel studied the market and laid out several programming options with their expected costs and benefits. The usual format was a five-day-a-week, half-hour animated series that was sold or syndicated to as many stations as possible. Such a series, which required sixty-five half-hour episodes to fill thirteen weeks before going into reruns, typically cost $250,000 an episode. But this was 1986, and there were too many programs competing for the same time slots. Even the ones that had made it had begun to bore their viewers, and the overall ratings were sinking, which meant the cost per viewer was rising. He considered a daily show ($16 million) too expensive for Tyco and a weekly show ($3 million) too infrequent to succeed.

The group at Tyco was intimidated. The cost seemed prohibitive, but they doubted their line could succeed without television; how else would they explain the fantasy? They finally decided to have Garfinkel produce an animated videotape about eight minutes long, telling the story of Dino-Riders. The tape would give them a chance to see how the three-dimensional concept translated into two dimensions, and they could have someone take the tape to the annual broadcasters' convention to see if the market seemed receptive. If they couldn't sell the series, they could always use the tape as a sales tool.

Throughout the summer and into the fall, the product-development and marketing people were, as they put it, "crashing" to have the line ready to show at the February Toy Fair. By September it had become obvious to everyone but Woody that B.C. was growing too large for him to manage alone. Members of Tyco's marketing department actually function as product managers, and when Woody had started at Tyco, his responsibilities had included only Super Blocks and personality telephones. Now he was overseeing two entirely new product lines that the company would be launching at Toy Fair: Super Dough, a copy of Kenner's Play-Doh, and Tuffies, a line of stuffed watchdogs. Super Dough had to be monitored especially closely because Tyco planned a big television advertising campaign for the product. Television promotion adds more risk because a company has to build up larger inventories in anticipation of high demand from the commercials.

Woody understood that he was overloaded, and he knew that

gaining a marketing director, who would be reporting to him, was in effect a promotion. But he also knew things would never be the same. Giving up primary responsibility for Dino-Riders was like giving up full-time parenthood and getting partial custody. It might eliminate some of the day-to-day aggravation, but it would put him one step removed from the real action.

Woody became the classic manager in the middle, and he was never completely reconciled to his position. As senior marketing vice president, Jim Alley would get the glory of speaking for the company. Woody would have enjoyed that. Neil Werde, Woody's new subordinate, would manage the product's day-to-day business and get the company plaudits if the product did well. Woody would have liked that too. As it was, Woody was in the middle, which he hated.

He had worked on the project harder than on anything else in his career, and he knew he had contributed a great deal to the concept and the product line. He also knew that the gratification of doing his job well was supposed to be reward enough. But he was only human, and he liked recognition as much as anyone else. So for the next year or so he would tell his colleagues, "There's enough credit to go around for everybody." He only wished he could convince himself.

It turned out better than he had anticipated. Before Neil had started on Dino-Riders, Woody had worried that he would become a glorified messenger, just conveying information and decisions back and forth between Neil and Jim. Instead, Neil did not start on the project until after Toy Fair 1987, and when he did, he and Woody quickly became a dynamic duo, feeding on each other's craziness.

Neil Werde is the quintessential New Yorker. More specifically, that special breed the Brooklyn boy. Fast-talking, quick-witted, streetwise with a hint of a swagger, Neil has always been in a hurry. At the age of sixteen, while still in high school, he found a job at an advertising agency through an intern program, and he has been working ever since. He was married right after high school, moved to Manhattan's East Village (the shabby, drug-infested poor cousin of adjacent Greenwich Village), and took night courses at the New School of Social Research while he worked during the day. When his wife realized her ambition to be a writer by landing a job as an assistant editor of *Screw* magazine, the pair felt as if they had made it to the heart of the New York scene.

Within two years Neil, now all of eighteen, was at one of the hottest toy companies in the business, Mego Corporation. As the company's first promotion director, he made twenty-five thousand dollars a year and could not believe his good luck. At first his actual duties most closely resembled baby-sitting: he escorted Marvel Super Heroes to stores and shopping centers, chauffeuring Spider Man around in his car and flying around the country with the Hulk. He spent seven years with Mego, and his responsibilities grew beyond escort service to marketing, where he worked on several action-figure lines. He was not in the company's inner circle, but he was nimble enough to find another job just five weeks before Mego crashed to an ignominious end, even for a toy company. In 1982 the company declared bankruptcy, and shortly afterward its president and attorney were convicted of wire fraud. Several jobs later Neil arrived at Tyco to work on vehicles, but when the Dino-Riders project required another person, he was the obvious choice.

In November Dick delivered another blow. He called Jim and Woody into his office. "We are not going to Toy Fair with Dino-Riders," he announced. "We're not ready. Let's sit back and wait. Instead of April, we'll ship it in December as we originally planned." He knew how crushed they would be and tried to soften the news. "We'll make a big deal of introducing it in the fall. But for now, let's hold back." Knowing that one of their biggest fears was that Hasbro or one of the other giant firms might beat them to the market, he also assured them, "If we find out at Toy Fair that somebody has something like this, we'll rethink the decision. But right now, we're going to hold it."

The entire team was heartsick. They desperately wanted to unveil Dino-Riders in three months. They had kept their stupendous secret for eleven months already and could not imagine holding it in almost another whole year. They had labored over it daily—it seemed as though that was all any of them ever talked about—and they were terrified that the competition would get there first. The real reason the delay was so painful, however, was that they could hardly wait to show it off to the rest of the industry.

By December they had adjusted to the delay and were deeply involved in creating the characters and the story line for the videotape. Once they began to work on the story, the conflicts inherent in the needs of toys versus television began to emerge. Tyco's story line had focused on the relationship between the characters and the dinosaurs rather than on the conflict between the Sauresians (or, after they lived on earth, Dino-Riders) and the Rulons. They were creating a dinosaur-based action-figure line; the dinosaurs were the focus, and the action figures and accessories were the extras. Woody's original marketing plan had not even included figures until the second year.

Garfinkel told them that the relationship between people and animals would be too static to provide the necessary drama. They had to concentrate on the people. "The dinosaurs are pawns, but respected, like a royal dog is to its master," he explained. "There can still be personality differences. Rin Tin Tin is different from Lassie. But in the end, dinosaurs are dinosaurs. I want to find the hubris in my characters that will provide dramatic tension."

To write the treatment (a description of the characters, environment, and philosophical underpinnings for the drama) Garfinkel hired a highly recommended comic-book artist he had never met. Paul Kirchner, a thirty-four-year-old art-school dropout, had written stories for *Heavy Metal*, an adult fantasy magazine, and had freelanced for a number of toy companies over the years. In fact, he had designed an action-figure line of toy soldiers for Mego the year Hasbro brought back G.I. Joe. Unfortunately, G.I. Joe returned in 1982, which was also the year Mego declared bankruptcy, so Kirchner never collected the twenty thousand dollars Mego owed him.

From the first time the two men met, Garfinkel's personal enthusiasm about the project was obvious to Kirchner. "I'm really busy at work," he explained as he drove Kirchner to Tyco's headquarters, "and I don't have time for another thing. But this is so exciting I couldn't refuse the offer. It's just like a fantasy I had as a kid."

At Tyco the group showed Kirchner their background story,

some dinosaur models, and a pile of sketches depicting Rulon and Dino-Rider characters, costumes, weaponry, and accessories. They had already created some evil Rulons by brainstorming from the phrase *scum of the earth*, and they offered him three categories: snakes, sharks, and insects. The lowliest troops would be the Antmen.

As he listened to the presentations, Kirchner soon realized that Jay Garfinkel was not the only one whose personal enthusiasm exceeded his professional interest. Woody Browne cared most about the dinosaurs' integrity as dinosaurs. He wanted them portrayed as untamed, natural creatures, neither domesticated pets of the Dino-Riders nor snarling comrades of the Rulons, but simply animals. He feared animation's tendency to anthropomorphize and was determined to champion and protect the beasts from becoming caricatures that talked, used their legs as arms, and carried on like Mickey Mouse, Scooby Doo, or Bullwinkle.

Jim Alley and Lee Volpe were more interested in the Dino-Rider characters. Jim often relaxed by listening to tapes of the J. R. R. Tolkien books, so he shared Lee's vision of heroic warrior elves. Lee had developed an elaborate underlying philosophy and made a point of cornering Kirchner at lunch to bombard him with ideas. "I see the Dino-Riders as sort of alien MacGyvers," he explained. (MacGyver is a TV character who uses arcane scientific knowledge in ingenious ways.) "They're inventive, creative, simple to the point of elegance. The Rulons will use technology to their advantage, whereas the Dino-Riders will be drawn to the natural, the organic, basic kinds of mechanisms. In fact, I'd like to see them use more slingshots, things like that."

Lee enjoyed talking to a fellow artist because he knew Kirchner could understand his plans to communicate these qualities visually through colors, shapes, and styles. The Rulons' costumes and weapons would be in purples, blacks, greens, and reds. Each color had meaning. In the action-figure world, purple is usually a villains' color; red and black are universally used as colors of evil and malevolence; and green was the natural outgrowth of the kinds of creatures they were using for the

Rulons. The Dino-Riders would wear shades of blue, mauve, and silver, colors that are usually associated with heroes and that Lee also happened to consider more organic. He also planned to utilize color to denote rank among both sides. The leaders of each group would wear the most intense colors, and the costumes for characters lower in the hierarchy would grow succeedingly paler.

In keeping with the Dino-Riders' organic nature, their uniforms, helmets, bodies, weaponry, and architecture would be drawn with soft curves, sleek construction, and flowing lines—a sort of futuristic, aerodynamic look. By contrast, the Rulons would favor hard angles, weightiness, straight lines, and technological solutions. Their uniforms would display a triangular motif and be very symmetrical. The Dino-Riders were more sophisticated. "You'd expect raw symmetry of a simple mind," Lee explained, "but the Dino-Riders are more intelligent. The asymmetrical designs in their costumes and accessories reflect their more advanced intellectual level." Lee did not have to tell Kirchner that none of these details would be wasted on their audience. They both knew that children's capacity for noticing and remembering details far exceeded any adult's.

Kirchner listened and took it all in. He considered himself a conduit for everyone else's visions; there were certainly enough visions to go around without any additions from him. Unfortunately, some of their concepts were mutually exclusive. Garfinkel heartily disapproved of warrior elves. "I don't believe in stereotypes," he began [an opening that usually precedes a *but*], "but this is not a heroic character. There are certain idiomatic expressions, visual as well as verbal. In film, for example, a dissolve usually means time is passing. And there are some idioms in looks. A strong, heroic character is typically a blond, Aryan type. You have very little time to tell your story, and you don't have time to get bogged down. You can't deal with a short, dark character as the hero without taking more time to set it up."

Kirchner relished the assignment and had his first draft ready a few days before Christmas. He had tried to incorporate everyone's ideas, but the net result of all the intellectualizing was . . .

Everymyth. All the original ideas and disparate approaches could be discerned, but somehow the sum of all these parts sounded strangely familiar—sort of a combination of the *Iliad, Ivanhoe,* and *The Last of the Mohicans,* plus a healthy dose of *Star Wars.* In other words, archetypal characters interacting in stock situations.

"Everyone seems to like to feel he's being subtle," Kirchner observes. "But you can't make it like a Bergman movie. Even though everyone wants to make his characters unique, you have to use them fairly simply. So you still come up with the wise old man, the callow youth, the rascal." He changed Sauresians to Valorians—much easier to say if you have a lisp—and, predictably, they looked like Norman conquerors: "tall, slender and refined in appearance." Led by their philosopher king-scientific genius Arturus, they communicated by mental telepathy, which they called "The Path." Arturus relied on a wise, but blind, old counselor, Mind Zei, who possessed second sight. Kirchner described Mind Zei's granddaughter, Serena, as "a regular woman of the 80's in 65,000,000 B.C.," but her special healing powers put her right back into the traditional female nurturing role. Ironoke was the "armorer, quartermaster and sergeant-major," and Elkin, the male ingenue, was "ready and willing but not quite able."

Villains always seem to worm their way into their creators' affections, and the evil Rulons were no exception. According to Kirchner, they formed "an alliance of four warlike species whose modest goal is the domination of the entire populated universe." The key to their power was "the technological horror of the Brain Box, which surely deserves a place in the museum of malevolence beside the rack, the guillotine, and the Zyclon B gas chamber." The Rulons were led by Mogg, who ruled by fear. "His machinations are unfathomable, his cunning insidious, his fury terrible, and his lust for conquest insatiable. Mogg is Attila the Hun, Joseph Stalin, and Darth Vader rolled into one."

Lest Mogg seem too attractive, Kirchner added not one but two tragic flaws. In times of defeat, "his rage seems somehow impotent and petty." Also, the "possibility of drying out is the one thing that can cause Mogg to panic. It is his Achilles' heel."

Hasbro's library of classics. Still enjoyed today, Tinker Toys were introduced at Toy Fair 1913. Raggedy Ann was created in 1914 by political cartoonist Johnny Gruelle for his terminally ill daughter. Playskool's wooden blocks date back to 1917. Frank Lloyd Wright's son John devised Lincoln Logs in 1916.

Toys then, collectibles now. Ideal Toys created twenty-eight models of Shirley Temple's face before company executives were satisfied. Costume is from *Stand Up and Cheer*, 1934. Lionel catalogs have been enticing children since 1903. This one dates from 1924.

Favorites from the 1930s. Louis Marx licensed popular characters like Amos 'n' Andy, but he also created his own. The Marx Merry Makers bear a striking resemblance to an already-famous mouse. Charles Darrow never imagined that MONOPOLY would become the bestselling board game in history.

Future assassins of America, or just kids having fun? As long as children have been asking for toy weapons, adults have been arguing about their long-term effects. Daisy's Defense Force Kit is just what a boy needs for the backyard shootout pictured below.

The Tyco team. *Clockwise, from upper left:* fearless leader Dick Grey, mature marketing executives Woody Browne and Neil Werde, inspiration man Jim Alley, and creative product development chiefs Mike Hirtle and Lee Volpe.

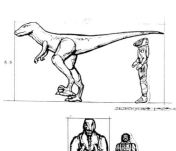

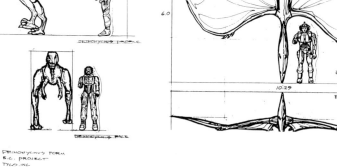

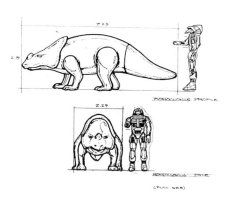

Museum-quality authenticity. "Dr. Bob" agreed to serve as spokesperson for Dino-Riders because he was impressed by the accuracy of Tyco's dinosaur models.

Before and after, 65,000,000 B.C. Pursued by the evil Rulons, the Valorians crash to earth where they Harness the Power of dinosaurs to continue their fight for survival.

Xavier Roberts, father of the Cabbage Patch Kids. At Babyland General Hospital in Cleveland, Georgia, "doctors" inject the cabbages with imagicillin, cut the stems with an easyotomy, and spank the newborn Cabbage Patch babies.

Seeing triple. Mattel's original Barbie from 1959 (*left*) had become Perfume Pretty Barbie by 1988 (*top right*), but Hasbro attacked with Perfect Prom Maxie (*center right*), a high school girl "much younger" than Barbie. Mattel retaliated in 1989 with Teen Dance Jazzie (*bottom right*), Barbie's cool high school cousin.

Microchip mania. Electronic toys range from radio-controlled cars to talking bears like Teddy Ruxpin. Mike Tyson's Punch-Out!!, launched in 1987, is still one of Nintendo's bestselling games.

CEOs need their friends. Alan and Stephen Hassenfeld hold Bumblelion and Big Bird. Charles Lazarus holds Geoffrey Giraffe. Table 18 holds (*counterclockwise from front*) Ruth and Elliot Handler, Sylvia and Merrill Hassenfeld, Fred Ertl, Bernie and Lillian Loomis (Kenner), Lionel and Bette Weintraub (Ideal).

His and hers. More trucks are bought for girls nowadays, but few girls wanted Madballs. Not many boys have clamored for She-Ra Princess of Power or My Little Pony (in Abra-Ca-Dabra costume).

A real American hero. In 1964, 11½-inch G.I. Joe was available in four costumes. Today he has multiplied into an extensive fighting force of 3¾-inch action figures, vehicles, and weapons. Shown here are Sgt. Slaughter's Marauders attacking in their Equalizer and Armadillo tanks.

Action-figure attack. Before the products were available, IOUs for Star Wars toys sold out at Christmas. He-Man and Masters of the Universe exploded after the product starred in its own TV series. GoBots transformed from robots to vehicles. Today Teenage Mutant Ninja Turtles fight for life, liberty, and a slice of pizza.

Hitching corporate wagons to stars. Basing toys on even the most venerated figure cannot guarantee success. Ideal's Baby Jesus doll was one of Toyland's biggest failures, while Mickey Mouse came from the movies, Garfield came from the comics, and Strawberry Shortcake came from nowhere to generate millions of dollars in merchandise sales.

Christmas in Toyland. FAO Schwarz, the Rolls-Royce of toy stores, braces for the season when the retailers usually sell 60 percent of their $12 billion annual volume.

Mogg's troops were the Sharkurrs, the Cobra Warriors, and the Antmen. Heavily muscled and known for their strength, the Sharkurrs were led by Hammerhead. Fangthorne, leader of the Cobras, was subtle, sly, and conspiratorial; constantly trying to usurp Mogg's authority, he was also "sycophantic, fancying himself Mogg's right hand man." The dull, plodding grunts of the military force, the Antmen, were led by Antor, who "makes up for his lack of intelligence and imagination by his dogged devotion."

Kirchner also created personalities, vehicle systems, and weapons for eight dinosaurs, among them Nike the *Deinonychus*. A fast-moving carnivore, Nike would be used extensively by both sides for general transportation and as a fast attack vehicle. Terry the *Pterodactyl* and Don the *Pteranodon* both flew, whereas Clone the *Monoclonius* and Top the *Triceratops* served as tanklike vehicles. The Valorians utilized Doc the *Diplodacus*'s strength and size to build a mobile command center and battle station with attached containers that looked like supply pods but opened to unleash a variety of lethal rockets. Biggest and best of the dinosaurs would be Tyrant the *Tyrannosaurus rex*. The one serving as Mogg's personal battlefield command post "makes a thunderous, unearthly roar. Try to imagine a bengal tiger on LSD with his tail slammed in a car door." The *T-rex* was so fierce that capturing one and fitting it with a Brain Box invariably cost several Antmen their lives.

Jay Garfinkel sent the draft to Tyco, but his covering comments exposed his real agenda. Clearly, he was not going to let everyone else have all the fun. "The names of the characters are a marketing issue," he wrote. "The names presented in the treatment are good comic book names, but not all of them are good animation or toy character names." Garfinkel explained that names should be memorable, personality- or task-oriented, and "have potential for being a buzz word." Just to be sure they understood, he enclosed a few examples: a page and a half of typewritten names in two columns, "Good Guys" and "Bad Guys." As he hunched over his typewriter banging out names like The Reaper, Terminator, Sgt. Gloom, and Dr. Doom, had the USIA executive kept a piece of paper handy to throw over his list in case someone walked in? Garfinkel had obviously labored hard to come up with "Good Guys" such as Potshot, Sharpshooter, Moondog, and Sundog, but his "Bad Guys" were even more impressive. Sludge, Rampage, Gore, Blow Torch, and Leech were catchy, but Nit Wit and More-On were inspired.

It was in tackling the thorniest issue—the nature of the dinosaurs—that Garfinkel was truly masterful. He wanted to make the best piece of animation he could, and to do so, he believed the dinosaurs needed to talk. Knowing the strength of the opposition, he cleverly couched his proposal in terms most likely to appeal to the toymakers. "Dinosaurs are what is being marketed," he wrote. "Action figures are the giveaway. The dinosaurs must talk for there to be a bond between the audience (i.e., children, viewers, purchasers) and the character." He offered telepathy as the vehicle. "Since the Dynoriders [sic] are the only ones who with their high intelligence/sensitivity, possess telepathic powers, only liberated dinosaurs . . . are seen as speaking. Only free dinosaurs have developed personalities. Enslaved dinosaurs are no more than transformed fighting machines who are brutish and growling."

They all met to go over the treatment the day after Christmas 1986. As Woody said, they would rather have been at home by the fire, but it was not a bad way to celebrate the anniversary of Jim's vision. They were all impressed by Kirchner's treatment— which was not surprising, since he had incorporated all their suggestions. Their universe had come alive, and the characters bore recognizable personalities. The problem was clearly going to be to keep the dinosaurs from having too much personality, and they argued for a long time about letting the dinosaurs talk. Woody held out longest, but he finally capitulated and agreed to let Kirchner try it in the second draft.

Kirchner finished the new version by January 5, and the dinosaurs were completely transformed. If a dinosaur were to be used by the Dino-Riders, Kirchner created one as a unique character with a name, distinctive personality, and speaking manner—important for animation. Clearly trying to satisfy both the pro- and anti-talking constituencies, Kirchner explained that "dinosaurs aren't actually 'talking' after all, except through the Dinoriders [sic] (who communicate telepathically) so the effect is a bit like the dog owner who knows exactly what his pet would say and how he would say it if only he could talk."

The *Pterodactyls* were now all Terrys, with a special one called Gimlet, "a bit of a kvetch" who liked to give advice and did not hesitate to offer an "I told you so" when his unheeded wisdom turned out to have been correct. The Dino-Riders' Clone (for *Monoclonius*), Sarge, was grumpy, stodgy, and "not terribly talkative, even for a dinosaur." Their Doc (*Diplodocus*) was a fussy, opinionated, fiercely maternal female called Big Bertha; and a baby *Diplodocus*, Slip, had been added to provide a humorous dinosaur. "Like a puppy, lovable but always getting into mischief," he would be clumsy and too young for speech, but he could make "adorable bleating baby sounds." Top gun of the Dons (*Pteranodons*) was Spitfire. With the "understated suave manner of a David Niven character," he kept a stiff upper lip (beak) and tossed off lines like "that'll show the blighters, eh what?"

The entire Tyco group was appalled. Their museum-quality, historically accurate dinosaurs had been turned into . . . *cartoon* characters! Had product development spent months of time and unprecedented sums of money painstakingly building models from the skeleton out only to see their treasured replicas turned into cavorting Disney characters? What did he think this was supposed to be, *Fantasia*?

"Take out the names," they told Kirchner in disgust. "Take out the talking. Concentrate on the characters and leave the dinosaurs alone."

Kirchner went back to his studio. This time he assigned the characters ages. The Dino-Riders leader, now named Questar, was twenty-five. Serena was seventeen but mature for her age. It was a tough job, but as requested, he made the Rulons even more vicious than before.

This draft, finished January 18, was supposed to be final, b. . Tyco's advertising agency had to get in its suggestions too. Cy Schneider believed that Kirchner should focus more on the leader. Questar was less clearly delineated than the Rulons' leader, now named Krulos, and Schneider predicted that the good-versus-evil struggle would ultimately come down to the two leaders. He also thought it made sense from a product standpoint. "If a child wants or can afford only two characters, it should be easy for him to select one good one versus one bad one."

Schneider also noticed a merchandising opportunity the others had overlooked. Why have the characters press their fingers to their foreheads to communicate telepathically when they could use some merchandisable device? He suggested a medallion that they could wear on a chain around their necks. Then when they needed it, they could "hold it in front of them and concentrate on it. . . ." He also suggested that if Tyco planned to organize a Dino-Riders club or society, the medallion would make a good giveaway. Additionally, a club might offer members half-price admission at all the country's natural history museums or a calendar with twelve pictures of dinosaurs.

They liked the medallion and decided to call it the AMP, for Amplified Mental Projector. Since Kirchner had to do one more draft to include it, they threw in a few last requests. They had debated a long time among themselves on the question of love interest. As Bob Lurie delicately put it, "Should Serena have carnal knowledge of the leader?" They finally decided to maintain her maidenly status but push her age up to twenty-three, just in case.

As the drafts piled up, the characters became less complex, more formulaic, and more combative. Instead of a philosopher-king, Questar became more an intellectual warrior. Mind Zei grew less obviously handicapped and more forceful, like a Kung Fu master. Gunnur was described as the Ernest Borgnine character. Contrary to their original suggestion, the man-against-nature theme almost disappeared, and the Rulons were never going to be allowed to cooperate with the Dino-Riders, even during a natural disaster.

When they had begun, the members of the Tyco group had concentrated on the dinosaurs, and by the time the treatment was finished the dinosaurs were about the only element that remained close to their original concept. The few dinosaur characters who appeared over and over would have nicknames (like Terry for a *Pterodactyl*), but in general the dinosaurs would be known by their scientific names and would still retain their natural characteristics.

Most important, not one of them would ever sound like David Niven.

12

THE GOOD, THE BAD, AND THE UGLY . . . NOT TO MENTION THE DECEPTIVE, THE VIOLENT, AND THE SEXIST

WHILE JIM, NEIL, WOODY, AND BOB SAT around discussing Serena's sex life, the farthest question from their minds was the morality of using a television program to sell their product. Television was an important marketing tool, and they would have considered themselves irresponsible if they had not explored the possibility of a television show for their action-figure line. Their biggest concern about television was its prohibitive cost. As long as it was legal, they could leave the ethical issue to Peggy Charren.

Peggy Charren is the founder of Action for Children's Television (ACT), an organization that works to improve the quality of children's television. An influential advocate and astute spokeswoman, Charren is an unceasing critic of toy-based programs, which she calls thirty-minute commercials. She is probably the best known of the many child advocates who monitor the toy industry and its products.

As producers of goods for society's most vulnerable population, toymakers are expected to behave more responsibly than manufacturers of goods for adults. Adults presumably know

186

how to use products safely, are competent to make informed choices, and understand the selling purpose of advertising. Young children do not think about safety, consider commercials entertainment, and cannot perceive flimsiness in an object even when they handle it in a store. Toys that fall apart cause children disappointment. Unsafe toys can cause children permanent injury or even death. Toys that reflect violence, sexism, racism, and stereotypical thinking promote those values. Toy advertisements that deceive create disappointment and cynicism.

Child advocates monitor toys and other children's products because children are not equipped to do it for themselves. They emphasize children's innocence and lack of experience, noting that children are impressionable and therefore easily deceived and exploited.

Toy industry and advertising people frequently scoff at this portrayal. They like to characterize children as little adults, claiming that real adults vastly underestimate children's powers of discrimination. Not surprisingly, some of the people who insist that child advocates underestimate and overprotect children are the same ones who insist that they themselves are big kids.

Even if both sides could agree on a definition of a child's perspective or limitations, many of the complaints about toys would remain unresolved. How durable a toy should be, how safe it should be, whether it promotes good values, and where the line lies between showing off the product in a commercial and overglamourizing it are often matters of judgment, even when self-interest is factored out. Adults cannot even agree on what "good values" are, so they are certainly not going to come to a consensus on which toys promote them.

Toy companies have been advertising on television for almost forty years, and they have been under fire for virtually the entire time. Even the most callous advertisers agree that children are a more vulnerable audience, and consequently children's television advertising is governed more stringently than other advertising. The rules for toy advertising are even stricter than the rules for advertising other children's products. Toymakers complain loudly about this, but they bring it on themselves. The compression of their primary selling season into a few short months creates enormous pressure to move their products while they have the chance, and even the most scrupulous have trouble resisting the temptation to make their commercials as compelling as they can. With so much clutter and so little time, someone is always testing the boundaries of the permissible, and the minute a concession is granted to one, everyone else wants it too.

Hasbro is known for its marketing prowess, which it needs to sell the millions of units of product necessary to maintain its high sales volume. The company is also known for aggressive advertising, for testing the limits on commercials. Hasbro is the largest and, in that sense, the most successful toy company in the United States. If Hasbro makes an unusually violent or exaggerated commercial and then sells more toys, its customers, the retailers, pressure the other manufacturers to do the same—if they are not already trying it on their own.

"Give me a Hasbro spot," a buyer tells an advertising executive who has just shown him a commercial designed for network airing. The buyer thinks the spot is too tame, too unexciting. He wants more action, and the spot is changed to make the product move by itself.

Overly imaginative commercials are hardly a new problem. "It seems that it is almost impossible for some of our leading manufacturers to put a toy on television without misrepresenting it," wrote the advertising manager of Aurora Products in a trade publication article thirty years ago. He described a commercial showing a toy airplane flying throughout most of a sixty-second spot, with the disclaimer "not a flying toy" flashed on the screen, but not spoken, at the end. "My youngster is only 5," he quotes a disgruntled father as saying. "He cannot read. It's a helluva thing to spend $15 on a toy and then see my kid sit down and cry because it doesn't fly like the one he saw on television."

Heartless advertisers like these generated so much parental resentment that the National Association of Broadcasters (NAB) added Toy Advertising Guidelines to its code in 1961, giving the toy industry its earliest regulations. It urged advertisers to avoid using overly dramatic presentations that glamorized products, the words *only* or *just* when giving price information, and hammering sales messages.

Three years later the NAB's Code Authority had to expand its list of prohibited practices to counter all the new ideas manufacturers had devised for commercials: dramatizing toys in a realistic war atmosphere; demonstrating products in a way that could encourage harmful use or unsafe actions; describing a price that was not widely charged; suggesting that owning the toy would make a child better than his or her peers or that not owning it would invite ridicule; implying that optional extras were part of the original purchase; creating the impression that the toy came fully assembled when it did not; neglecting to mention that batteries were needed but not included.

By 1970 ACT had begun to pressure both the Federal Communications Commission (FCC), which regulates broadcasters and sets policy for programming and advertising, and the Federal Trade Commission (FTC), which regulates advertising with respect to deception, fairness, and substantiation, to tighten the rules on children's advertising and programming. Finally in 1978 the FTC called hearings to consider two issues. One was whether television advertising directed at young children was deceptive and should therefore be banned. The other was whether commercials for sugared foods should be banned or, alternatively, counteracted with advertisements about balanced nutritional practices.

The hearings produced mass hysteria in Toyland, Cerealland, and just about every other industry that advertised to children. More than 130 witnesses testified on both sides of the issues, including toy and cereal executives, psychologists, sociologists, consumer advocates, and representatives of every conceivable professional organization from chocolate candy manufacturers to dentists.

In the end nothing happened. The FTC conceded that advertising to children under six could be considered deceptive because children that young generally did not understand the persuasive intent of commercials. But the agency could find no practical remedy. Children under six constituted only a small portion of the audience for every program except "Captain

Kangaroo," and banning children's advertising for one program was ridiculous. Banning advertising on other programs for a minority of the viewers was deemed unfair and impractical. To Toyland's great relief, the matter was finally dropped in 1981.

The following year the NAB code was declared in restraint of trade, so each of the three major networks devised its own code. They all followed the NAB code fairly closely, but advertisers and their agencies soon detected differences among the three networks' standards departments. ABC was considered the toughest, so sometimes the companies' advertising agencies sent a proposed commercial to ABC first.

Independent stations have become much more important than networks for children's advertising and children's programming over the last few years, and many companies use them exclusively. A group of independent stations often delivers more viewers per advertising dollar than the networks, and they have other attractions. With only a few exceptions, the independents have no clearance people, giving advertisers much more freedom to be creative: agency people like to speculate about scenarios lurid enough for the independents to turn down. One of the most noticeable differences between network and spot (locally bought or syndicated) toy commercials is the island shot at the end. Networks require toy advertisers to include a five-second shot at the end of their commercials, showing the product all alone and unadorned so that children can see what is really being offered. That is a large chunk of time in a twenty-eight-and-a-half-second spot and certainly accounts for some of the erosion in network advertising. Under the press of competition with the independents, the five-second isolation shot had slipped to three or four, at least at NBC, but the shot is still obligatory in all network toy commercials.

Networks also restrict animation in toy commercials to one-third of the total time, and they do not allow it to be interspersed with live action. Cereal and food companies have much more latitude, but the networks' rationale is that children know that raisins cannot really dance, but they do not know what a particular toy can or cannot do. Even so, a number of toys that cannot dance alone in the children's home appear to dance unassisted on television.

After watching a few spot commercials, anyone can discern the toy commercials that were never intended for network airing. Animation and special effects abound, interspersed with live action. Children often enter games, which come alive around them. Dolls do all kinds of miraculous things. Disclaimers sound like "batteriesnotincluded," or "eachsoldseparately," only faster.

Other than the FTC, there is no enforcement agency with teeth. TMA members voluntarily "conform" to the code of the National Advertising Division of the Council of Better Business Bureaus, whose Children's Advertising Review Unit (CARU) monitors children's commercials. CARU responds to complaints from children who are disappointed when the toy cannot do what it did in the commercial, from competitors who complain about the same thing, and from its own observations. Some of the offenders are toys posed in positions that children cannot duplicate, vehicles that drive on television where they cannot go in real life, dolls that walk by themselves only on television, transformable robots that seem to transform faster than fingers could possibly move them, toys that fly without fingers visibly holding them, and multiple toys that seem to come as a set but must really be bought separately.

The cases follow a predictable pattern. CARU complains to the advertiser about the deceptive or overly glamorized portrayal of the toy. The advertiser explains that such a technique is quite common, sometimes adding that the child audience can easily separate fantasy from fact. Then, without conceding wrongdoing but in the "spirit of cooperation," the advertiser agrees to withdraw the commercial, explaining that its run is finished anyway, that it has been discontinued for marketing reasons, or that the mistake was made inadvertently by its agency. Then the company promises that it will be more sensitive to such concerns in the future. Since the process takes months, the commercial tends to run its full schedule anyway.

By 1983 Peggy Charren had become so frustrated with the state of children's commercials that she petitioned the FCC to require broadcasters and cable companies to insert an inaudible electronic signal at the beginning and end of all advertising. This "Children's Advertiser Detector Signal," ACT's release explained, "would pave the way for the development of inexpensive reactive devices that parents could attach to their TV sets to automatically block out commercials during children's programming." The idea, outlandish to begin with, seemed pathetically optimistic in view of what the FCC allowed later the same year.

In 1983 Mattel was nearing forty, but the company still retained its pioneering spirit. As a result of Mattel's efforts, the toy companies found themselves able to expand from thirty-second to thirty-minute commercials. Mattel successfully syndicated an original animated program based on its action-figure line He-Man and the Masters of the Universe. The program, which ran five days a week beginning in September 1983, was wildly successful, and the product line's sales exploded over the next couple of years.

Mattel had tried once before to run a program based on a line of toys, when it underwrote a 1969 program based on its Hot Wheels line of die-cast cars. After a competitor complained, the FCC slapped it down, deeming it a "program length commercial." By 1983 the climate had changed. Then-President Ronald Reagan's commissioners believed that the marketplace, not a group of regulators, should determine programming. The chief commissioner lifted both the ban on toy-based programming and the longer-standing limitations on the number of minutes of commercials allowable in children's programming. When he defended the decision on the basis that the marketplace would present viewers with alternatives in the form of cable stations, Peggy Charren assailed the remark as a "let them eat cable" philosophy. Since cable is pay television, it is unavailable to poor children, who presumably could benefit most from constructive programming.

Once the He-Man program was allowed, the free-for-all began. Within a year other toy companies were flooding in, trying to duplicate Mattel's success. Toy-based programming soon ran practically every other children's program off the air. By the 1986–87 season there were about forty toy-based series on the air, but the shows were so repetitious that their ratings were falling. The networks had refused to run the programs at first, but many of the independent stations preferred them. They knew the toy companies would be advertising the products elsewhere as well, which they believed would help the programs' ratings.

The syndicators bartered the program to the stations in exchange for some of the programs' advertising time, which they then sold to national advertisers. Sometimes advertisers, media buyers, and stations all worked together. The only question apparently not asked was how good the program was. In many cases the answer was, not very.

At one point, for example, DIC Enterprises, producer of animated programs based on Coleco and LJN toys, teamed up with Bohbot & Cohn, now Bohbot Communications, which is the media-buying agency that buys all television time for Toys "R" Us and many of the manufacturers. Bohbot & Cohn convinced stations to take programs DIC had produced, in return for Bohbot's promise to place Toys "R" Us, Coleco, and LJN spot advertising on other shows on the station. (One of the few rules that seems to be followed in the industry is that commercials for a product do not appear on that product's program. Even that has happened on occasion—"accidentally.") In some cases the quid pro quo went even further. In return for taking its "ThunderCats" program, the syndicator, Lorimar, offered stations a percentage of LJN's ThunderCat toy sales. Some stations agreed to the arrangement, and others considered it unethical.

ACT has tried since 1983 to convince the FCC to declare toy-based programs thirty-minute commercials, which would put them out of business because they would have to be purchased as thirty minutes of advertising time. The agency has so far refused. Defenders of the programs note that entertainment-merchandise tie-ins have been around for years. They also insist that the programs have to be entertaining or they would not last. Charren does not dispute the validity of program-merchandise tie-ins, but she has argued that the new programs, developed concurrently with the product lines, are exploiting children. Previously, licensed toy merchandise was based on programs, characters, comic strips, movies created primarily to entertain. Toy-based programs, like thirty-second commercials, are entertaining, but their primary purpose is to sell, or at least showcase, the product; that is why they are created. Charren also believes the programs take advantage of children's innocence in a way that would not be attempted with adults. "Can you imagine a TV series about Kleenex for adults?" she asks.

In 1987 Mattel proudly announced a line of interactive toys based on a character called Captain Power. Using toy weapons and vehicles, children would be able to shoot at a Captain Power live-action (real people as opposed to animation) television program and affect the action on TV. When she first heard about it, Peggy Charren thought they were kidding. She was outraged that Mattel would add insult to injury by creating two classes of viewers for its "thirty-minute commercial"—those with and those without the toys. And, worse, that Mattel would encourage shooting at the television set. In the end, the show failed and so did the toys. Mattel pushed too much product onto its customers, so when they could not sell it through quickly enough at retail, they stopped buying Captain Power from Mattel.

As reprehensible as many consider toy-based programming, subordinating the needs of entertainment to the needs of toy-makers is not new. In 1951 Tess Trueheart, after waiting years to marry Dick Tracy, had to wait fifteen months instead of the usual nine to have a baby. Ideal Toys had licensed the right to make a doll based on their baby, but it was due in February, which Ideal considered a terrible time to introduce a new doll. The artist, Chester Gould, agreed to delay the birth, and that summer Bonnie Braids finally made her appearance. (Bonnie was popular, but she was not the hit that another Dick Tracy baby character, the daughter of the repulsive B. O. Plenty and Gravel Gertie, had been in 1947. When Ideal's Sparkle Plenty doll, complete with long golden tresses, appeared on July 28, 1947, she caused an immediate sensation. Stores sold ten thousand Sparkle Plentys in the first five days, a huge number at that time.)

In 1961 Walt Disney announced that for the first time in history a movie, his new *Babes in Toyland*, was going to feature toys especially manufactured by Disney licensees. In fact, Dis-

ney's 1954 television program, "Disneyland," and his 1955 "The
Mickey Mouse Club" were promotional tools for his Disneyland
amusement park, which was under construction at the time.
Mattel created several toys specifically to appear on "The
Mickey Mouse Club."

Peggy Charren is only one of Toyland's critics. Many find the
shows' violent content as objectionable as their selling purpose.
Instead of watching Tom and Jerry outwit each other, children
watch an array of characters repetitiously shoot an array of
weapons in each others' direction and drive or fly around in an
array of vehicles—all available at the nearest toy store for reen-
actment of the fighting. But these programs are really only the
latest battleground in a very old war.

The fact that children, especially boys, have been so fascinated over the years by war and fighting has produced one of the
longest-running controversies in the history of toys. Adults as
well as children have always loved playing with toy soldiers, cap
guns, miniature weapons of all kinds. The perennial question
about such toys—and the television programs based on these
action figures—has always been, Do they encourage violent
play? And does allowing such toys imply approval of fighting?
Or do the toys (and the programs) provide an outlet for an
inevitable interest without necessarily creating militaristic or
violence-prone adults?

The arguments against war toys, and toy guns in particular,
range from philosophical to political, from psychological to
practical. At the philosophical level some adults believe that if
they allow war play or provide their children with toy guns or
weapons, they are implicitly supporting violence or war. Given
the many imitative activities that parents would not dream of
encouraging—stealing and drug or alcohol abuse, for example—they wonder why instruments for shooting, stabbing, and
killing should not be similarly barred from their homes. During
the 1960s and early 1970s the nation was so sickened by the
Vietnam War that sales of combat toys fell off dramatically. Toy
weapons and war toys traditionally sell strongly when nations
are at war, but the Vietnam War was an exception. As soon as
the war ended, sales rebounded.

Even among adults who believe that guns have constructive uses, many are concerned about the violent nature of American society. They worry that the products built around conflict—action-figure lines such as G.I. Joe and He-Man, as well as toy weapons or military vehicles and accessories—encourage violent tendencies and overly aggressive play. The link between such toys and the daily television programs that promote them, they believe, prolongs children's interest to the exclusion of other activities that might otherwise attract them. Their concern also extends to video games in which children "kill" and "hit" their victims dispassionately.

The most practical objection to toy weapons is that they can present real physical hazards. Children and adults playing with toy weapons have been killed when they brandished realistic toy guns at people who felt threatened and shot back in seeming self-defense. There are now many local ordinances banning realistic toy guns, and late in 1988 Congress passed national legislation requiring that the barrels of realistic-looking weapons be marked with an orange plug. Toy-gun manufacturers had already begun a voluntary program of "de-replication," and the TMA supported the law. The irony, as members of the industry like to point out, is that toy guns do not kill anyone. They wonder why so much legislation is devoted to banning toy guns while real ones are still relatively easy to obtain.

Defenders of toy guns and war-related toys allow their children to play with them for a number of reasons. Many adults who played with guns as children do not consider themselves dangerous or violence-prone and therefore see no reason to deny similar playthings to their own children. Many parents deplore their children's militaristic tendencies but do not believe that such toys will do lasting harm. A number of people, including many who use guns either professionally or for sport, tend to consider gun play a healthy outlet and an opportunity for adults to teach children safe practice and respect for the potential danger of firearms.

Other categories of toys evoke some of the same objections. Giant hypodermic needles have prompted protests that drug addiction was being treated as a joke. Gross toys always offend some adults, which undoubtedly enhances their appeal to children. AmToy, a toy division of American Greetings Corporation, created a 1986 product called Madballs, rubbery balls in such shapes as Oculus Orbus (an eyeball) and Screamin' Meemie (a face with a large, protruding tongue), which were a tremendous hit with elementary-school boys. When AmToy tried to capture the same market with a My Pet Monster line of stuffed creatures, they failed. The monsters may have been too endearing; there was nothing cute about Madballs.

When Nabisco, Inc., maker of Oreo cookies and Ritz crackers, bought Aurora Products in 1971, it was bewildered to find itself the target of public demonstrations and a threatened boycott. Aurora had been in the monster business for ten years, and monsters had been very good to Aurora. Monster kits had boosted its sales from $8.7 million in 1961 to $13.7 million the following year. Two of its most popular products were a Movie Monster series, featuring the Hunchback of Notre Dame (which resembled Anthony Quinn), King Kong, Godzilla, and Frankenstein, and a series of models based on figures in Madame Tussaud's Exhibitions, the famous wax museum in London.

The staid cookie company's executives were mortified when twelve demonstrators, including one dressed as a hangman, appeared at Nabisco's Madison Avenue headquarters to protest the Monster Scene kits. Chanting "Sadistic toys make violent boys" and carrying signs that read "Sick Toys For Children Make A Sick Society!" they explained that they found the Hanging Cage and the Pendulum (in which a seminude woman was strapped to a platform under a guillotine) extremely offensive and that they considered the Vampirella, Pain Parlor, and Gruesome Goodies kits almost as objectionable. Nabisco's top managers had managed to get themselves out of town to an important biscuit convention, but their embarrassed subordinates assured the demonstrators that Nabisco would cease production on what the demonstrators called "torture kits."

That same year The Godfather Game, packaged in a violin-shaped box, drew protests from the Italian-American Civil Rights League, an Italian-American congressman, the mayor of New York, and the *New York Times*. The object of the game, "to

take control of a racket—bookmaking, extortion, loan sharking
or hijacking—in as many neighborhoods as possible," worried
critics, who feared both the perpetuation of an ugly stereotype
of Italian gangsters and the proliferation to children of ideas for
undesirable activities.

Stereotypes are especially worrisome in toys because they may
constitute the child's only exposure to the group in question. In
that sense, all toys are educational. In 1986 Coleco halted production of its Nomad Desert Warrior when the American-Arab
Anti-Discrimination Committee protested that it depicted Arabs
as terrorists. Although Coleco responded that the figure was
portrayed as having "no country he calls his own," the committee pointed out that he had Middle Eastern features and head-
dress and carried a nametag written in Arabic—and that the
packaging description labeled the figure a "treacherous desert
warrior," a "sneak," "a man without honor," and "deadly as a
desert scorpion."

Black dolls have been included as a matter of course in many
doll lines for years, but black parents and educators now worry
less about a scarcity of black dolls and more about the frequency
with which black children prefer white dolls. Today there are
several companies, run by black entrepreneurs, devoted to promoting role models with which black children can identify
through dolls, not simply black versions of white dolls.

The appropriate role toys can or should play in transmitting
values can be as controversial as the values themselves.

> GRACE DOLL: I used to be a little tiny person inside my mommy's
> tummy, now I'm all big.
> PHIL DONAHUE: Translated, don't kill me in my mommy's
> tummy, don't allow abortion.

Grace is a "pro-life" doll manufactured by Praise Unlimited
for adults who want to give such products to their children to
promote fundamentalist Christian values (a very limited
market). Appearing on the same February 1988 "Phil Donahue
Show" was Jack Chojnacki, president of Those Characters From
Cleveland (TCFC), the successful mainstream toy- and charac-

ter-licensing firm owned by American Greetings Corporation. TCFC had just created a line of dolls called Special Blessings for Kenner to sell to the mass market. Four soft dolls in soft clothes, named Angela, Matthew, Christina, and Abigail, can clasp their hands and kneel, courtesy of Velcro. Chojnacki explained that TCFC had developed the line in response to "mothers asking for this series of dolls . . . [that] can have a fun and friendly way to share the faith between mother and children." Some members of the audience considered even the Special Blessings dolls objectionable propaganda.

Sometimes the values transmitted are so outrageous that observers can only assume, charitably, that the adults in charge must have gone to sleep. In 1989 both Western Publishing and Milton Bradley offered board games for girls, based on the idea of dating. In Western's Girl Talk Date Line the players choose two cards, one denoting a girl and the other a boy, and see whether they would be a good match. They try to determine who would make a good couple by finding people with common interests. The winner is the first player to get dates for all her friends and then herself. It may not be the activity one would choose for one's daughter, but at least the game suggests that relationships should be based on common interests and that helping one's friends is important.

Milton Bradley, the reputable game-industry leader, came out with a game called Heartthrob, which could have been written for "Saturday Night Live." First the players choose the date they like best on the basis of looks. Then they get a fact about his attributes that will help them determine whether he would be a "dream date." "So what if he's boring, he's the 'football team captain' and he 'drives a Porsche,'" says the description in the company's catalog. A girl in the commercial gives another reason that a player should want to go out with him: "He's rich!"

For such games and for innumerable other products, toy companies also earn the charge of promoting sexism. The large toy companies would have trouble refuting it, although they defend themselves by arguing that they follow trends, not set them. They "only sell what the market wants."

There is no doubt that much of Toyland is divided by gender. Everyone talks about girls' toys and boys' toys, and large companies such as Mattel and Hasbro even have separate vice presidents for the two categories. Many of the toys designated girls' or boys' are exaggeratedly feminine or masculine in design. Even if no more than one square inch of one of these toys is exposed, it is easy to tell whether it is intended for girls or for boys by the color or pattern alone. The differences are that predictable.

Overall, the situation is not so bad as it sounds. The toys attributed to one gender or the other make up only a portion of all toys. Toy categories not defined by gender include preschool toys, games, puzzles, books, videotapes, riding toys, activity toys (Etch A Sketch is an example), athletic equipment, crafts, and electronic and nonelectronic learning toys. Specific products within each of those categories may be targeted toward girls or boys—a puzzle may portray Barbie, for example—but in general the appellation girls' or boys' toy really belongs only to categories of toys that are overwhelmingly preferred by one sex or the other. Girls' toys include dolls and doll accessories, some crafts, and, beyond the preschool years, stuffed animals. Typically considered boys' toys are action-figure lines, toy guns and other weapons, toy vehicles, noneducational electronic games, and some other crafts, such as models.

That is not to deny that manufacturers—and buyers—assign sex roles. Brooms and mops are certainly not considered boys' toys, and electric trains have been marketed to girls only recently although girls have longed for them for years. (In 1957 Lionel Trains completely missed the point when it responded to a number of letters from girls wanting trains. It offered them a pink locomotive pulling a lilac hopper, boxcars in buttercup yellow and robin's-egg blue, and a sky-blue caboose. A complete flop, the set was quickly discontinued and is now prized by collectors because of its rarity.) In theory, the toy companies should be happy to sell any product to both sexes; it would double the size of their potential target market. In practice, they maintain the divisions, fearing that an eight-year-old girl will spurn a product she believes is liked by boys and vice versa.

Electronic toys are an interesting case. Electronic learning toys and musical toys have remained fairly gender-neutral, but video games and hand-held electronic games have been vastly more popular with boys (and young men). Knowing that the product appealed more to boys, the designers built most of their games around themes that appealed to boys—sports, combat, space—which in turn made them even less appealing to girls. (It is also regrettable that girls are not more interested in space or sports; smaller companies make products that try to lead their markets, but the large ones do not.)

Once the target market is defined, even if a product itself could be enjoyed by children of both sexes (and it is difficult to imagine one that could not be) the manufacturer tends to design the specific product to be as appealing as possible to that target. Girls get pink, purple, lavender, blue, ruffles, frills, horses, flowers, hearts. Their products have been known to induce gagging in adults, but when Mattel designed She-Ra, Princess of Power, the action figure was not well received by little girls until Mattel "pinked it up." Boys get their toys black or silver, fast, scary, macho, gross, violent.

According to the conventional wisdom, if a toy is aimed at the six-to-twelve age group, targeting a product to both sexes is suicidal. But sometimes manufacturers are surprised. Hasbro introduced a product called a Pogo Bal, a ball surrounded by a disk, which looks like a solid version of Saturn. Children stand on the disk, gripping the ball between their feet, and bounce as if they were on a pogo stick. Hasbro assumed it would appeal primarily to girls and gave it to its vice president for girls' toys to supervise. Even so the company made the Pogo Bals in bright colors and showed both boys and girls in its commercials, and both sexes bought it.

Toymakers like being socially responsible, but they have no interest in making products they cannot sell. Hasbro's vice president for girls' toys, Maurene Souza, has found herself, more than once, trying to lead her customers where they are not ready to go. "I have had such good ideas over the years," she muses. "I wanted to bring out a tool kit called Handy Girl. . . . I thought it would be great." But when Hasbro tested tools on real little girls, the idea failed. What the research tells Souza repeatedly is that little girls want to groom themselves, their dolls, their horses. Barbie has a computer, but her bridal gown always outsells her suits.

Without doubt, the large toy companies cater to little girls' desire to be sex objects and little boys' interest in killing everyone. To get the volume, they gravitate toward the lowest common denominator, and that does not result in toys that encourage nurturing behavior in boys or assertiveness in girls. Even so, there are plenty of mass-marketed toys that are harmless at worst and could even be described as beneficial. Barbie is frequently condemned as Toyland's most pernicious role model, yet psychologist Bruno Bettelheim told Mattel that Barbie is an excellent vehicle for girls to weave all kinds of fantasies in play therapy.

Every adult sets different priorities in evaluating toys. There is only one on which everyone agrees: unless a toy is safe, nothing else matters.

13

SAFETY PATROL

Toys that maim and kill continue to flood the marketplace and
invade our children's safety.
> —Ed Swartz, Press Conference, December 6, 1988

"THERE IS A LAWYER IN BOSTON," SAYS a TMA
spokeswoman, "who puts out a list at Christmas of toys he
thinks are unsafe. I can't remember his name."

Everyone in Toyland would like to forget the name of Ed
Swartz. He is a formidable adversary, an inflammatory crusader
given to flights of scathing rhetoric. He names names, publishes
books, and holds an annual press conference the first week in
December to announce his choices for the ten worst toys of the
year. He encourages parents to "ferret out the dangerous toys
that may be lurking in their toy boxes" and all but portrays toy
manufacturers as heartless child killers. Then he wonders why
they will not debate with him on television.

Swartz also happens to be a product-liability lawyer. The
citizens of Toyland unvaryingly recall his occupation, even
though they have trouble remembering his name. Accusing
companies of making unsafe products is how he makes his

living, they say. Swartz responds by saying, "Guilty. Now let's look at what I say."

What he says can be found in his 1971 book *Toys That Don't Care*; his 1986 update, *Toys That Kill*; and the press releases that precede his December press conferences. "The CPSC [Consumer Product Safety Commission] knows that toys that can choke, strangle, lacerate, burn, poison, shock, blind, and otherwise maim and kill our children continue to pollute the marketplace and infest our homes," he warned in 1985. For an industry whose literature refers to the possibility of a child's being strangled by a cord as an "unpleasant accident," this is strong stuff.

Swartz is accused of grandstanding and draws protests from the TMA for waiting until December to announce the toys he considers hazardous. He has heard it all before and describes the usual industry response to his list. The TMA spokesman, he notes, "will concede that one or two of the toys on my list are violative of the standards, and the next line will be 'why wasn't I told sooner?' as if I were a paid consultant to the toy industry. A $7.5 billion industry can afford their own safety cops. . . . I'm not a full-time Ralph Nader. I write textbooks. I give lectures. I try cases and train other lawyers to try cases. What else do you want me to do? The answers are in there. Maybe the names are new, but the generic hazards have been there for many years and they know my position on those toys. . . . And the TMA president wonders why I didn't tell him about his problems earlier. I think it's an obscenity that he has to admit he doesn't know these things himself, that he has to rely on my wisdom to tell him what's wrong."

He is grandstanding, of course, but even messengers with questionable motives may bear valid messages. "The best opportunity for me to teach safety is when I've got people's attention, and that's what bothers them. I do have their attention. I can't get people into my office to talk about toys in June or August. The holiday time is when the media have the most interest, and understandably so. That's when the buying public has the most interest."

Swartz evokes from toy-industry people the same response

they would give a rattlesnake: horrified fascination. Articulate and charming in person, he is outrageous, shamelessly melodramatic, and extremely effective in court. Any attorney who can get a jury to award $139,632 to an eleven-year-old boy who lacerated his penis when playing horsey on a vacuum cleaner is not to be taken lightly. (With the permission of the defense attorneys, Swartz pulled three hot dogs out of his pocket and fed them to the vacuum cleaner in court.)

A litigator who can extract $1.1 million from Rand McNally on the grounds of "negligent publishing" is rightly feared by his adversaries. Swartz represented a seventh-grade girl who was scarred from an explosion during chemistry class when she left a beaker of methyl alcohol too close to a Bunsen burner. Her textbook had not advised her to keep methyl alcohol away from fire. "It is clear that danger can lurk between the covers of textbooks," he told the jury. "The very instruments of learning can be the instruments of danger and even death."

In 1987 Swartz hit the product-liability lawyer's version of a home run. Not only did he defeat Fisher-Price, one of the most highly respected companies in the toy industry, but he won the largest settlement in the history of the industry. Furthermore, he won the case from a jury in Buffalo, New York, Fisher-Price's home area, on behalf of a foreign national. The product in the suit was a toy the company has sold for over twenty years, Little People: peglike figurines that fit into its play sets and vehicles— farms, schoolbuses, fire trucks. It is one of the mainstays of Fisher-Price's product line.

The case was tragic. In 1971 a Little People figure lodged in the throat of a fourteen-month-old Canadian boy, Iain Cunningham. Both parents were home, but neither could dislodge it, and the boy was unable to breathe. While his father drove to the hospital, Iain's mother tried to resuscitate the child through the nose. They saved their son's life, but the boy suffered brain damage so severe that it rendered him permanently retarded. The court awarded Iain's parents $3.1 million, and the parties later settled at $2.25 million.

Swartz won the battle but lost the war. Fisher-Price did not issue a statement, and the decision received little publicity. More disappointing to Swartz and other consumer advocates, the company made no plans to change or recall the product, and the CPSC neither banned nor issued a warning about the toy, which does conform to all existing regulations. Comments a Fisher-Price spokeswoman: "We don't think he [no name, as usual] is an objective critic of the toy industry. With respect to the product, the Little People figures offer about as much safety to the consumer as any manufacturer can provide when they are used with proper supervision and within the proper age range. Fisher-Price has been selling Little People figures for over twenty years. We have sold over 670 million of them. Out of that number there have been four serious injuries reported to Fisher-Price. With one exception the children were less than the two-to-six age range prescribed on the box. . . . The particular figure in three of the incidents has not been in line for a number of years, and in the fourth, the figure was not identified. We felt that the number of serious accidents compared to the number sold was no worse than random coincidence."

She did not add that other Little People sets previously pre-scribed age ranges as low as eighteen months. Nor that the company has now added a warning to purchasers that the toys may be hazardous to children who still put things in their mouths.

The regulation with which Little People comply is called the small-parts rule. It requires that any toy intended for sale to children under three be large enough to prevent a child who puts it in his or her mouth from choking. The small-parts rule covers not only whole toys but also parts of larger toys that might become detached through normal use and abuse.

There are two problems with the small-parts rule. First is the standard itself, which a number of people both inside and outside the toy industry consider inadequate for protecting chil-dren from choking. The other is that the absence of a labeling requirement allows toy companies so much latitude that they are free to use ambiguous wording on the packaging.

Whether a part is appropriate for sale to children under three is determined by a measuring device called a small-parts, or truncated, cylinder. If any portion of the toy or toy part sticks out of the cylinder, then that toy or toy part complies with the regulation and is deemed large enough to be safe for children under three. The cylinder looks like something designed by committee, which it was. The tube is one-and-one-quarter inches in diameter, but the base slants at a forty-five–degree angle. The length of the interior space varies from one to two-and-one-quarter inches. That means that narrow toys or toy parts will tend to sink deeper and have to be longer to comply, and fatter parts can be shorter because they will not slide so far down into the cylinder.

The small-parts rule became effective in 1980, but the CPSC has continued to receive reports of fatalities caused by toys that conform to the standard. Late in 1987 the professional staff began studying the standard and the accident rates to determine if the statistics indicate that the standard is inadequate, or if the accidents should be considered isolated incidents. The professionals also wished to empanel a group of physicians to offer them a medical rationale for a possible amendment to the standard or other remedial strategies to address the problem. Throughout 1989, however, the CPSC operated with only two commissioners out of an authorized five, so it was unable to garner the quorum one of the two commissioners considered necessary to empanel a medical panel. (President George Bush nominated a third in October 1989.)

The absence of a warning requirement in the small-parts regulation means that the rule is almost a secret. The regulation bans the sale of noncomplying toys to children under three but does not require that such toys be marked with a warning. It is even relaxed about determining which toys should be covered by the rule. According to the regulation, the criteria to be used to tell if a product is for the under-three-year-old child are "the manufacturer's stated intent (such as on a label) if it is a reasonable one; the advertising, promotion, and marketing of the article; and whether the article is commonly recognized as being intended for children under 3."

Toys that fail the small-parts test are often labeled Ages 3 and Up or For Children 4–6 or whatever the manufacturer chooses to say, giving the purchaser no hint that the label is there because the toy is considered hazardous for younger children. Adults buying toys usually assume that the age label on a package is there to assist them by suggesting an appropriate age span for the child with average intelligence or dexterity. That is done, after all, for many children's items, such as books, board games, and clothing. Since adults frequently consider the child for whom they are buying the toy smarter or more coordinated than average, they do not hesitate to buy an item for a child younger than the "suggested" age range. They have no idea that the label is a "warning" that the toy is considered hazardous to younger children.

The small-parts hazards of some toys—small doll accessories, for example, or tiny cars—are obvious, but many are not. Many toys that could not possibly choke a child have parts such as limbs or buttons that break off easily and are quite ingestible. Some manufacturers choose to add labels that read something like "Small Parts may be Hazardous to Children under Three Years Old," but such warnings are optional.

Even toys that do conform to the regulation can cause accidents, of course. The Fisher-Price spokeswoman was correct in asserting that the number of Little People accidents was low enough to be attributable to random occurrence. But the severity of the incidents was high—death in the other cases. Other companies faced with those accidents might have chosen to withdraw or redesign the product.

In 1977 Parker Brothers launched a new type of product, Riviton construction toys for older children, ages six to twelve. The company was very proud of Riviton, flexible plastic pieces that could be locked together with rivets to make vehicles, buildings, or just sculptures, and described the product as "a toy that makes toys." Parker Brothers had already sold 900,000 units of the product by April 1978, when the company received a report that an eight-year-old boy had died from ingesting a small rivet. Parker Brothers, which had never heard of one injury caused by any of its products, was shocked. In developing the toy the researchers had considered the possibility, but they had been assured that accidental death from ingesting small objects was very rare among older children.

Parker Brothers and the CPSC investigated the incident and finally determined that it had been a freak accident. Even so, Parker's management began to investigate ways of adding some chemical to the rivets that would make them taste bad enough to deter children from putting them in their mouths. That November they received another call. A nine-year-old had died, also through product misuse. At that point Parker Brothers felt it had no choice but to withdraw the product, and the employees came in during their Thanksgiving vacation to plan the recall effort. The company tried to contact all the purchasers of the toy to exchange Riviton for another toy, and it ultimately reached about half the owners. Many of them refused to return their sets. The children liked the product and believed that they knew how to use it safely. Backed by their parents, they refused to be penalized for what they considered freak accidents stemming from unsafe practices.

Ed Swartz's pronouncements to the contrary, the manufacturers and importers want safe toys, for financial as well as for humanitarian reasons: they do not want to be sued. The large companies have full-time quality-control people responsible for safety as well as for overall quality, and they take pride in their work. They subject their products to all kinds of abuse tests, trying to make them very safe and reasonably durable, "reasonably" being a value judgment because there is always a price/value trade-off. Sometimes toy companies even advance the science of safety. Mattel invented a way of making toy parts radio-opaque so that if they are swallowed they will show up on x-rays, and the company offered to share the technology with the rest of the industry. Not only did the company receive several hundred inquiries from other toy companies, but several manufacturers from outside the industry were interested as well. One manufacturer planning to make plastic revolvers thought the technology could be useful for making plastic guns visible in airport metal detectors.

Responsible toy manufacturers even think about what they call "connotive content." Explains Bob Jezak, Mattel's vice president of product integrity, "We wrestle with arguments about subjective things. Like, is selling a toy gun encouraging someone to use a real gun? We asked, should Barbie wear a seat belt in her dream car, and I said yes. We also monitor our commercials for safe practices. When we were having human figures dropping through a castle in our Masters of the Universe line, we asked ourselves if we needed to have a net underneath. After we looked at playgrounds, swingsets, things like that, we decided it was not necessary."

In spite of the industry's good intentions, there are plenty of hazards. Stuffed animals ripped open for inspection reveal anything from crushed walnuts to razor blades that careless factory workers trimming threads have dropped in. Responsible companies have installed metal detectors specifically to monitor the contents of their plush products. Counterfeit products often flout safety as well as trademark laws, but the American toy industry has also produced its share of products with sharp points, sharp edges, or excessive lead content in the paint. Many of the problems are inadvertent; a toy may unexpectedly pinch when moved a certain way, for example, or a point may puncture skin even though it conforms to the CPSC's sharp-points regulation.

Manufacturers also face constant complaints about the flimsiness of their products. Plastic action-figure headquarters and dollhouses particularly irritate parents because they are expensive and still break quite easily. Toymakers sometimes defend themselves by saying that the public has unrealistic expectations about price/value trade-offs, but in moments of candor most will admit that at times even they have been known to produce junk. Sometimes the toys come apart the way they do because manufacturers cannot figure out any other way to make the product safe.

The American toy industry as a whole has a very good safety record. The vast majority of toy-related injuries are not caused by inherently unsafe toys. Of the thirty-seven toy-related deaths reported to the CPSC for 1987 and the first nine months of 1988, for example, sixteen children died in accidents associated with riding toys, most when they rode them in front of cars or into swimming pools. Balloons (seven) and balls and marbles (six) accounted for the majority of the deaths caused by aspiration or ingestion that were reported to the agency.

Toymakers have grown more sophisticated in the past twenty-five years, both in making toys safer and in dealing with regulators. In 1969 Congress passed the Child Protection and Toy Safety Act over the toymakers' anguished protests, opening the way for stronger federal regulation. When hearings on the legislation began in 1966, *Toy & Hobby World* thundered that if the proposed law were enacted, "an injustice of the greatest magnitude will have been needlessly perpetrated against the American Toy Industry." The editors even had the effrontery to add, "We are on firm ground because we could not uncover one bit of valid evidence of any existing hazard contained in a toy produced in the U.S." Perhaps they were telling the truth—in the narrowest sense—since a huge proportion of the industry's toys are produced overseas. In the manufacturers' defense, some of the statistics entered into testimony were wildly inaccurate or ignorantly misinterpreted to depict a callous industry producing killer toys. Not surprisingly, the bill sailed through Congress; in the House of Representatives the vote was 327–0.

The most difficult period for the manufacturers was in the early 1970s, when the "consumerists" hit their stride. Memories of the activists' shoot-first-ask-questions-later methods during that era still rankle toy people. The Food and Drug Administration (which regulated toy safety until the CPSC took over in 1973) published banned-toy lists without communicating with the manufacturers, changed its safety criteria frequently without warning, and generally confused the industry, which had no idea how to comply or what was coming next.

Although the consumer-protection movement has quieted down, toymakers still complain about "consumerists," and consumer activists still complain about them. Said Ralph Nader in "Buyer's Market," a consumer advisory, in 1987: "There is a tremendous gap between dangerous, expensive toys that soon bore children and inexpensive, safe and perennially interesting toys presently available. If parents interpose themselves between their children and that manipulating, intrusive television set and its ads, rational rejection of bad toys will prevail in favor of good toys." He left out only "bad" plastic versus "good" wood. The kind of thinking that equates safety with play value and low price, or danger with television advertising, understandably infuriates toymakers. It also confirms their suspicion that many activists' criticism stems more from an antibusiness philosophy than from objections to specific offenses.

When Ronald Reagan took office as president in 1981, the toy industry dared to hope the days of banned-toy lists and inflammatory publicity were over. Aaron Locker, the TMA counsel who has been traveling to Washington for the toy industry since 1954, advised caution. "The regulatory climate is not necessarily limited to one political party," he explains. "The Democrats give more money to the agencies, but when that happens, the agencies find that there are other things to go after besides toys. They devote more money to product safety, which means they go away from toys. When the Republicans are in and cut back on the agency, they [the CPSC] begin to whip the hell out of the toy industry—which, after all, is a very favorite whipping boy because nobody likes to be against toy safety. They know they can proceed with a lot of congressional support and immunity."

Over the years the toy industry has become somewhat resigned to its fate as a political football. So has the CPSC. In 1987 the CPSC chairman embarked on a joint exercise with the U.S. Bureau of Customs called Operation Toyland, which consisted of "blitz operations" (Locker called them West Coast and East Coast pogroms) in the ports of San Francisco in July, Los Angeles in September, and Newark in November. Agents of the two organizations seized shipments of toys coming into the country to check for safety violations.

The total value of the goods seized during the spot checks amounted to $3.85 million (1987 domestic retail toy sales: $12 billion), but, as CPSC Commissioner Terrence Scanlon explained, "far more important than the dollars involved is the fact that none of the 1.5 millon plus units confiscated will fall into the hands of unsuspecting children. . . ."

While the country undoubtedly slept easier knowing that $3.85 million worth of dangerous toys had been kept out of innocent children's hands, the timing of Operation Toyland might have given some people pause. Shortly before Scanlon announced his successful forays, New Jersey Democratic Congressman James Florio, chairman of the House Reauthorization

Subcommittee on Commerce, Consumer Protection, and Competitiveness, had targeted Scanlon, calling him "brain dead" and the agency "a wimp."

Operation Toyland did nothing to raise Scanlon's standing with the ambitious Florio, who frequently criticized the CPSC as inadequate consumer protectors (and who managed to get elected governor of New Jersey in November 1989). When Scanlon testified before Florio's committee on funding reauthorization for the CPSC, the congressman told Scanlon that resigning could be his greatest contribution to product safety. "Lawmakers Label Product-Safety Chief Hazardous to Consumers," proclaimed the *Washington Post*. Scanlon evidently maintained his sense of humor, because CPSC staff members felt free to stop him in the hall and ask him how it felt to be brain dead.

All this posturing is directed toward the consuming public, which innocently assumes that the necessary regulations are in place to minimize hazards from toys and maximize toy safety. In fact, the average parent lacks the information to evaluate toys knowledgeably, and the other interested parties cannot agree on how much to regulate and how much choice to leave up to the consumer.

Toymakers assert that too much regulation takes away parental choices and amounts to the government's taking over the parents' job. They prefer voluntary standards for themselves and urge adults to participate in the selection, inspection, and maintenance of their children's toys. Their position assumes a high level of adult knowledge and intelligence, which would seem to suggest that they also support a strong labeling system so that adults can understand hazards in order to make informed choices. That is not their position, however; they like the labeling requirement the way it is. Furthermore, industry publications on safety stress the importance of parental supervision while children are playing, conveniently ignoring the fact that one of the primary uses of toys is to amuse children when adults are not playing with them.

Consumer advocates, on the other hand, are paternalistic. They assume that adults possess little information, leave their children unsupervised while the children play, and cannot always be trusted to make intelligent choices. Activists support strong regulations to protect children from the toys they personally deem undesirable or unsafe, even at the cost of some parental liberty. "Is it supposed to be open season on kids with stupid parents?" thundered Swartz at one of his press conferences. He was referring to a child's ride-in car that could travel five miles an hour, a speed Swartz considered unsafe. He also considered the car's battery hazardous. Although the car was so expensive that no child would have one unless an adult bought it, Swartz wanted the CPSC to ban it to prevent adults from making what he considered an unsafe choice.

Ultimately, the standards for toy safety, like other regulations, emerge from negotiation. Since perfect safety is impossible to regulate and unattainable anyway, any standard is going to be an imperfect compromise. The final results of the negotiation are determined by such real-world factors as the strength of the competing interest groups, the political climate, the persuasive powers of the individual lobbyists, and even the nature of the latest toy accident.

14

FEBRUARY–APRIL 1987
How Toymen Put the Pieces Together

THE 1987 TOY FAIR WAS ALMOST UNBEARABLE for Tyco's Dino-Rider team because they were so worried about what they might see. As Neil Werde put it, "Anytime we heard about anything, someone had to go investigate, especially if it began with a *D*." That year there was quite a bit of activity in the category beginning with *D*, but they had already heard about most of the products and convinced themselves that none of them posed a threat. Dinosaurs were clearly a trend, however, and they wondered how long it could last.

The industry was overdoing it, as usual. Commonwealth Toy's Dinomites line had plush, sleepy-eyed Dinosnores that snored when rocked; Dinobones, which featured glow-in-the-dark bones; and velourlike Dinoeggs, in which a dinosaur hatched from an egg and could change from a dinosaur back into an egg again. Larami Corporation offered TimeOSaurs, "Soft Dinosaur Friends that tell you the time" (furry wristbands with turquoise and purple plush dinosaurs on watch faces). Intex advertised "Dinosaurs & Die Cast! Two hot categories from Intex," and a company called Cardart featured a set of Dinosaur

215

cards for children to paint as greeting cards. United Media sought licensees for its Tiny Dinos property by Guy Gilchrist.

The cuddly products were easy to dismiss; they were not aimed at Tyco's market. But Hasbro and Mattel both offered dinosaur-related action-figure lines. It is never fun to contemplate taking on market leaders: not only do they have deep pockets, but they have muscle. The Tyco group knew that, all things being equal, retailers facing a choice between a dinosaur line from Hasbro and one from Tyco would tend to buy Hasbro's. Hasbro had the action-figure experience, Hasbro had more money to spend on advertising, and, most important, Hasbro had the only two action-figure lines on the list of the twenty top-selling toys, Transformers and G.I. Joe. Success like that created more than credibility with buyers; it created leverage. A generous order for a company's weak or unproven lines may be rewarded with shipments of the company's hard-to-get products, and conversely, a customer who does not support the less desirable lines may have trouble getting the hotter items.

Tyco was relieved that Hasbro's Definitely Dinosaurs line was being marketed under its preschool division, Playskool. Four of its dinosaurs duplicated Tyco's, and each came with its own storybook and one Cavester friend. The Cavesters, who looked like professional wrestlers, were rounded and squatty, as befitted toys safe for preschoolers, and wore bright, fantasy-colored "skins." The dinosaurs' hides were tinted in similarly fanciful shades, varying from purple and lavender to bright greens, oranges, and blues.

Mattel had added dinosaurs to their five-year-old He-Man and Masters of the Universe action-figure line, which did compete with Tyco for the same market of four-to-eight-year-old boys. Mattel was sending He-Man back to Preternia, a prehistoric version of his usual abode, Eternia. Aided by "He-Ro, the most powerful wizard in the universe, Eldor, his mentor and teacher, and Turbodactyl and Bionotops, his mighty dinosaur allies in battle, He-Man would fight against the evil dinoreptilian kingdom and the dreaded Tyrantasauras Rex" from whose chest a wind-up creature called a "mecha-drone" could emerge.

To anyone else it might have seemed that Dino-Riders had

some serious competition: people with dinosaurs . . . traveling back in time . . . making friends with nice dinosaurs and fighting against the fierce ones that were allied with the enemy. But the products, fielded by companies ten times Tyco's size, fazed Dino-Riders' creators not at all. "Cavemen with dinosaurs," they chuckled derisively when they saw Hasbro's Cavesters. "All kids know that people and dinosaurs didn't live at the same time . . . that's so hokey." Some of Tyco's dinosaur species missed each other by a similar time period (dinosaurs roamed the earth for about 135 million years, and species came and went), but the Tyco group considered that immaterial. "What's a few million years more or less?" they asked each other. Mattel's product idea also elicited their contempt. "Things coming out of the dinosaur's stomach! Can you imagine? How realistic is that?" they sneered. The fact that their Dino-Riders communicated with dinosaurs telepathically through medallions was entirely different.

Maintaining an intelligence network on dinosaurs was hazardous but exciting. Neil found *New York Times* press tags on the floor one day, so he put them on and toured as many showrooms as he could fit in. He had to hurry back because Tyco was having an outstanding Toy Fair. The company's radio-controlled cars had been hot for a year and showed no signs of decline, and the Super Dough play sets were very well received. The Flower Makin' Basket included flower-scented bud extruders for making multicolored flowers that could be arranged in a plastic "wicker" basket. Squeezers consisted of a skull and two other gross heads that allowed children to extrude Super Dough through bloodshot eyes and other cavities.

Less successful was Tyco's first attempt in the plush category. The Tyco people quickly saw that Tyco was far from the only company trying to mooch some pooch dollars away from Tonka's canine version of Cabbage Patch Kids. Plush puppies that needed adoption from the pound, Pound Puppies were a much more acceptable "doll" for little boys who wanted to nurture something soft but were too embarrassed to carry a doll. They replaced Cabbage Patch Kids as the industry's bestselling toy and generated $156 million for Tonka in 1986.

In response, the industry had unleashed such a plethora of pooches that Toy Fair 1987 resembled a fantasy version of the Westminster Kennel Club dog show. At Chosun's showroom there were History Hounds, including Abrahound Lincoln, Bitsey Ross, Pocahoundas, and even Spaniel Boon in a coonskin cap. J.P. Rufio, a poodle that wore sunglasses and a T-shirt and contained an audiocassette recording of one of his "remarkable adventures" from "The Rufio Trilogy," had an unusual advisory board of twenty students from three Harlem schools. For aspiring doctors and hypochondriacs, a Boo Boo Pooch was just the thing. Its "seven minor aches and pains ranging from a bumped head to a bruised tail" could be treated with its personal first-aid equipment, which included an ice bag, an adhesive strip, and a sling.

In such imaginative company, Tyco's first "action plush" entry, Tuffie, "Your Fearless Friend," began to look a little forlorn. Tuffie had one dark eyebrow that stretched over both eyes, giving him an appropriately fierce expression ("dogs that are lovable enough to be your best friend and bedside buddy, yet are tough enough to protect you from the 'scaries' "). Action-gear accessories allowed boys to dress the dog as a sailor, a cowboy, a sergeant, or as Karate Tuffie, and the packaging, which displayed the dog in front of a cardboard doghouse, was innovative and attractive. Best of all, the dog's jaw could grip things when its owner squeezed its neck.

In spite of all of its competition, the group at Tyco liked their dog Tuffie so much they had a hard time figuring out why the buyers passed it up. Some of the salespeople decided that the trade had no more appetite for boys' plush dogs, but Jim Alley said it was all his fault: he just wasn't any good with emotional toys. Not until a few months later did they conclude that maybe a dog that bit things when you strangled it was not so great a product as they had originally thought.

Toy Fair lasts ten days, but the Sunday in the middle is usually fairly quiet, and Tyco used the lull to present Dino-Riders to the creative people at its advertising agency. Although its introduction had been postponed, the line was still on an overtime schedule, and Tyco wanted the agency people so excited by the concept that they would go back to Los Angeles and throw themselves into the project.

That was exactly what happened. The copywriter on the account, Garth DeCew, is a temperamental twin to Lee Volpe—both love to wax eloquent on grand philosophical questions—and Garth got the idea immediately.

"I *love* it!" he proclaimed as Lee showed the line. Much later he speculated about why he had responded so positively. "There was this tall, thin guy in product development who really created those babies, and I felt very strongly about his childlike enthusiasm. I think that's important in this business. A professor of mine once said that there's an aspect of our personality and character called the exceptional child. That's the ability to react to things as a child would react, with a sense of abandon and honesty, and the ability to walk away from all the things society teaches us and let the spontaneity happen. I think that's the source of creativity. Joy and enthusiasm and humor and all those things that are creative come from the ability to tie things together in ways that are not traditional. And that is what this guy was exhibiting. He loved his work."

By the end of the meeting, the guy who loved his work was downcast. Jay Garfinkel was at the meeting, too, and Dick Grey gave him the final go-ahead to spend $200,000 to produce an eight-minute videotape based on Paul Kirchner's treatment. That was great. But Dick also made the final decision about the Dino-Rider characters, joining Cy Schneider and Garfinkel, who advocated muscular He-Man character types rather than aliens. Garth allied himself with Lee and argued in favor of the warrior elves, but they were outranked. The well-trod path of superhero types was the safer choice, and Dick was not interested in piling gamble on top of gamble. Dino-Riders finally and irrevocably joined the ranks of the macho that day, and that was the end of Michael Tut.

With Toy Fair 1987 behind them, they all redoubled their efforts to get the project ready on time. One of Neil Werde's responsibilities was setting up a Dino-Riders Fan Club ("Send four proofs of purchase to the following address . . ."), and he wanted to hire a genuine paleontologist to write the club newsletter. They had discussed the idea of hiring a spokesperson to use for media events, and Neil thought a real scientist could give club members actual new information about dinosaur findings. Besides, a genuine academic would emphasize the products' authenticity.

Tyco contacted several paleontologists whose names were most prominently mentioned in news reports of dinosaur findings, and Neil, advertising vice president Bob Lurie, and Tyco's outside public relations agent, Bruce Maguire, set out to interview them. Their first candidate was Dr. David Weishampel of Johns Hopkins University, a tweedy, pipe-smoking professor with patches on this elbows, whom they considered extremely academic.

Then they met Dr. Bob. Robert Bakker, forty-two, B.S. Yale, Ph.D. Harvard, is one of the best-known paleontologists in the field; he is usually one of the experts called for a quote when new information about dinosaurs appears in the popular press. His book *Dinosaur Heresies* had offered the world a radically different vision of the primordial world of dinosaurs. One of the leading proponents of the theory that dinosaurs were warm-blooded, brightly colored, and lively, Bakker had supported his hypotheses with scientific data and had illustrated his book himself with elegant line drawings.

On paper he sounded perfect for the job. A professional who retained the enthusiasm of an amateur, Bakker had always loved sharing his knowledge with children. He had no objection to the commercialism of the venture because he saw it as an opportunity to reach a larger audience. He was willing to associate himself with the products because he was impressed by Tyco's attention to detail and insistence on authenticity. Furthermore, his job with the University of Colorado Museum allowed him enough time to get away for media tours.

In practice, there were a couple of problems. First, Dr. Bob was more than a trifle eccentric. The son of fundamentalist Christians, he claimed to have been such an effective street preacher during college that he had been called Dr. Doom. His parents were ardent creationists, but it was his mother who had taken him to the Museum of Natural History in New York, where, as he puts it, he was "infected with the childhood disease" of dinosaurs. When he failed to recover and in fact chose dinosaurs as a profession, his parents were not pleased. Family relations cannot have been helped by the fact that he kept getting married and divorced—he has married four times.

Then there was his appearance. Though mild-mannered and pleasant, Dr. Bob wore his graying hair hanging untidily past his waist and topped it with a floppy hat. At the introductory luncheon at a restaurant, he flipped his mane over his face, put his glasses on over his hair, and went into his Cousin It from "The Addams Family" routine. Although Bakker is a brilliant scholar, his penchant for the outrageous makes him wildly unpredictable. Bruce Maguire was appalled at the thought of trying to control this whimsical genius (who was well aware of the effect he had on his audience).

The marketing people could not resist Bakker, however, and decided to take the risk. Rejecting Weishampel, whom they always describe as "the one with the elbow patches," the Tyco group believed that if Bakker respected what they did, he would be wonderful both with the press and with children. Bakker himself was pleased at the agreement, although once he realized how uncomfortable he made Tyco's public relations agent, he made a point of tormenting him with threats to misbehave and embarrass the company. Just to be safe, Neil and Bob kept him away from Dick Grey for almost a year.

In March Woody and Neil had to prepare yet another presentation of Dino-Riders. This time they were going to show the line to the outside consultant who had brought Tyco the ideas for Super Dough and the Flower Makin' Basket, industry giant Bernie Loomis. (In fact, since Loomis had been president of Kenner for a number of years, Kenner promptly sued both Tyco and GLAD—Loomis's company, Great Licensing And Design— when Tyco introduced Super Dough, for stealing its classic product, Play-Doh. Kenner lost when the judge ruled that its "confidential" idea of pushing two colors of Play-Doh through an extruder was not unique enough to warrant the protection of the courts.) Besides bringing Tyco new products, Loomis had agreed to evaluate and help review products the company was developing internally.

Woody and Neil were completely intimidated. As Woody described it, "We're going to present this thing to somebody who knows more about what we're trying to do than we do . . . I mean, Bernie Loomis: see Toys 101, 102, 103 and any other mention of toys in the Western world."

They even made up a mantra. Anytime Bernie Loomis was mentioned, one of them would chant "Looooommmmm." Not only did they dread making fools of themselves, but they were worried that "Looooommmmm" would suggest all kinds of changes so that he could put his own imprint on the line. They liked Dino-Riders the way it was—it was theirs.

Contributing to their nervousness was the fact that as many times as they had presented Dino-Riders, they had never shown it in a formal presentation. Their meetings at Tyco, though formal by company standards, had always been fairly casual. In other toy companies, and in other industries where entertainment value and customer appeal are important, presentations are often entertainment in themselves. Both Woody and Neil had participated in such so-called dog-and-pony shows, and they wanted to look professional when they showed the line to one of the top professionals in their industry.

To tell the story of the fantasy, which they agreed would be the hardest part, they decided to use the commercial storyboard their advertising agency had just sent over. A storyboard is a series of sketches laying out the visual sequence of a commercial in comic-strip form. They circled about thirty of the frames and told an artist from Tyco's art department to enlarge and mount them. It took him an entire weekend.

Meanwhile, they worked on a narrative. One of them would recite while the other slowly flipped the drawings to give the illusion of the story's unfolding. They had problems from the beginning. It was physically impossible for the flipper to flip fast enough to keep up with the narrator, and even when the flipping lagged behind the narrative, it was much too fast for the audience to see anything of the drawings.

They tried it the other way, t-a-l-k-i-n-g v-e-r-y s-l-o-w-l-y, but that did not work either. By then they were both on the floor in hysterics. By the time they picked themselves up, they had figured out that they had too many illustrations. Once they discarded half the carefully enlarged drawings, the narrator was easily able to talk at a normal speed.

When Woody and Neil finally presented Dino-Riders to Looooommmmm, that estimable personage could not have been nicer. He said only positive things for the first few minutes, so that by the time he added, "I think I can help you," they were relaxed and receptive. Loomis's question immediately pinpointed a weak spot, and even Woody and Neil were impressed. He asked them why they were planning to offer six different items at the same price point. They were packaging all three medium-priced dinosaurs (the *Deinonychus, Pteranodon,* and *Monoclonius*) with two figures and weapons in both Dino-Rider and Rulon assortments. "Why would the kids buy two of the same dinosaur?" he asked. "Why don't you add something to half of them and push the price up a little?"

Woody and Neil liked his idea and felt jubilant that they had sold the famous Bernie Loomis on their concept. "His reputation had definitely preceded him," Woody recalled later. "I had met him a couple of times, but not that he'd remember. Now he does, of course. Now he calls me whenever he has a crisis. I've taught him everything I know."

Actually, the snow job came from the other direction. "I didn't love the concept," Loomis confessed months later, "although I thought it was okay. But I could see how excited they were, and I didn't want to discourage them."

Loomis's suggestion took them further than he had envisioned. Lee decided to add value by giving the Rulons traps to capture dinosaurs. But his comment also started them thinking. Even with the traps they were still offering the same three dinosaurs. New ones were out of the question at that late date, but maybe they could find some way to alter the three existing ones into other species. The product-development group went back to the list of dinosaurs and found that, in fact, some of the various species had had remarkably similar bodies. They realized that they could fit the *Monoclonius* body with a new head and turn it into a *Styracosaurus.* The *Pteranodon* could be converted to a *Quetzalcoatlus.* Once the creatures were painted different colors, the similarities would be evident only to the close observer. Only the *Deinonychus* had no close counterpart, so they kept both Dino-Rider and Rulon packages for Nike.

The next time he was at Tyco for a new-products review meeting, Bernie Loomis offered another idea that became one of the centerpieces of the line. As they showed him the new dinosaurs and traps, Woody, Neil, and Jim were complaining about the high cost of television programming and the low level of viewer interest. Jay Garfinkel was finishing the eight-minute videotape, but the cost per viewer was becoming so prohibitive that even if Tyco could sell it, they weren't sure they wanted to have a program. On the other hand, if they didn't get on television, how else could they get their story across to the kids?

"Instead of a program, why not do a videotape?" Loomis suggested. "You already have eight minutes. You could sell it in the toy stores with the other videotapes." It was a novel approach and a wonderful solution. Right then they decided to sell it at their cost and attach a sticker saying something like Special Value to keep retailers from marking it up to regular videotape prices. If they printed half a million tapes and the kids who bought them made another 500,000 copies for their friends, Tyco might reach an audience of about 2 million, assuming two children in a family. They also agreed that offering the tape at cost justified their tacking on a couple of commercials for other Tyco products.

The marketing and product-development people were not the only ones at Tyco racing against time. While they were deliberating weighty issues such as warrior elves and talking dinosaurs, the engineers were toiling away at their drafting tables, painstakingly designing the molds for each part of every toy.

Both the marketing and the engineering groups agree that they are temperamental opposites. They even agree on how they differ. They just disagree on how they define their differences. To the marketing people, engineers are "the kind of guys who buy square sedans. No styling . . . you know, 'If it takes you where you want to go, who cares what color it is?' " The engineers consider themselves realists and think of the marketing people as "blue-sky boys"—prima donnas who have all the fun and get all the credit. The view from the engineering department is that they pore over their blueprints, figuring out how to make the dinosaurs look the way marketing wants them to look, move the way marketing wants them to move, last as long as marketing says they should last, and all at a "reasonable" cost so that the products can be sold at the price marketing has set. Oh, and by the way, they should hurry because marketing needs everything yesterday.

Tyco's engineering vice president, Don Martin, knows that nobody loves an engineer—except perhaps another engineer. "I know we're a necessary evil," he admits. "If the rest of the operation could do without my department, I know they'd be delighted. We're always the bearer of bad news—'This is what the product has to cost,' 'There will have to be a delay'—whatever. As far as marketing is concerned, after they make their decisions, everything else is in the way. To them, it's 'Here's the product, here's the name, here's the box, so when can I have it?' Creativity can't be time-studied, and I understand that. But it's still hard to take.

"Marketing and new products [product development] come up with the products, and even if they're a month late, they still want everything ready to ship by a certain time. Engineering comes up with a schedule [which covers several months and is very detailed], and if I miss that date by even a day I hear about it from everyone. But if new products misses by six weeks, no one says anything. There's not even a ripple." He sighs resignedly. "But I understand."

Don Martin may be exaggerating, but only a little and not about the pressure. In the promotional-toy category the commodity in shortest supply is time. Tyco and its competitors care about costs, but time is frequently more important (within reason). Trends move quickly, so the marketing people always want the products on the shelves as soon as possible.

The engineering department translates the product-development department's "works like, looks like" models into manufacturable products. Each new product requires individually designed tooling (molds), and the simpler the design, the lower the cost. Sometimes a small alteration in design can save considerable costs, so engineering, product development, and marketing negotiate constantly about the design. "That curl in the tail is not going to sell one more dinosaur," the engineer will protest to the designer, "and it means an extra part." The designer may insist that it is a very important curl. The arguments are not just about aesthetics; they are also about strength, durability, or how much abuse a product should be engineered to withstand.

Tyco's manager of quality assurance is Jerry Rasor, a gentle, pleasant man who worked for most of his career on General Electric's rocket systems—he even spent a couple of years at Cape Canaveral. Now he checks on blocks, dough, and dinosaurs, and he enjoys the little products just as much. Since Tyco is a small operation, he is in charge of both product safety and product quality. He considers some of his decisions concerning product quality just common sense. "You look at the price of a product," he explains. "If it will cost the consumer ninety-eight cents, you expect maybe eight to ten hours of play. A fifty-dollar toy should last a lot longer and be more reliable." Quality is never cheap, and finding the right price is a delicate decision. Sometimes the decisions are argued all the way up to Dick Grey.

When a product goes to engineering, the engineers usually come back to marketing with questions like "How long do you want it to last?" or, more specifically, "How long do you want the *Torosaurus* to run on one battery?" They want a specific answer. The engineers do not want to hear "A long time," which is a marketing kind of answer. They are hoping for "Seven hours," or something at least reasonably specific.

The marketing people, who do not like to deal in such specifics, sometimes pick their answers out of thin air. Then they get annoyed when the engineers return to tell them, "Here's the *Torosaurus*. We have it running for seven hours on one battery. But it will cost you fifty dollars to produce." If marketing had planned to sell it for thirteen dollars, they mutter about death by overengineering and add more audibly that they would prefer to have a few hints about cost/benefit trade-offs before they reach into the air for their numbers. As a result, marketing people tend to drop things on the engineers' desks and try to get quick cost estimates—which engineers do not like to give because there are too many variables.

When they designed the battery-operated dinosaurs, the engineers had to determine the size of the motor each would need. The motor had to be powerful enough to propel the creature around and make it do everything it was supposed to do (such as roar), and it had to be durable enough to last for the desired life span of the product. But the motor could not be so powerful that it would drain the batteries in an unacceptably short time.

Even when they could extract more specific definitions of "desired life span of the product" and "unacceptably short time," the engineers could use them only as targets. They still had to guess which motors would produce them. Although the engineers make educated guesses, they never know if they are right until the first successful samples, called first shots, can be put together from all the parts. The process often takes several tries because the molds usually need adjusting. Companies typically wait three or four months between the time engineering releases its designs to production and the time they see the product run.

For the engineering and quality-control areas, the making of the Dino-Riders line moved along relatively smoothly. The fact that everyone was always behind schedule was just normal procedure. The only exception was the Affair of the Rug.

When the engineers first received models and patterns for the dinosaurs, they began to ask their usual nitpicking questions. One of the questions, sandwiched among many, was, "Do you want the motorized dinosaurs to walk on the rug?" They were told no and designed the four walkers (*Torosaurus*, *Triceratops*, *Diplodocus*, and *Tyrannosaurus rex*) accordingly.

When the samples began to come in, marketing had a change of mind. No one remembers exactly how it happened, but suddenly the dinosaurs, which had been engineered to walk with a lumbering gait, whose heads swung naturalistically from side to side, whose price was coming in on target, were deemed unsatisfactory. When they were placed on a rug, they could not walk. Marketing said they had to walk. A larger motor was installed in Hong Kong, where the samples were being tested, and the word came back: "They can walk on the rug."

Everyone was relieved and thought the problem was solved.

Then the samples arrived in New Jersey, and they could not walk on the rug. Complaints to the Hong King office were met with, "Well, they walk on *our* rug." Engineering tried a number of remedies and failed. A dinosaur that could walk on the engineering rug would be found immobilized on a marketing director's rug. And once it worked on marketing's rug, it could not negotiate the presidential pile in Dick Grey's office.

The controversy raged for several days. Finally, Jerry Rasor went out and bought a piece of gold, medium-pile rug and declared it the Official Rug. When the animals could walk on it, he ruled, they could "walk on the rug." Furthermore, to prevent the usual East-West communications problems, he had the rug cut in half and sent one piece to Hong Kong so that Tyco's testing could be conducted under globally identical conditions. Thenceforth only walking tests conducted on the Official Rug would be considered valid.

Consistency really was important, because the dinosaurs not only had to be able to walk on the rug, but they had to continue walking for a certain number of hours before the battery ran out. ("How long do you want it to run on one battery?") And the walking mechanism itself had to last many more hours before wearing out. ("How long do you want the toy to last?") To answer all the "how long" questions, people actually sat and watched little dinosaurs walk to the edge of the rug and picked them up or turned them around and watched them walk back, monitoring their progress for hours. These tedious tests were conducted in Hong Kong, where labor costs are lower. Even so, the testers ran many samples at the same time, so the tests looked like little dinosaur stampedes across a golden plain.

Although they did not patent it, Tyco's engineers did push back the frontiers of the science of dinosaur rug walking. They found in the course of their experiments that the life of the product was significantly affected by whether the dinosaurs walked with or against the nap of the rug. Unfortunately, the information has been lost. No one thought to record it at the time, and no one showed any enthusiasm for repeating the tests.

The final product turned out to be so high in quality that it more than fulfilled—it surpassed—the Official Rug specifications. Everyone in the marketing, product-development, and engineering departments remembers the day when Lee's long arm reached around an office doorway and set two *Diplodocuses* down on the rug.

When the arm withdrew, the two little dinosaurs marched sedately across the room, over the plush presidential rug, all the way to Dick Grey's desk.

15

CREATORS, COPYCATS, AND COUNTERFEITERS

ON THE FIRST WEDNESDAY OF TOY FAIR, toy inventors traditionally visit the toymakers' showrooms. They go to gaze with pride at their creations, to glare in disgust at the manufacturers' inferior executions of their spectacular ideas, to choke enviously at their competitors' achievements, and to moan to themselves when they see their half-developed projects already out on the market.

The toy manufacturers are ambivalent about professional inventors. They rely on them because they cannot generate enough ideas in-house, and outsiders bring them fresh vision. But many, particularly the employees who consider themselves creative, envy the inventors. Outsiders can bring in an idea (a one-page treatment, a simple line drawing, a crude sculpture, or even a concept tossed off in conversation) that makes them millions of dollars. The standard inventor's 5 percent royalty comes off the top, out of the product's sales.

The inventor's job looks so painless while they, the poor corporate drones, do all the real work in exchange for their puny salaries. Inventors do not have to discuss every little detail with the product-development department. They do not have to argue with the engineers or yawn through boring meetings. Inventors do not screen licensing agents or packagers. Nor do they sit all day at production studios while two seconds of a thirty-second commercial are shot over and over and over. They never have to stay up all night revising budgets and trying to squeeze yet another penny out of the cost. All inventors seem to do is deposit hefty royalty checks at their local banks.

The vision of reaping more of the benefits of their work leads many marketing, design, and development people to go out on their own as independent toy developers. Most of them soon find, however, that being a successful inventor is less glamorous than it looks. The waiting, especially, looks different from the other side.

From all but the top inventors, manufacturers may hold an idea, often for months. They may pay a retainer—sometimes as much as $30,000–$50,000—but many times they pay nothing. They take a long time to decide because if they buy the idea, they may have to invest $2-3 million developing the product, including a healthy advance against royalties to the inventor. Meanwhile, the inventor's mortgage comes due regularly, medical bills accumulate, meals are a daily necessity, and 5 percent of nothing is, sadly, nothing. So back many an aspiring inventor goes, to a salary with benefits. The rewards are much lower, but so are the risks.

Some of the industry's most successful toys have been created not by the professionals who place enough inventions to make a living at it but by complete outsiders with one good idea. Pound Puppies, Trivial Pursuit, Cootie, Pictionary, and Slinky were created by amateurs. Silly Putty was an accident. As in the record business, many artists have one hit in a lifetime. Many toy companies avoid dealing with amateurs in spite of the possibility that they may miss the next blockbuster, and some refuse to see them at all.

Meeting with the established inventors is time-consuming enough, and the professionals do not waste their time with typical amateur's mistakes, such as creating a game that has already been invented or targeting a market that does not exist.

But time is not really the problem. The toy companies are insatiable idea consumers, so they would make time to see the amateurs if they did not also fear them. It is to protect themselves from lawsuits that so many of them ban amateurs, or at least amateurs without agents.

Even professional inventors sign waivers before they show their ideas; the waivers include an acknowledgment that the company may already have seen or be working on a similar idea or product. (That is why inventors keep logbooks documenting the dates of their ideas: so that they can prove the timing of their creations' origins in court.) A company may reject an idea from outside for any number of reasons, including the fact that it is already working on something similar, and it often chooses not to give the inventor a reason. Both parties know that ideas can and will be duplicated and cannot be patented, so they have to trust each other. Amateurs are not part of this community, however. Often unaware of the frequency of innocent duplication, they can be a litigious lot, and they scare the corporations. As one executive who sees inventors describes them, "They walk in hiding something under their arm and say, 'I've got a great idea for a toy for you to make, but I'm not going to show it to you because I'm afraid you'll steal it.' "

The toymakers' aversion to amateurs is understandable, but it erects an additional barrier against outsiders. The frustrations are not difficult to imagine, although few designers would go to such extremes as a twenty-four-year-old New Yorker named Wilbert Anthony McKreith did in July 1983. When Mattel refused to see him, he barricaded himself in the Beverly Hills Hotel and threatened to blow himself up unless someone arranged a meeting for him with the president of Mattel. After a hotel evacuation and four hours of negotiations, the bomb in his briefcase turned out to be a Bible, and McKreith never made it in to Mattel.

Stealing is not unknown among professionals, of course, and lawsuits claiming theft proliferate. The usual line in Toyland is "A patent is just a license to sue." The government only grants a patent; it is up to the holder to protect it. One New Jersey inventor even specialized in litigation: he would buy patents and then sue makers of similar products for infringement. The companies generally treat inventors honorably, which is in their own interest. They need a constant flow of ideas, and if they steal from the source, they will be cut off from the supply. Theft of intellectual property is difficult to prove, however, and what an inventor may consider stealing the company may define as inspiration.

The professional inventors' community is largely invisible to the outside world. Inventors do not sign their creations, and any credit (or opprobrium) from the general public flows to the company. The final product often owes much of its success to the contributions of others anyway, and the inventors do not seem to mind their anonymity. If their products are selling, they enjoy the kind of credit they get at the bank.

The range of inventors is as broad as the range of products they create. There are flamboyant showmen, market-niche seekers, seasoned pros, artistic types, technological wizards. The real professionals, the ones the toy companies see regularly because they all want to be the first to see the good ideas, are the ones who are consistent. To use the industry's favorite baseball analogy, the real pros do not hit home runs every time, but they can produce singles and doubles consistently. Even the most well-established inventors have to be able to take rejection—on about 90 percent of their ideas. They like to show their favorites to the largest companies first because the bigger firms can make more of an investment and tend to create broader product lines and costlier advertising campaigns around a concept. An idea for a truck may result in a pair of trucks at a small company, for example, while at Hasbro's Playskool the same idea may be turned into trucks, cars, and a bus.

Two inventors in New York have been splitting the royalties on the game Connect Four for years, well over $8 million by now. Psychologist Howard Wexler was working for one of the industry's first independent inventors, Ned Strongin, when the two invented the vertical–tic-tac-toe game played with checkers. They disagree about who did what, but they are locked together in a royalty agreement forever. Now estranged competitors, they both continue to turn out ideas year after year.

Marvin Glass & Associates, in Chicago, reigned as the largest and most prestigious toy-design firm for forty years, until its partners split the firm in half in 1988.

In Connecticut, Avi Arad takes calls from France, Israel, and San Francisco, switching each time to the caller's native tongue. When toy-company executives dream about going out on their own, Avi Arad is who many of them would like to be. One of the most successful independent inventors in the business, he may bring a company nothing more elaborate than a drawing of a package or a list of the items that would make up a product line he is proposing. He sometimes shows a sample or a commercial. Sometimes he brings nothing at all, just a few words about an idea, and he may be very well paid for that idea.

No wonder everyone wants to be Avi. Accomplished performer that he is, he makes it look easy.

Like a character from Leon Uris's novel *Exodus*, Arad was born on a ship docked in Cyprus in 1947. He rejects the title inventor: "Inventing is the light bulb, the microprocessor, penicillin—I can't think of any toy that changed humanity." He defines his job more as marketing than invention: using an ability to recognize what people will buy. Aided by a foreigner's perspective, he watches the American culture and attempts to translate it into products that fill a gap in the market—about fifty a year.

Like other independent inventors, Arad bases some of his product suggestions on holes he perceives in a company's product line. He showed Bouncin' Babies, miniature dolls that could crawl and move their heads, to Lewis Galoob in December 1987. Galoob wanted a doll, but it had to be small. The company was still closing out a large talking doll, Baby Talk, and it did not want to compete with itself. Galoob liked Bouncin' Babies so much that it showed the product at the 1988 Toy Fair and shipped it early enough to sell $2 million the first year, making it the number one promotional doll in 1988, except for fashion dolls.

Another inventor/product developer, in New York, has had one of the most flamboyant careers in the industry. Genius, charlatan, or rascal, depending on who is describing him, Marty Abrams is undeniably controversial.

While still in his twenties, Abrams transformed his family company, Mego, from a nearly obscure importer of cheap rack toys (those toys that hang near stores' cash registers to encourage impulse purchases) into one of the top companies in the industry. Eleven years after he took over, the company went into Chapter 11 bankruptcy. Chapter 11 is hardly unusual for a toy company. What was unusual in the case of Mego was that bankruptcy was only the second-worst thing that happened that year. Five months earlier Abrams and four others had been indicted for stealing from the company.

Mego was an exciting place to be in the 1970s. The company had been around for eighteen years, but it was brought to life in 1971 when Marty became president. Mego had expanded beyond rack goods to low-priced versions of industry leaders like G.I. Joe and Barbie (Action Jackson, Dinah-mite), but its products had begun to lose sales to even lower-priced knockoffs. Abrams thought he could do better with original products and convinced his family to allow him to spend large sums—often $100,000 plus 5 percent royalties—to cash in on the celebrities, real and fictional, he sensed would be marketable.

He was good. By 1975 Mego's toys based on Superman, "The Waltons," *Star Trek*, and *The Wizard of Oz* were generating sales of $50 million with earnings of $4.4 million. In 1976 Mego produced Sonny and Cher dolls (Cher came with false eyelashes and a choice of thirty-two costumes especially designed by Bob Mackie, the real Cher's favorite designer) and a Muhammad Ali doll that could be pugilistically posed in a miniature boxing ring. Mego was not the first to license celebrities, but it was the leader in the 1970s.

There is skill as well as luck in choosing the right licenses. Instinct and timing are crucial, but Abrams hedged his bets by buying a wide range of celebrity licenses every year on the assumption that he would be right on at least one or two. In one year Mego featured Farrah Fawcett-Majors, Diana Ross, The Captain and Tennille, a new Growing Hair Cher, Wonder Woman, and a very large King Kong. Abrams also appreciated the value of publicity and loved launching his products with lavish events. To introduce the Sonny and Cher dolls, he staged a dinner dance for a thousand guests at the Waldorf-Astoria, complete with music by Lionel Hampton and personal appearances by the dolls' namesakes.

Even in an industry that relishes eccentricity and flamboyance, Marty Abrams stood out. Wags liked to say that the company name was a contraction of "Marty's ego," but Abrams always demurred, modestly insisting that the name originated from his younger brother's habit of tugging at his father's coattails and saying, "Me go, too."

When the end came, it came quickly. While Mego grew, Abrams spent money freely. Then the company had a pair of bad years (combined losses from 1980 and 1981 exceeded $44 million), and the creditors began to close in. During the same period an investigation of pilferage revealed a five-year pattern of selling merchandise off the books for cash. The warehouse manager, William Stuckey, was convicted of charges that he and "unidentified co-conspirators sold $60,000 worth of returned or damaged goods. He went to jail for ninety days and paid a $10,000 fine.

The U.S. attorney's office went after Mego the following year, and Stuckey turned prosecution witness. Abrams and four others (Leonard Siegel, Mego's former general counsel, two other Mego executives, and the head of a trucking company with which Mego did business) were indicted for defrauding the company and its shareholders by selling inventory and using the proceeds to enrich themselves and to bribe others. Before they could go to trial, Mego, with debts of $50 million, filed for bankruptcy protection.

After a seven-week trial and four days of jury deliberations, Abrams and Siegel were found guilty of fifteen counts of wire fraud and one count of false filing of federal corporate income-tax returns. The others were acquitted. The two appealed and the appellate court split the decision, sending the case back to the original judge, who sentenced them each to five years' probation and $5,000 fines. Siegel was suspended from the bar for two years, and the irrepressible Abrams was soon back in the toy industry.

In 1986 Abrams joined three brothers named Gentile to form Abrams/Gentile Entertainment, adding film and theatrical production to his toy-development activities. Besides marketing the film *Dirty Dancing*, Abrams/Gentile has developed and sold several major toy lines, with varying degrees of success. Coleco took an action-figure line based on Rambo, which failed. Another action-figure line, Visionaries, which featured holograms on every product, brought Hasbro modest sales. Hasbro also bought FAZZ, a line of cosmetics that could be worn as jewelry, and FAZZ sold very well.

Throughout his years in the business, Marty Abrams has fascinated the industry. Some people detest him, and others like him very much. No one denies his talent. "When he is channeled and controlled, he does great," one veteran opines. "Some people are just not meant to control the finances." Abrams, forty-seven, has several projects in the works at all times and is convinced that his best years are yet to come.

At the other end of the country and the other end of the spectrum is the dean of toy inventors. He started on his own in Chicago, joined forces there with Marvin Glass, and then went out to California, where the sunny climate reflects his mild geniality.

If there is a Santa Claus, he is alive and well and working in Los Angeles's San Fernando Valley. Eddy Goldfarb, a gentle man with twinkling blue eyes, thinning white hair, and the personality of Kris Kringle in *Miracle on 34th Street*, has been inventing toys since 1948 (or long before that, who knows?). Like many inventors, he does not consider his job work. "I've never worked," he chuckles, "except for three months once to buy liquor for my wedding."

Goldfarb has sold ideas for dolls, mechanical toys, electronic toys, and vehicles to Mattel, Revell, Ideal, Kenner, and many others. Among them were Kerplunk, an action game with sticks and marbles; Melody Madness, a musical version of the game Concentration; Baby Beans, little dolls named after varieties of beans; and Stompers, small off-road vehicles. He has had products in every Toy Fair since 1948.

Even as a child, Goldfarb knew he wanted to be an inventor. The only question was what he was going to invent. After World War II he began experimenting with plastics, and he and his wife sent letters soliciting model-making work to twenty-five different companies. One of the letters landed on the desk of an unsuccessful toy manufacturer named Marvin Glass.

Glass had produced toys during the war, but his manufacturing business had failed when he had tried to branch out into Christmas tree ornaments. By the time Goldfarb's letter reached him, he was selling toy ideas to other manufacturers. Glass could sell and Goldfarb could invent, so they decided to join forces. Ironically, Glass, who died in 1974 and left his name on what became the preeminent design firm in the country, never invented a single toy, but he was the only toy "inventor" ever to achieve recognition outside the industry. He managed to take credit for everything, but his real talents lay in salesmanship, showmanship, and extracting creativity from others and in his unerring instinct about what would sell in the marketplace.

When he met Glass, Goldfarb had already invented several toys, and Glass placed three of them immediately. A cheerful Chicago insurance entrepreneur named Dave Traeger, who had gone into the toy business for fun, took two of the toys to New York to find an established manufacturer. The two products were the Busy Biddy Chicken, a hen that laid five marble eggs when its head was pressed, and the Merry-Go-Sip, a domed plastic cup topped by a little merry-go-round that spun when a child drank from the cup through a straw.

Traeger came back from New York empty-handed and irritable. All the large operators had rejected the cup, telling him that parents would not want their children to play while they ate. "They can't all be right," he insisted stubbornly to Goldfarb and Glass. "If they're unanimous, they must be wrong." He manufactured the cup and the chicken himself even though the process was complicated and expensive, and his instincts were right. When the three took their "line" to the 1948 Toy Fair, the Merry-Go-Sip was an instant sensation, described on "Voice of America" and in many newspaper and magazine child-care and health-care columns. The cup was a hit because parents were willing to do anything to get their children to eat or drink, especially when the drink was milk. Even the fact that the dome tended to split down the middle did not deter them; they just ordered more domes. Typically, Glass could not resist trying to boost sales at Toy Fair by handing out pictures of two nude models drinking from the cup.

The Busy Biddy Chicken was successful as well, but Goldfarb's third invention has lasted even to this day. Eddy Goldfarb is the man who invented wind-up chattering false teeth. Glass sold them to a novelty company, Irving H. Fishlove, and more than forty years later Fun, Inc., Fishlove's successor, still makes them. The patent ran out in 1967, but Fun still supplies more than 80 percent of the domestic market for chattering false teeth.

Goldfarb went on to invent a number of other tooth-related items (he doesn't know why he was so interested in teeth), and a few years later he left for California.

Back in Chicago, Glass began to build his operation, starting with a handful of talented employees who were almost as eccentric as he. One was a gifted but embittered sculptor and painter whose motto was "Every morning I walk out on the roof and I spit on the world." Another employee once chased Glass out of the studio wielding a hammer and threatening to kill him, although no one can remember why. Glass relished confrontation, bullied his employees, and fired and rehired them all periodically. According to a number of ex-employees, he would cheat them out of royalties if he could, and he was careful to get his name on their patents. He could also be loyal and generous once he formed an attachment.

Manipulative, predatory, and sexually voracious, Glass was also brilliant and charming. His act of boyish helplessness was so effective that people bent over backward to come to his aid, and he excelled at getting and spending other people's money. He was married five times, twice to the mother of his daughter. This wife was intelligent and strong willed and helped Glass as much as he would allow. His other wives included a Playboy bunny and an ex-dancer, both much younger than he.

Glass, who read four or five books a week, had great intellectual capacities. Living in Chicago was something of a trial to him because the exploits of Hugh Hefner, who was both friend and role model, confronted him almost daily. In an attempt at sybaritic living, he gutted an old coach house in suburban

Evanston and installed a sauna, a Jacuzzi with a liquor dispenser, Tiffany lights, an elaborate stereo system, and paintings by Picasso, Chagall, Dali, and Rouault. He maintained two chefs, one for Chinese food only, although he ate little and drank no alcohol, subsisting largely on cigarettes and coffee. Like Hefner, he kept Playboy bunnies and other young women around.

Glass went through a stage in his fifties when he kept threatening to commit suicide, and he carried around an object (it may have been a stone) that he insisted was the cyanide he planned to use to kill himself. His family and friends finally succeeded in getting him into treatment, and he spent years in analysis but never found peace.

Like many in the toy business, Glass was obsessed with secrecy (ideas are the most portable property in the world), so the security at his headquarters reflected his usual extravagance. Visitors passing through iron gates were scrutinized by closed-circuit cameras. Once inside, they were almost always restricted to the outer offices, which were sumptuously furnished, not with replicas of successful toys, but with paintings by Chagall, Bernard Buffet, and LeRoy Neiman and sculptures by Remington.

Vigilance did not end with the Remingtons. Windows in the work areas were papered over; employees were bonded and sworn to secrecy and instructed to reveal nothing about the firm, even to their spouses. According to former Glass intimates, the work areas were bugged. Only three sets of keys were made for the triple-lock doors, and the holders of the other two sets did not know each other's identity.

Glass died of cancer in 1974, and his friend and associate Anson Isaacson took over as managing partner of the organization. Isaacson was a well-respected, sane executive, and it seemed that the era of excess was at an end. Two years later, however, an employee walked into the offices with a pistol and killed Isaacson and another partner standing in Isaacson's office. He then proceeded to the back area, where he killed one designer and wounded two others. After that he killed himself, although it took four bullets to do the job. He had a list of fourteen names in his pocket, and the police conjectured that the thirty-three-year-old designer/engineer had thought other Marvin Glass employees were plotting to kill him.

After that the atmosphere calmed considerably. Five partners ran Marvin Glass & Associates in a businesslike way (if such a description can be applied to people who play with toys all day), but it was never the same loony place without Glass.

Glass's obsession with secrecy is shared by most of the industry, even if his methods were more dramatic. Imitation is a fact of life in Toyland, just as it is in every other fashion-oriented industry, but the manufacturers never stop trying to prevent it. Russ Alben swears that when he was the Carson/Roberts copywriter on the Mattel account, he once attended a meeting at Mattel's headquarters at which he was told to face away from the windows when he talked because spies with telescopes might be in a nearby office building trying to read his lips.

There are some toy people who think secrecy during the development stage is ridiculous because most of the copying occurs after a product proves successful. It makes sense: why copy a product that has an 80 percent chance of failure when by waiting a little longer you can knock off a proven success? Much of the copying is neither illegal nor even unfair. A trend, after all, cannot be a trend without a host of imitators either buying the same product and/or selling it. Copying ranges from legitimate competition (Hasbro's Maxie could pass for Barbie's twin sister) to criminal counterfeiting (fraudulent merchandise passed off as the real thing). In between is the vast gray area where most lawsuits take place.

The accusations are patent infringement, trademark violation, and a host of other practices banned as unfair competition. Packaging is frequently imitated and the imitation challenged. Companies that make a business of manufacturing look-alike products—and some of those companies are quite large—may consult a patent attorney before they make a product, but patent attorneys sometimes cannot help. The outcome of such lawsuits can be difficult to predict because judges vary in their ideas about what constitutes legitimate competition and what crosses the line into deception or infringement.

If there are always a few toy companies in Chapter 11 bankruptcy, there are always far more suing each other. Kenner and American Greetings went to court to try to prevent Dan-Dee Imports from selling its Good Time Gang bears, whose tummy graphics bore a suspicious resemblance to the tummy graphics of their Care Bears. When Hasbro attempted to sell a line of Slime Time digital watches for boys, Mattel sued it for using the word *Slime* because Mattel had been selling green Slime (a gelatinous substance) for years. When Tonka produced Super Naturals, its hologram-based action-figure line, at the same time Hasbro produced Visionaries, *its* hologram-based action-figure line, Hasbro called foul (Marty Abrams had shown the concept to both companies). Conan Properties spent years insisting that Mattel had stolen its Barbarian character Conan, charging that He-Man was really Conan "disguised in a blond wig." Tyco was sued by Lego when it created Super Blocks and by Kenner (maker of Play-Doh) when it launched Super Dough.

Those are legitimate competitors taking their chances by copying each other. Many trademark violators jump into a fad with a quick product, grab their money, and run before the law catches up. By the middle of 1989 Batmania was rampant. Although Warner Communications had licensed one hundred companies to make about three hundred items, an estimated quarter of the merchandise on the market was unauthorized. Warner and its licensing agency held a press conference in July and displayed thousands of bogus Batman items. Gilt-edged properties such as Walt Disney and Jim Henson characters lose millions of dollars a year to sales of unlicensed products.

Copycat products are especially profitable because they require no development, advertising, or promotion costs; knockoff operators benefit from marketing expenditures on the originals. Manufacturing is easy because start-up costs are low and production can be contracted for at established factories.

Security during manufacturing is virtually impossible. Many "American" toys are manufactured overseas, often in factories in Hong Kong, China, Taiwan, and Korea. Not only do the contract manufacturers work for more than one toy company, but they often run production lines for several different companies simultaneously. That means legitimate toymakers can see what their competition is doing without much difficulty. It also means unscrupulous competitors can get samples fairly easily and begin knocking them off. Some operators even use the legitimate manufacturers' own molds to make illegitimate copies. Some retailers contract for copies themselves. "There are no secrets in the toy business" is one of Toyland's maxims, but the manufacturers continue to devise elaborate security precautions anyway.

Some copycat producers wait to see what is popular before choosing what to knock off. Others find out which products will be given heavy promotional campaigns and begin producing the items concurrently. Toymakers maintain tight security at Toy Fair in hopes that they can at least delay the inevitable imitation, but some of the good ideas in one showroom on Toy Fair's opening day can be found in several others by the end of the week.

Copying can be actionable imitation or legitimate competition, but counterfeiters are clearly thieves. Companies spend millions of dollars every year protecting their products and trademarks against fraud. Not only does fake merchandise cut into their sales, but it endangers their good name. If consumers believe the product they purchase is the genuine item, they will blame the legitimate company if something goes wrong with it. Licensers retain the right of approval on every product they license because consumers consider the property a brand. Shoddy Garfield merchandise reflects on the rest of the Garfield products because consumers do not distinguish between the manufacturers of different Garfield items. Poor-quality counterfeits can ruin the market for the legitimate products.

Counterfeit products can also be hazardous to consumers' health. Counterfeiters are not interested in safety regulations. Their products routinely flout the rules about flammability, strength of seams, or content in soft toys; for sharp points, loose parts, tensile strength, or chemical content in rigid toys; and for the percentage of lead in painted toys. A large number of counterfeit Cabbage Patch Kid dolls were treated with such toxic chemicals that some California children trying to restuff one had to have their hands treated for chemical burns.

Several detection agencies pursue pirates, but Jack Fox is one of the leading counterfeiter catchers for the toy industry. He left Mattel, where he was director of licensing, to form Commercial Counterfeiting Control, Inc., in 1984. Also a former investigative reporter, Fox runs operatives all over the world, using decoys, disguises, and his own accumulated knowledge to trace illegal products. He attends toy fairs and trade shows, looking for toys before they get into the stores, and works backward toward the source when fakes show up on the market.

In 1984 Original Appalachian Artworks hired New York patent attorney Jerry Dunne to run an anti-counterfeiting program. Cabbage Patch Kids merchandise generated about a billion dollars a year wholesale in 1984 and 1985, and the manufacturers' shortages were irresistible to counterfeiters. Dunne hired a firm of four investigators who pretended to be suppliers for flea markets, and the illegal merchandise kept them busy for several years. They had to expand the team and once even used the wife of one of the original investigators. A six-foot blond, she roamed the streets of New York in a short skirt, fishnet stockings, an elaborate wig, and heavy makeup, cracking her chewing gum, buying as many "CPs" as she could, and ducking into restrooms to take voluminous notes every time she left a supplier. Dunne's team then tracked the suppliers to their warehouses and presented them with court orders to confiscate the dolls. The team also conducted stings in New Jersey, California, Texas, and Florida.

The high point for Dunne was the FBI raid. He had gone to a New York City federal judge for a seizure order, but the judge, who had a little girl of his own, was outraged by reports of the toxic chemicals used on many of the counterfeit dolls and wanted Dunne to take the case further. He suggested trying to get the U.S. attorney's office to go after the suppliers on criminal charges: counterfeiting is a federal criminal offense. (Dunne later conjectured that the judge might also have been concerned that the investigators were about to stumble onto an ongoing FBI operation.) The FBI, while not happy to enter the case at such a late stage, agreed to cooperate. The investigators spent the next few days maneuvering and stalling the supplier while they got the proper papers and prepared the federal agents.

Dunne's investigator and the supplier were supposed to drive trucks to a vacant lot in Brooklyn, where they would transfer the dolls. But to stall the vendor during the preparations, the investigator kept increasing the size of his doll order. By the time everything was ready, his order was so large that his supplier told him he might as well come to the warehouse. Getting access to the warehouse was a lucky break, but since it was in Perth Amboy, New Jersey, he had to stall the supplier again while the FBI reorganized the raid through its Newark office and Dunne found a New Jersey judge to sign the seizure order. Then they went in, pistols ready, just like in the movies.

The raid was exciting, but Dunne was never really in danger. His investigators were. One of the flea-market suppliers they caught was a Taiwanese national whom the Immigration Service wanted to deport. The man had a wife and children in the United States, so in exchange for cooperating with Dunne's operation, he was allowed to stay. Since the word was out that he had been caught, he was able to pretend that he had retired from crime and passed his contacts' names along to a friend. The friend was really one of Dunne's investigators.

Pretending to work for the Philadelphia Mafia, the investigator followed one trail to California, where he engineered a meeting at the office of a big distributor. When he arrived, he set down a briefcase full of one-dollar bills—covered by a few layers of tens—and prepared to negotiate. Suddenly the distributor reached into his desk, pulled out a Beretta pistol, and pointed it at the investigator. The investigator thought the game was up— and all because of a bunch of dolls—until the distributor spoke. "Can you use any of these?" he asked calmly.

Practically fainting with relief, the investigator coolly asked to see the gun. The distributor, who thought he was dealing with a gangster, removed the clip before he handed it over. Like characters in a comedy routine, they traded the clip and the gun back and forth a few times, neither wanting the other to have both at the same time. Even then the danger was not past, because the investigator had to maintain his cover. Fortunately, he knew enough about the going rate for contraband guns to be able to negotiate plausibly.

When he finally managed to bring the discussion back to Cabbage Patch Kids, he convinced the distributor that he was in a hurry for a large quantity of dolls but insisted that the seller call the warehouse to reserve them. The investigator had situated himself where he could see the telephone, so he watched upside down as the man dialed, and he memorized the number.

Although he was working with the U.S. Customs Service on the doll search, Customs does not deal with guns, so the investigator notified the Bureau of Alcohol, Tobacco, and Firearms about the contraband Berettas. Then he gave the warehouse's telephone number to Customs so the agency could find out its address. When the Customs agent told him it would take a couple of days to trace the telephone number, he looked at the government employee pityingly and called his partner in New York. A few minutes later his partner called back with the address (the investigator refused to tell Customs his source), and they went in to seize the dolls.

They were surprised by what they found. The fight to protect American children from counterfeit Cabbage Patch Kids had never lacked drama, what with FBI raids, deportation threats, hazardous chemicals, and gunrunning. But even the hardened investigators were stunned by the weirdness of mutilation: when they raided the warehouse, they found the dolls, but they had all been decapitated. To foil the authorities, the smugglers had taken the heads to one location and the bodies to another. The investigators had found the bodies. Now all they had to do was find twenty thousand counterfeit Cabbage Patch Kid heads.

16

THIS LITTLE COMPANY
WENT TO MARKET

Steve Shank bought Kenner Parker to cover up a bad year at Tonka. It's called how to put your company on the line because you failed. They were heading straight south.
                                        —Wall Street analyst, April 1988

Donald Kingsborough told a room full of analysts that under no circumstances would he sell equity below the offering price. Then, four months later, he did it.
                                        —Another Wall Street analyst, April 1988

Analysts are very dangerous people.
                                        —Bernie Loomis, February 1988

ON JULY 17, 1987, NEW WORLD ENTERTAINMENT Ltd., a grade-B television and movie company, offered $41 a share for Kenner Parker Toys, a combination of Kenner Products in Cincinnati and Parker Brothers games in Beverly, Massachusetts. Kenner Parker, maker of Play-Doh, Care Bears, Monopoly, and Sorry, did not want to be owned by the producer of *Godzilla 85* and *Reform School Girls*. The toy company cast about for

some way to stave off New World's advances. It explored a leveraged buy-out by management; it sought protection against a
hostile takeover in the Massachusetts courts; it filed a complaint
with the Securities and Exchange Commission, alleging stock
manipulation. Nothing worked. Still the unwelcome suitor per-
severed.

By the end of August, Kenner Parker announced that it had
entered negotiations with unidentified parties, and a month
later it had a white knight. Stephen Shank drove up in a yellow
Tonka truck and claimed the prize, paying $51 a share, or a total
of $610 million, to save Kenner Parker from a fate worse than
debt. By December the acquisition was complete. Kenner Parker,
an independent toy company for two years, was independent no
more.

About two weeks later another publicly held toy company
faced its final moments, when control of Worlds of Wonder
passed from its chairman and founder, Donald Kingsborough,
to the Oakland, California, bankruptcy court. It was an ignominious conclusion to a short but glorious performance. The
company had not even been in existence for three years, and its
story was already up to Chapter 11.

So ended the lives as public companies of two of the industry's
major players. It was a dramatic year, even by promotional-toy-
industry standards. The financial analysts who follow toy stocks
were disgusted with Tonka and furious at Worlds of Wonder.
The only really happy investors in Worlds of Wonder were the
ones who had guessed right and sold the stock short. They had
found the best way to make money on toy stocks in 1987.

Many in the toy industry consider public ownership of toy
companies a curse, particularly because the large public companies rely on the promotional business for their volume. They
believe managing the volatility of a toy company is difficult
enough without keeping an eye on the stock market and worrying about the price swings in the company's stock. "Wall Street
is a disease," says Bernie Loomis, who has worked for or with
publicly held toy companies for the past thirty years. He
watched from the inside as Mattel and, later, General Mills' Toy
Group put their figures and their operations through contor-

tions to make themselves look good for the financial community. Loomis believes that the stock market exerts a destructive influence. "It's a very dangerous industry, a very misunderstood industry. Analysts tout the stock, and then in some way they become part of management. Then if the company doesn't deliver, they say, 'Management let me down.' It's an all-too-frequent story, and it's certainly not a toy-industry exclusive. We become slaves to the quarterly earnings reports and do dumb things to achieve them. It's a dangerous incentive."

Loomis was part of Mattel when it did some of those "dumb things" to keep its stock price up. No one would disagree with him that the unrelenting pressure to report favorable earnings adds yet another layer of stress on an industry that does not need it. Toy companies already contend with volatile sales patterns, short product life cycles, and only one major selling season a year. Most of the public toy companies have no choice but to rely on promotional products, even though they are the most volatile: that is where the potential for big volume lies. Even with large volumes, orderly earnings growth is very difficult for a promotional toy company to achieve. Hasbro has reduced its volatility because it has been able to reduce its dependence on promotional toys by increasing its roster of staple sellers and remaining very lean. Tyco has increased its business by acquisitions, but the bigger it gets, the more difficult it will become to sustain high growth rates.

Difficult though the demands of public ownership may be, no one forces a toy company to go public. And, once it goes to the public capital markets, it is hardly fair to blame Wall Street analysts for doing their job of monitoring its performance. Toy-company analysts really do have a more difficult task than many of their peers because sales of promotional toys are so unpredictable. Much as they may resist at first, the analysts inevitably find themselves joining in the game of predicting hits and flops, because the bottom line in the promotional business is so largely determined by hits. In spite of the companies' wild fluctuations (or maybe because of them), the toy analysts all relish following the industry. "If they didn't pay me to cover the toy companies, I'd do it for free," one after another will say.

They love the zaniness. They like looking at goofy stuffed animals that talk and cars that change colors. They try to teach themselves to factor out the optimism, but they too get infected; it is hard to avoid when the impact of a hit can be so enormous.

That optimism is dangerous to the investor in toy companies because analysts already have a bullish bias. They want to recommend stocks. They have to recommend something. Otherwise, who needs an analyst? The investor is caught, therefore, between industry projections, which with a few exceptions range from optimistic to ridiculous, and the analysts' tendency to look for a winner. Loomis is right when he says the analysts get angry at toy companies' managers if things go wrong. Because the analysts are rooting for them.

With a showman as persuasive as Donald Kingsborough, the analysts find maintaining their objectivity even harder. One analyst told another that even when WOW was clearly in trouble, he forced himself to stay away from his office for four hours after a meeting with Kingsborough. "I didn't want to be near a phone where I could talk to clients until the spell wore off," he explained. "I knew he had to be exaggerating, but after listening to him for a couple of hours, I thought he was God."

For a while it did seem as though Kingsborough could do no wrong. He had founded Worlds of Wonder in February 1985 with one product, a talking bear named Teddy Ruxpin. That bear generated $93 million in sales and $8 million in profits by the end of the company's first year. Worlds of Wonder was a star, and almost before Teddy R. could finish saying "Hi, my name is Teddy Ruxpin," Kingsborough took his company public. Going public was always an integral part of his plan; he had even chosen the name Worlds of Wonder so that it would translate into the stock symbol WOW. What he actually got was WOWI, but WOWI was not bad either.

Whether it went up or down, WOW always lived up to its name. The initial public offering of 6.2 million shares was priced at $18.00. As they say in the toy business, the shares flew off the shelves. The stock jumped immediately to $24.75 and closed the first day at $29.00 Unfortunately, WOW peaked early—extremely early. Its first day on the market was its best.

After that, as they say in the stock business, the shares went south.

The investment community never expected WOW's migration to be permanent. The company's second year was even more spectacular (sales of $327 million and earnings of $18.6 million), and analysts continued to recommend it even after it began to lose money. "I followed it all the way down to $2," confessed one dejectedly in January 1988, a month after WOW declared bankruptcy. By then it was even lower.

Not surprisingly, Donald Kingsborough, only thirty-seven when he started WOW, had utilized his persuasive personality to build a career in sales. By the time he became the sales manager for Atari in 1983 he had sold skin lotion, eight-track stereos, and a number of other products, including Atari's Pong video game. Those who knew him then agree that Kingsborough was already an aggressive salesman and an astute marketer who followed the cardinal rule: listen to the customer. His detractors add that part of his effectiveness as a salesman was that after he listened, Kingsborough would promise whatever the customer wanted to hear, whether he could deliver or not.

The toy business came knocking at Donald Kingsborough's door. He had left Atari when it was sold in 1984, and a company called Alchemy II approached him with an idea for a toy. Alchemy's founder had helped design the robots at Disneyland, and he wanted to market a toy version, a furry little bear called Teddy Ruxpin that housed a cassette player in his back and moved his mouth and eyes when he talked. Mattel, Coleco, and other established toy companies had rejected the toy; they had not recovered from their electronic-games problems, and they wanted no part of an expensive high-tech toy.

Kingsborough loved it. He thought children would relate to it not as a piece of electronic equipment but as a stuffed animal that responded when they talked to it, like the robots they had seen at Disneyland and other amusement parks. In January 1985 Kingsborough licensed the rights to the bear, formed WOW, hired people he had known from Atari, and flew around the country raising $15 million to produce Teddy Ruxpin. He planned to change the bear's name, but he found that children liked it, so he tinkered only with Teddy's appearance. By the time Teddy Ruxpin emerged from the factory, he was chubbier and, in Kingsborough's opinion, cuter.

The company had missed the 1985 Toy Fair (the employees did not even know what Toy Fair was), but by giving several distributors a little stock in his company, Kingsborough managed to enlist them into pushing the toy hard, and they convinced retailers to take a chance on the product. Teddy Ruxpin became the hit of the 1985 Christmas season, and by the end of March 1986 WOW had sold 1.5 million units. Kingsborough was hailed as a genius, and he reaped the benefits—almost $9 million for about 11 percent of his stock—when the company went public less than three months later. Kingsborough attributed his success to his unique approach to toymaking, which he believed was going to make WOW a very special company. The established toymakers did not understand technology and feared it, he explained. He would harness it. WOW was going to establish a unique market niche by finding toys or games that children already liked and improving them with state-of-the-art technology. The investment community loved it.

Kingsborough might have added that he believed in improving sales by adding promotion. He hired a public relations firm, which set up personal appearances for Teddy Ruxpin in cities all over the country. Kingsborough was on all the major talk shows, such as "The Tonight Show" and "20/20." Kingsborough and his marketing vice president, Paul Rago, spent every week from October through December traveling to different cities to fulfill a crowded schedule of radio and television talk shows, Ronald McDonald House events, and hospital visits.

Having led the toy lists at Christmas, WOW flew triumphantly into its first Toy Fair with yet another exciting product that seemed to prove Kingsborough's genius in adding technology to traditional toys. Several of the WOW executives had been sitting around Kingsborough's swimming pool trying to come up with an idea for the company's next product line. They were reminiscing about their favorite childhood games when Kingsborough started teasing Paul Rago about cheating at tag. The two had grown up together, and Kingsborough insisted that

Rago had always claimed he had not really been tagged and had made up all kinds of excuses to avoid being "It."

Rago suddenly asked the group what they would think of a toy that enabled kids to tag each other from a distance by shooting beams of light. They thought it sounded great, like being Buck Rogers or Luke Skywalker. After months of research, Lazer Tag evolved as a game in which opponents shot infrared beams at each other. Although the company's researchers never managed to make the light beam visible as they had hoped, they made cheating impossible by having each player wear a sensor that beeped and flashed when it was hit by the beam.

At Toy Fair 1986 WOW took over the basement of the St. Moritz Hotel, sent limousines downtown to bring the buyers up to its exhibit, and entertained lavishly. To expand on the talking-bear concept, WOW also introduced Talking Mother Goose, Talking Mickey Mouse, and Talking Snoopy. Its Teddy Ruxpin sales were still booming, but WOW's star that year was Lazer Tag. It had competition. LJN, a subsidiary of the entertainment company MCA, had a remarkably similar product called Photon. Since neither company had its television commercials ready, the buyers could not decide which to buy, so they ordered both.

Today the Lazer Tag commercials are famous in the toy industry because they were so elaborate, so powerful, and, most of all, so expensive—about a million dollars apiece. Other toy companies and advertising agencies sneered at WOW for spending so much: toy commercials usually cost $50,000 to $100,000, and many of them run even less. Without doubt the commercials were extravagant, but they were also stunning. If WOW had been able to deliver the merchandise it promised, the spots might have seemed like a better idea.

Although the company had not one employee with toy-industry experience (as they boasted at the time), its executives combined many years of marketing experience, particularly in electronics. One of their earliest decisions was that they would market Lazer Tag to teenagers. They considered Lazer Tag a natural for teenagers, and they figured that by selling to teens they could pick up two markets for the price of one. If teenagers wanted the game, WOW would get the younger children without advertising to them; they would want to emulate the adolescents.

The company began stirring up interest with teasers on MTV in July. It followed up in the fall with demonstrations by celebrities such as Kareem Abdul-Jabbar and with college Lazer Tag tournaments. Those publicized the product, but the commercials were the key element. Run during events like NCAA championship games, they were supposedly set a thousand years in the future when Lazer Tag had become a high-tech game used instead of war to settle disputes. The spots depicted Lazer Tag competitions in a stadium packed with cheering spectators. One showed futuristic contestants battling each other in space suits and closed with the line "Lazer Tag, the game that moves at the speed of light. From Worlds of Wonder. Stadium not included." Another portrayed a match between the Americans and the Russians for the 310th annual Statue of Liberty Challenge.

The commercials were extremely effective—so effective that when Lazer Tag finally appeared in stores in August the supply was quickly cleaned out. For the second year in a row Worlds of Wonder had the hottest-selling toy at Christmas, but Lazer Tag was plagued by production problems—such as the gun's right half not fitting its left half—that the company delayed shipment for two months. That gave WOW's competitors the opening they needed. LJN got Photon sets into the stores and siphoned off much of the demand WOW had spent millions of dollars creating. When Christmas was over, the retailers told WOW to keeping shipping and it was not until the sets had begun to pile up for a couple of months that they all realized Lazer Tag had been a Christmas item. The demand was not going to carry over into the spring.

Kingsborough went to Toy Fair 1987 expecting to wow the world with yet a third exciting blockbuster toy, Julie, "the world's most intelligent talking doll." But in Toyland the third time is often a curse, not a charm. Even with all the megahits in the 1980s, no one produced new ones three years in a row. In fact, the third year after any big hit often spells trouble in the

promotional-toy business. In the first year the company chases
the demand, unable to make enough. In the second, production
expands to meet it. In the third, demand drops, the company is
too big, and the overhead eats up the profits.

Like Teddy Ruxpin, Julie featured synchronized eye and
mouth movements when she talked, but the twenty-three-inch
strawberry blond could do much more than play cassette tapes.
Julie could "read" certain words in her sticker activity book
through special sensors in her hand, and she could tell when her
batteries were running low. She could also speak—in theory—
more than one hundred sentences when cued by her owner,
through voice and word recognition. If she heard the word
hungry, Julie was supposed to say something like, "I'm hungry.
Let's eat." Or if she heard the word *melody*, she might sing
"Twinkle, Twinkle Little Star."

Even if enough children had wanted a very expensive doll that
would talk to them, Julie had problems from the beginning. To
recognize her owner's voice, Julie and the owner had to go
through a conversational training course, which often did not
work. Julie was just as likely to respond to the word *hungry*
with "Can we talk about your friends?" She also cost about $125
retail, an extremely high price for a doll. Julie's biggest problem,
however, was that she had too much company. Dolls were chat-
ting all over Toy Fair that year. They may have been less intelligent than Julie, but they were just as cute. Mattel's Baby
Heather could mature from a baby to a two-year-old—she even
grew teeth; Coleco's Talking Cabbage Patch Kids could talk to
one another; Galoob's Baby Talk doll came in both sexes; and
Playmates Toys' Jill used such advanced technology that the
company's president later sighed, "We should have just made a
rocket ship and gone to the moon."

Like Lazer Tag and Teddy Ruxpin, Julie was plagued by late
deliveries and expensive returns, which are common problems
with complicated toys, particularly if the company is inexpe-
rienced at manufacturing. Meanwhile, though the company had
more than tripled its sales in its second year, overhead had risen
even faster. By March 1987 its quarterly sales had risen 145
percent, reflecting the huge inventory of Lazer Tag toys now

sitting on the retailers' shelves, but earnings were down 86 percent. Expenses rose in every area—manufacturing, advertising, promotion, administration, development—at the same time retailers and WOW began cutting prices to move their overloaded inventories.

Knowing that the company had to diversify to spread the risk, WOW's product-development team was going in all directions. Before joining Worlds of Wonder, Paul Rago had developed Class Act, a line of hip school accessories including Stuff-It, a three-ring binder; Rack-It, a locker organizer; Got-It, a personal-dictation recorder; and Express-It, an answering machine for lockers. He licensed the line to WOW, but production was late and the company missed shipping in June, which is essential for back-to-school merchandise. Some of WOW's other products, such as Little Boppers (plush, sound-activated dancing versions of Teddy Ruxpin, Muppet Babies, and Walt Disney characters) sold steadily until the company ran out of supplies.

In April tragedy struck. An eighteen-year-old youth playing Lazer Tag in a Los Angeles schoolyard was shot to death by a sheriff's deputy responding to reports of armed prowlers. Lazer Tag had already been criticized for encouraging violence and unsafe play because players pointed the guns directly at each other. The California incident confirmed the critics' fears while dampening whatever consumer enthusiasm was left for the toy.

The company lost $10.4 million between April and June, its first fiscal quarter. The stock, which had drifted gently downward in 1986, began to slide.* Layoffs began in August.

At the company's annual meeting that October, angry stockholders questioned Kingsborough about second-quarter earnings, which he refused to divulge, and complained about insider selling. Kingsborough had sold 130,000 shares in July for almost $9 a share. By the time of the meeting the shares were below $4.

---

*Company insiders tried to sell some of their stock that spring but had to withdraw the offering. In June WOW raised $80 million through bonds, convertible into stock at $17.10 per share. Although the stock was below $14.00 by then, the price angered some investors because Kingsborough had insisted he would never sell equity below the stock's offering price ($18.00).

Soon after the meeting WOW announced the second-quarter figures: a $43 million loss.

The week WOW went bankrupt, the stock plunged below $1.

The bankruptcy court allowed the company to show at Toy Fair 1988, so WOW still had a chance to survive. As one of the marketing vice presidents remarked grimly, "Kids still like Teddy Ruxpin. They don't care what chapter we're in." Kingsborough applied his usual charm as the group showed its new and old products at the Waldorf-Astoria Hotel. The company was clearly trying to spread itself into less expensive, lower-risk products with Splatter Up, a water baseball game, and Skipstik, a jump rope with a bar in the middle. All the products were samples, however, and even when they liked the products, buyers hesitated to order. They could not believe WOW would get the money to produce the toys, much less advertise them.

WOW did get interim financing, and even some support from its customers, particularly Toys "R" Us. A month after Toy Fair Donald Kingsborough was finally forced out, although, as part of the agreement, he received $375,000 for a loan he had made to the company (ahead of the other creditors, who were owed over $200 million) and another $212,500 (according to *Toy & Hobby World*, for "emotional distress"). An outside financial consultant was brought in, and he hired Loren Hildebrand, a former Mattel executive, as chief operating officer. Hildebrand spent two months going around the country soliciting orders from buyers to get the company through the year. Layoffs mounted. Everyone from stockholders to Alchemy II sued. Somehow WOW survived, making it through Christmas 1988 all the way to Toy Fair 1989.

If WOW provides the toy industry's best lesson on the hazards of investing in a toy stock, Kenner Parker is one of the better examples of the tribulations of being publicly owned. By comparison with Worlds of Wonder, Kenner Parker in December 1987 should have been a happy place. It was no longer publicly held, but it was not in bankruptcy. At least not yet.

While WOW had been piling bad news on its shareholders, Tonka and Kenner Parker had spent the fall of 1987 entertaining the industry as Toyland's first players in the exciting game of

tender offers, hostile takeovers, white knights, and impoverish-
ment through leveraged buy-out.

Working at a toy company is never dull, but the employees at
Kenner Products in Cincinnati and Parker Brothers games in
Beverly, Massachusetts, were worn out. They could not figure
out why fate chose to single them out for cruel and unusual
punishment. They were prepared to contend with the ups and
downs of the business; fads are an integral part of life in the
industry. But why did their corporation have to pass from hand
to hand every time the game on Wall Street changed?

Toyland is not the only industry with fads. In the 1960s and
early 1970s diversification was considered the panacea for financial ailments, and conglomerates were actively seeking companies to buy. Toy companies were considered prizes and were
snapped up greedily. Quaker Oats bought Fisher-Price. Kidde
took on Ertl and Daisy. CBS bought Creative Playthings, Wonder Products, and Gabriel Industries. Warner Communications
bought Knickerbocker Toys and Atari. Food companies were
especially avid. General Foods bought Kohner. Consolidated
Foods bought Tyco. And General Mills bought Kenner, Parker,
Rainbow Crafts, Chad Valley, Regal Toy, and Lionel Trains.

Conglomerates did not live up to expectations. Managers had
trouble running such a diverse group of subsidiaries, and some
businesses suffered from the lack of independence. Diversification fell out of favor in the early 1980s, and the investment
community made its disapproval known in the usual way:
lower-than-expected stock prices. Companies got the point and
talked about "rationalizing" their businesses. Divestiture became the newest solution to corporate problems, and the
conglomerates began selling off many of the subsidiaries they
had bought ten years earlier.

No two toy companies followed the fads of corporate finance
more faithfully—and more involuntarily—than Parker Brothers
and Kenner Products. Forty-year-old Kenner and century-old
Parker Brothers were originally family-owned, family-operated
businesses. Then, still family-owned, they became professionally managed businesses. In the late 1960s General Mills bought
them and several other toy companies, organized them as a toy

division, and planned to boost their profits by applying their sophisticated marketing skills. The plan worked well for a while. But there were basic differences between packaged goods processes and entertainment business methods—especially the pace, because toy companies need to be able to move much more quickly. Eventually it became clear that toys were not cereal, that in fact the "grain grinders," as the unhappy toy people called their Minneapolis bosses, had actually milked the toy companies and left them in worse shape than when they had bought them.

For Parker Brothers the nadir was reached during the electronic-games boom. The company had exploded along with the rest of the industry, riding the first wave of hand-held games with one of 1978's biggest hits, Merlin. Parker also correctly forecast the market's decline and got out in time. When video games began to take over the country, Parker reverse-engineered the Atari machine and sold game cartridges based on popular coin-operated arcade games, as Atari had done. Led by Frogger, the company's cartridge business generated $74 million in six months—the last six months of 1982.

Then, although Parker Brothers sensed that the demand was weakening, General Mills forced its subsidiary to keep its earnings forecasts high and ordered it to fulfill them any way it could. Soon Parker Brothers was in trouble, paring meat from the bone as well as fat in order to deliver short-term profits to General Mills' bottom line.

General Mills had enjoyed its toy division's good times but had no patience with the lean years. The conglomerate put the toy division up for sale just before the 1985 Toy Fair. It must have been the right decision: the investment community approved. General Mills' stock climbed from below $50.00 to $65.25 in the next few weeks, so Parker, Kenner, and the other subsidiaries had obviously been a drag on earnings.

Toy Fair that year was a nightmare for the toy executives. The ten-day show is grueling under normal circumstances, and selling is certainly not made easier if one's customers are wondering who or what will be running the company in six months. Buyers hesitate to place orders when they have no idea which products will even be produced. The Kenner and Parker executives did not know any more than their customers.

Even this uncertainty would have been tolerable if they had been allowed to concentrate on selling their products. But the toy executives also had to show around another host of buyers: the kind who buy corporations. Competitors, investment bankers, competitors' bankers all came through. Just when the toy people wanted to be upbeat, these shoppers not only depressed them but drained their time and energy.

After all the visits from financiers, General Mills could not get the price it sought. Finally the company decided to spin the division off, and on November 1, 1985, Kenner Parker Toys went on the New York Stock Exchange. It was the fourth-largest American toy company, following Hasbro, Mattel, and Coleco. The employees were thrilled, thinking that they were going to control their destinies at last.

They did, for a while. Layoffs continued because the new company was in the red, but by the middle of 1987 Kenner Parker was profitable and strong. That was what made it so appealing to New World Entertainment. The Kenner Parker executives were alarmed as well as repelled by the high-flying young entrepreneurs who had just bought Marvel Entertainment. Harry Evans Sloan and Lawrence L. Kuppin, only in their thirties, had already built New World into a $400 million company, and they envisioned Kenner Parker making toys from Spiderman and all their other properties.

Once it became clear that none of its other defenses was going to work, Kenner Parker resigned itself to the embraces of a more palatable suitor. Tonka Corporation was only half the size of Kenner Parker, but at least it was a reputable toy company, and it was willing to pay.

Stephen Shank, chairman of Tonka, had been wishing for just such a partner. With perhaps the oddest background of the toy-company chiefs—he is a Harvard-trained lawyer with a degree from Tufts University's Fletcher School of Diplomacy—Shank had already planned to build Tonka into a larger corporation. The way he saw it, as the industry continued to consolidate, Tonka could be either a major player or a niche player but not something in-between. Two hits in a row, GoBot transformable robots and Pound Puppies, had boosted the truck company into the big leagues: 1983 sales, $88 million; 1985 sales, $244 million. But now Tonka was having trouble replacing the sales from its two megahits, which only reinforced Shank's determination to diversify by acquisition.

Shank had already tried several times that year. He had almost bought Ertl, another fine old midwestern toy-vehicle company, but that deal had fallen through. He had succeeded in buying Polystil, an Italian toy company. He had tried to establish Tonka as a presence in video games by signing up as the distributor for Sega, one of the smaller competitors of Nintendo. But Kenner Parker was obviously the perfect opportunity to grow and diversify in a big way, and it was not likely to come around again. What attracted Shank was not just the company's size, it was the stability of Parker Brothers' games.

As a result, two previously healthy companies went far into debt to make one bigger, unhealthy, highly leveraged company. It would be tight, but Shank believed it would be worth the risk.

The Wall Street analysts did not. They ridiculed the acquisition. They accused Shank of trying to cover up poor earnings. They insisted he would never be able to handle the debt load. They said he overpaid just to get Monopoly. They said the deal was a poor imitation of Stephen Hassenfeld's masterful 1984 purchase of Milton Bradley. Most devastating of all, they said to their investors, "Sell."

Steve Shank was not worried; he believed he was going into the deal aware of all the risks. Holders of Kenner Parker stock were happy because they made a tidy profit. (The holders included New World Entertainment, which pocketed about $20 million.) Some of Kenner Parker's top managers bailed out in their golden parachutes; the president took home an estimated $5 million.

Only the employees left at Kenner and Parker were doleful. Their independence was at an end once more. It was time to subordinate the interests of their individual operations to a Minneapolis parent—again. For those who had survived the layoffs there was nothing to do about it but go on with their business. They were going to be working off that debt for quite a few years.

As they worked on their Nerf games and their Real Ghostbusters and their Play-Doh and, of course, their Monopoly, every once in a while someone would speculate about what Wall Street's next exciting idea for improving corporations' finances was likely to be. Whatever it was, they had no doubt Kenner and Parker would be among the first to know.

17

APRIL–SEPTEMBER 1987
How Toymen "Go Hollywood"

GARTH DECEW, TYCO'S EXUBERANT copywriter at Bozell, Jacobs, gazed into space. He was dreaming of novel approaches for Dino-Riders commercials. It was his favorite occupation. He only wished he did not have to sandwich it in between the other forty commercials he had due, for Tyco's Super Dough, Super Blocks, radio-controlled cars, and racing sets. Not to mention the spots for his other account, a group of Chrysler dealerships.

Because Tyco could not count on having a television program to tell the story of Dino-Riders, Garth kept trying to summarize the story in a commercial. It was quite a squeeze, since the usual commercial is thirty (actually, twenty-eight-and-a-half) seconds long. He could pack more words and pictures into every second than anyone else he knew, though, so he was confident that if he could not say it in thirty seconds, he could surely do it in sixty.

As the spring wore on, however, Garth had to admit to himself that maybe even sixty seconds was not going to be enough. Then Tyco made it worse. To save money, the company wanted

him to salvage as much as he could of the animation from Jay
Garfinkel's videotape. Although the absurdity of the idea exasperated him, he dutifully studied the tape. He could see immediately that the footage would not lend itself to the demands of
a one-minute spot, but it took him a while to convince Tyco. "It
doesn't take a genius to figure out that if a guy took eight
minutes to tell his story, then the action just ain't going to be
fast enough to tell it in a minute," he explained. But the Tyco
people didn't want to discuss it from that standpoint; they
suggested that maybe Garth did not understand animation.

Eventually they decided on a revolutionary strategy. They
would show a full two-minute, animated version of the Dino-
Riders story on the day after Christmas. The cost of television
time dropped after Christmas, which would enable them to
afford two minutes to communicate the fantasy, and they would
"roadblock" the spot—show it on all three of the major networks. The date offered other advantages besides cost. Dino-
Riders would stand out because it would be appearing alone,
outside the clutter of pre-Christmas commercials. The spots
would undoubtedly have a large audience because children
would be home for the holiday vacation. Best of all, the kids
might already be bored with their Christmas toys and looking
for something to buy with their Christmas-gift money. December 26 began to seem like such a good time to launch a
product that they were surprised no one had thought of it
sooner.

In addition to the two-minute introductory commercial,
Garth had to write three thirty-second commercials, which
would advertise the products during the rest of the year. He and
the art director, Mike Phillips, kept searching for an innovative
approach. They would be judged on the effectiveness of their
spots, and they wanted fresh ideas to break through the clutter.
Then Dick Grey made it clear that he wanted them to follow the
traditional formula for action-figure commercials. Tinkering
with the successful advertising formula, no matter how inspired
the innovation, was a risk he considered unnecessary.

It was a frustrating situation, just like the Michael Tut issue.
The young men wanted to be original and creative, in order to

prove themselves. The decision makers were older and already well established; they just wanted to sell the product. Not that Dick Grey or Cy Schneider was insensitive or unoriginal; they were pros with a feel for product and years of marketing experience. They just had different priorities. Lee Volpe and Jim Alley had wanted elfin warrior Dino-Riders so that their Dino-Riders would be special and unique. Dick and Cy wanted He-Man–type Dino-Riders because such characters' appeal to children was already proven.

When Garth talked about innovative commercials, Dick Grey told him, in essence, if it ain't broke don't fix it. The boilerplate action-figure commercial begins with an animated clip from the product's television series and includes live children playing with the toy, an announcer describing their activities or the product, and sometimes the children talking, as well. That was what Dick wanted.

Garth resigned himself to conventional spots and went to work. He used an announcer to do most of the talking, on the assumption that a professional adult could pronounce names such as *Tyrannosaurus rex* faster and more easily than a child, although he spiced the spots up with some children's dialogue. Before they enacted a battle (the usual activity with action figures), the boys traded insults like "Eat rocks, Rulon" and "Take that, Snake Breath." Garth satisfied his own desire to underline what he called the product line's "epic proportions" by hiring a well-known Hollywood songwriting team, Mathew-Griffith, to write him some music with grandeur; he wanted something similar to the theme from *Star Wars*.

Once he had approved the final storyboards, Dick Grey rekindled the creative fire. He told Garth what a good job he had done and then added, "Okay, you've given me what I asked for. Now go back and do what you'd like to do." Garth could hardly wait. He and Mike Phillips were both fascinated by all the Dino-Riders' little weapons, so they created a dramatic commercial that featured them. They called it "Preparation for Battle" because it never showed the battle; it ended as the battle was about to begin.

"The whole spot would be close-up," explained Garth later.

"There would be no establishing shot at the beginning. Instead, it would have a rhythm—sort of a point, counterpoint of increasing intensity, with an irregular meter, like 'good-guy weapon,' 'bad-guy weapon,' 'bad-guy weapon,' and so on. You would hear Krulos say, 'Arm. Arm laser.' And a hand would reach in and set it up. Then a good-guy voice would say [the name of] a weapon. Then at the very end there would be a reveal of the two kids with these two armed dinosaurs. That way we would build up suspense because for the first two-thirds of the spot, no one would know what was going on. Then when they did, they would say, 'Oh, that's so neat! I have to have one!' "

Dick liked it. The sales department hated it, but Dick stuck by Garth and told him to shoot it along with the conventional spots. During the summer they ran out of time, however, so they only shot the conventional commercials. Woody and Neil attended every shoot, a boring duty. Whatever glamour there may be in filming commercials is dissipated in the first half hour. Then it becomes extremely tedious. Things always seem to go wrong. The same short take is shot over and over. But Woody and Neil never thought of missing a day. They did not want to leave the decisions to anyone else.

The two also spent the summer trying to put together the pre–Toy Fair show that Dick had promised them. All the major companies present their product lines to their major customers months before Toy Fair. These preview presentations have become so commonplace that they have acquired a name of their own: "pre–Toy Fair." Some are very elaborate, even though the buyers may have been consulted all along the development process and may be quite familiar with the products. The toy companies rely on the opinions of the buyers they respect, frequently changing or even killing a product if the trade is critical. If the response is unexpectedly strong, they may broaden the line or plan a larger advertising campaign.

Tyco had never had a pre–Toy Fair. The company's traditional sales posture was "Here are our products. Here are the commercials we're running. How much do you want?" Dick Grey consciously projects a businesslike image for Tyco. Once he was even quoted telling a financial analyst, "If you want to see the guys who wear the beanies with the propellers on top—the ones that design the toys—they're down the hall. I run this company to make money and that's my only interest." That statement provoked quite a bit of eye rolling around the company when it appeared in print.

Woody and Neil were determined to inject some pizzazz into this conservative tradition. Ignoring Dick's injunction, "No Hollywood," they set out to design a presentation that combined show-business flair with Tyco's no-frills image. The two began by assuming that they would put on a big show in New York and bring in Tyco's thirty largest accounts. When they looked at the cost of airfares, meals, and hotel rooms, however, they decided that it would be cheaper to take their show on the road. They could do four or five regional shows and bring in the buyers from each of those areas. Neil contacted Jan Ross, a New York producer of multimedia presentations, and explained Tyco's requirements. "We want a show that's going to be big and impressive, but it has to be mobile so we can take it all over the country."

Ross proposed a traveling version of the television program "Nightline." On the real ABC show, host Ted Koppel interviews people in other locations via monitor. Ross suggested they hire an actor who looked and sounded like Ted Koppel and tape him interviewing Tyco people. Jim Alley could talk about the Dino-Riders marketing program, and Bob Lurie could describe the advertising; the actor could pretend to interview them without their having to take time off to travel around with the show.

Neil, Woody, and Jim thought it was a wonderful idea and arranged for Ross to present the idea to Dick. This was not one of the times Dick sat through a presentation with a poker face. "Wait a minute," he interrupted. "I am not going to go out and try to sell a line of authentic, museum-quality dinosaurs and have them introduced by some goddamn fake Ted Koppel standing in front of the room pretending to be on 'Nightline.' " He said quite a bit more, but that was the main idea.

Then he reminded them that he did not want any "fake Hollywood." "Forget the showmanship," he told the three. "Just show the product. The buyers don't want to be entertained. They want to be sold." With that he practically swept them out of his office.

Woody and Neil were undeterred. They figured they had just not found the right format. They continued to struggle with the idea of a traveling show for a few more weeks, and then they gave up and went back to their original plan: they would bring the buyers to New York. But if they were going to go to that much expense, they decided, they would present the line to each account one by one, over a three-week period.

They still had not come up with an idea for a format when Garth flew in from California one day and gave them one. "I've been thinking about this presentation problem you're having," he told them breezily, "and I've written something that I think will do. I've boarded it out so you can see what you think."

He showed them the storyboard, and they liked it. Even better, Dick liked it. They liked the dramatic format, and they figured Dick liked it because much of the excitement was provided by the product itself and by the novelty of Tyco's marketing strategy. By then they were all convinced that by showing the two-minute spot, and doing it the day after Christmas, they were going to make history.

Garth suggested a huge curved screen that wrapped 180 degrees around the audience—even though the audience might sometimes consist of just one person. They would start by showing some Dino-Rider footage, following it with authoritative quotations about the enduring appeal of dinosaurs. Then Woody or Neil would demonstrate and describe the products, one by one. Once the entire line had been introduced, the marketing, advertising, and promotion plans would be presented dramatically on the screen. The finale would be the thirty-second commercials. After that the lights would come on, and Woody or Neil would answer questions.

Garth wrote the multimedia parts, including slides and portions of the animation, and Neil hired Ross's Corporate Theater Company to produce it. The sales department invited the buyers and scheduled the marketing people for five shows a day for three weeks in September. Woody and Neil spent August worrying that the samples would not be ready and pushing to get the commercials finished on time.

On the Thursday before their Monday opening, they were "going live," and Garth flew in to watch the dress rehearsal with Dick. They had hardly begun when both Garth and Dick began calling for changes. The second half to the multimedia presentation was not even finished, so they were improvising that part anyway. But when Woody and Neil began their portion of the show—demonstrating the product—Dick stopped them after a couple of minutes. "Wait a minute," he said, finally getting into the Hollywood spirit. "You guys are good-looking, but the buyers are not going to listen to you even though you are the experts. We need two models to come in and present the product."

This was Thursday. The buyers were coming Monday. Woody and Neil did not want models, but they assumed they could deal with that later. They finished what was left of the show, and then Garth began his complaints about the liberties the production company had taken with his script. To begin with, where was the music? He had planned the opening around music from Aaron Copland's *Fanfare for the Common Man*. The producer had cut that out completely. Garth insisted that it was essential and had to go back in.

He was also upset about the changes in the two-minute commercial. They had cut the introductory incantation, "Harness the Power!" But that was absolutely essential to set the mood. Even worse, they had changed the ending. The commercial was written to run like the teaser for a movie, and he and Mike had come up with what they considered a sensational ending. At the conclusion of the story, a *Tyrannosaurus rex* toy would burst through the animation. They were convinced that the viewers, lulled into thinking they were watching a commercial for a movie, would gasp with excitement and say, "Wow! It's a toy!"

Dick had not liked the ending at all. He had considered it unclear and confusing, and they had changed it to a quick pitch for the videotape. Garth contemplated his handiwork in ruins and went to work. "Trust me, Dick," he implored. "Put the breakthrough back for your presentation. It makes no fucking sense to do it any other way. I don't care what we decide later on about what goes on TV. But please trust me on this."

Dick relented and ordered that the music be added and the *T-rex* breakthrough reinserted.

After Dick and Garth had finished ordering alterations, Woody and Neil eyed each other bleakly. By now the entire program was in shambles, and they had to re-create the whole thing in the three days before it opened. What made it worse was that no one even sympathized. The two could see that to Dick these were only small touches to an otherwise finished product. He confirmed their impression when he walked up to Woody afterward and put his arm around him as if to congratulate him. "You know, Wood," he smiled encouragingly, "you're 90 percent there."

Meanwhile, as Woody tells it, "I'm losing more hair, and Neil's throwing up in the back room. I'm thinking, 90 percent there? We'll have to hire and train the demonstrators, rewrite the whole thing, including the script, rerecord the multimedia, and get our parts down. And this is Thursday. We know that Monday morning at nine o'clock the guy from Woolworth's is walking through that door and we have to be live. Onstage."

By the next day Woody and Neil were training three of their favorite models-demonstrators from previous Toy Fairs. Neil spent the rest of the weekend rehearsing them—*Deinonychus* and *Tyrannosaurus rex* do not always trip easily off the tongue.

They had only Friday for recording. Garth had left on Thursday for meetings in California with Chrysler, but he had promised to rewrite the script and read it over the telephone to Bob Lurie, at Tyco's headquarters in New Jersey by 9:00 A.M. Bob would get it typed, have it approved by Dick, and fax it to Woody and Neil in New York so that they could have the voice-over redubbed on the tape. They had a 4:00 P.M. booking at the recording studio and had hired Mel Boudrot, the highly paid announcer who did the Heineken commercials.

On Friday, 9:00 A.M. came and went. And 3:00 P.M. came and went. By early afternoon Bob Lurie, who had begun his career as a copywriter, was writing. Among his many calls, Woody called the advertising agency in Los Angeles and someone faxed what Garth had written between meetings to Bob, in New Jersey. Dick did not like it, and Bob kept rewriting.

When 4:00 P.M. came and went, Woody and Neil were frantic. They would not have a second chance for the studio or the announcer. Woody called Bob again. "I have to have it right now," he shouted into the telephone, "because I'm walking out this door and that's it!"

Bob dictated his new version to Woody, who scribbled it down, ran down the stairs, and jumped into a taxicab with Neil.

When they arrived at the studio, Woody called again. "It's still not approved," reported Bob. It was too late. They recorded what they had, including a few bars of *Fanfare for the Common Man* to placate Garth.

Hours after they finished recording, Dick finally approved a final script. No one ever mentioned to him that his final changes had not been included.

Monday morning came quickly, and they all felt as though they were opening on Broadway. Jim was there to welcome each group of buyers.

The film was as dramatic as they had hoped. It opened with the words *December 1987* whooshing toward the foreground as if hurtling through space. That shot was followed by a series of quick cuts of commercials for toys they all knew would be heavily advertised that Christmas season: Hasbro's Pogo Bal, G.I. Joe, and Transformers; Mattel's Barbie; Worlds of Wonder's Teddy Ruxpin; and others, mostly action figures. The pace of the cuts accelerated, underscored by a jarring cacophony of voices that increased in intensity to a crescendo, at which point they were overridden by dissonant music.

Then the screen went blank. A heartbeatlike ka-thumping began, and the words *December 26, 1987* appeared. "It's December 26, 1987," intoned the announcer. "The noise has stopped. Toys are being exchanged. Holiday-gift money is being spent. But kids are still watching television, a wealth of children's holiday programming. It is in this captive, virtual vacuum of children's advertising that Tyco will launch Dino-Riders with an unprecedented two-minute minispecial."

With that, the fearsome face of the *Tyrannosaurus rex* appeared on the screen in the middle of the Dino-Riders logo. The two-minute background story began, accompanied by "Harness the Power . . . DINO-RIDERS!"

The Tyco team was thrilled.

After the multimedia portion, a demonstrator stood in the still-darkened room. Like a magician's assistant, Neil or Woody handed her the products through a curtain, one by one, until the entire product line was arrayed in front of the buyers. Then they showed the thirty-second commercials and Neil or Woody came out to answer questions.

Before they let the buyers talk, however, they gave a simple pitch. It had three messages.

One: "Eighty percent of the products you're looking at are production pieces off the tooling." That told the buyers that the tooling was finished, which meant that Tyco was committed to the project. Since Tyco was showing finished products, availability was not likely to be a problem.

Two: "We're going on television whether you buy the product or not." The fact that the samples were tooling samples added to the believability of this promise. Since Tyco had already made the financial commitment to tooling, the company was going to want to support its products.

Three was a plea: "Please buy it. But at a small level. Just enough per store to get it onto the shelves. We would like a thin veneer of product in every store in America. And then, if we are so dumb that this is not going to work, you won't be hurt. If we can't pull a thousand dollars a store of product off your shelves with $2 million worth of innovative advertising and programming, then we don't deserve to be successful anyway."

They bought it.

18

COMPLIMENTS OF THE TRADE

"Where's that doll with makeup?"
"Here's one."
"No, that's not the right one."

"Scott, put that back."

"Are they kidding? $49.95? It'll fall apart in a week."

"No interactive toys. The only thing we'll interact with is people."
"And no batteries."

"Oh, look at this. It's just like the one we had."
"No, it isn't. Ours was wood. This is plastic."

"Jennifer, get over here right now or you're getting nothing for Christmas, do you hear me?"

"I'll never grow out of my Barbies. I'm saving them for my children when I grow up."

THE AISLES ARE ALMOST IMPOSSIBLE to negotiate, clogged with shopping carts piled high with dolls, cars, stuffed animals, electronic games, board games, athletic equipment, Pampers. The shelves are messy piles of misplaced merchandise. The electronic demonstration dolls do not work. The voucher pockets for the most popular video game cartridges are frustratingly empty.

A shopper approaches the front of the store wishing she were in the supermarket. At least there she could pass the time in the checkout line by reading one of the store's magazines.

What happens, however, stuns her.

There is no wait.

The cashier is cheerful.

The charge goes through without a hitch. The manager is hovering to okay it.

She wonders if she is asleep. Is it or is it not three and a half weeks until Christmas?

It is. She is at a Toys "R" Us. And more often than not, at Toys "R" Us, the system works.

There is a joke in the toy industry about the ever-diminishing number of independent manufacturers and retail stores. Time: the future. The manufacturers and retailers have merged so many times that there is only one toy seller, Hasbro, and one toy buyer, Toys "R" Us, left. Every February they meet to hold Toy Fair, and Toys "R" Us buys Hasbro's merchandise.

One year, however, Toys "R" Us looks at Hasbro's line and says, "I don't like it." So Toys "R" Us doesn't buy it—and that is the year they have to call off Christmas.

Hasbro may lead the toy industry, but no one assumes it will remain number one forever.

The predominance of Toys "R" Us is unprecedented, and everyone assumes it is permanent. The chain now accounts for about a fifth of the industry's sales; its chairman's stated goal is 50 percent. But those who know him suspect privately that hard-driving Charles Lazarus really wants 100 percent.

Toys "R" Us is not just an outstanding toy chain. It is one of the best retailing operations in the world. Its aggressive founder and chief executive officer pioneered the concept of a toy supermarket, and his success has been imitated but never duplicated. Under his leadership its managers seldom make mistakes, and the company has prospered. The financial community loves it. In 1987, Lazarus was the nation's highest-paid executive, earning $69 million, largely because of stock gains. He is married to his second wife, prominent sex therapist Helen Singer Kaplan; their children have dubbed them the Toy King and Sex Queen. "Between sex and toys, we have all the pleasure centers covered," Dr. Kaplan once told *Time* magazine.

Toys "R" Us has succeeded because its managers look for the optimal solution and pursue it conscientiously. By mid-1989 there were 404 Toys "R" Us stores in the United States, all of them within a day's drive of one of the company's regional warehouses. It transports the merchandise in its own fleet of trucks, all of them adorned with the smiling face of Geoffrey Giraffe, the company's mascot.

Location is crucial in retailing, and Lazarus has remained closely involved in site selection for his stores. His staff members use demographic data to choose the markets and then situate the stores near major malls and major highways to take advantage of the traffic. The stores are not inside shopping malls because the real estate cost per square foot is cheaper outside. Using freestanding sites also enables them to provide ample parking directly outside the stores, so that customers will not be discouraged from making extra, unwieldy purchases. Tough negotiators, they extract the maximum in their real estate deals.

The stores' floor plans are all the same so that personnel can be shifted from store to store and go right to any department. Disposable diapers, sold at a discount to attract the allegiance of young parents and pull-in traffic, are artfully placed at the back of the store so that customers always have to walk the length of at least one toy-filled aisle to get to them. Toys "R" Us is the largest seller of disposable diapers in the world. The stores also discount all infant-care items. Lazarus instituted a liberal money-back, no-questions-asked return policy years ago when he realized that the loudest customers managed to get refunds anyway. He reasoned that if they did, everyone else should too.

One of the most critical elements of the company's success is largely out of sight of the consumer: its superb use of technology. By utilizing information systems, the company almost eliminates the human element in making buying decisions. Over the years it has installed sophisticated reporting systems that track the sales of each store's twenty-two thousand items (SKUs, or stockkeeping units, in industry parlance). The stores are so large that they can accommodate the entire product line of every major toy company—and quite a few of the smaller ones. Toys "R" Us puts the merchandise on the shelves and lets the customers vote with their dollars. Sales determine reorders.

Because of its volume, Toys "R" Us receives an enormous amount of data and often picks up sales patterns and trends ahead of the competition—and ahead of its suppliers, with whom it sometimes shares information. Still, Toys "R" Us is not infallible. It does not take every product made, and occasionally it misses a winner. In 1988 the chain had no Koosh Balls, a successful new product introduced by a fledgling operation called OddzOn Products.

Charles Lazarus grew up in the retailing business. His father owned a bicycle shop in Washington, D.C., which Charles took over when he returned from World War II. He added children's furniture and called the shop the Baby Supermarket, but he soon realized that he was not going to get much repeat business. Once a family bought a crib, it did not usually buy another one. He looked around for something purchasers buy repeatedly and decided on toys.

With his father and brother-in-law, Lazarus opened his first Children's Supermarket in 1956. He realized almost from the beginning that he could turn the seasonality of the retail toy business to his advantage. At that time department stores were the biggest outlets for toys, but they expanded their toy departments for the Christmas season and shrank them immediately afterward, aiming for empty shelves by January 1. Lazarus figured that by stocking toys all year round he could afford to carry a wider selection. He could buy cheaply because he could buy in generous quantities and build volume with low prices. Since he did not have to clean out his inventories by January 1, he was able to buy continually and warehouse the merchandise.

Although he did not stock as much during the rest of the year, off-season sales were steady enough, and he gained an advantage over his competitors because he was able to get an early reading on what was selling.

Discount stores were in their infancy then, and Lazarus modeled his store after one of the earliest general-merchandise chains, Bargaintown U.S.A. As an early associate recalls, Children's Supermarket was the typical discount operation of the time—"pile 'em high, sell 'em low." In the original stores they simply stacked the merchandise, adding shelves later. Now Toys "R" Us tells manufacturers very specifically what it wants in packaging: rectangular containers with product information on all sides, because its stores are largely self-service. Its suppliers are happy to comply.

One of the most famous characters in the toy business joined Lazarus in those early days. In 1958 Lazarus had just opened the third Children's Supermarket, in Rockville, Maryland, and was about to close one of the older outlets. Sy Ziv was a Philadelphia jobber (a wholesale and factory representative). The two often worked together on Lazarus's orders from about eleven to midnight, after Lazarus had closed the stores for the night, and they had come to know each other well. One night, after Ziv had come back from buying toilet paper for the Rockville store, Lazarus said, "Why don't you come down and work here?"

He helped with everything from buying merchandise to stoking the coal furnace. By the time he retired in 1984, Sy Ziv, like quite a few other Toys "R" Us employees, had become a multimillionaire. For most of his twenty-five years with the company, Ziv served as the senior buyer and merchandise man. For many years he was one of the most powerful men in Toyland, and manufacturers trooped steadily to his office to show him their new products. In those days the opinion of Toys "R" Us was the opinion of Sy Ziv, and grown men quaked at the thought of what might happen when they brought their treasures for him to see. They also respected his judgment, because he was considered one of the best product people in the industry.

Impulsive, impetuous, profane, and opinionated, he was often outrageous, and Sy Ziv stories abound in the industry. While very generous with advice and with help in finding people jobs, Ziv had a few bad habits. In particular, he was known for throwing samples (which are often worth thousands of dollars) on the floor, at the wall, or anywhere else if he didn't like them. When Mattel showed him the product that eventually became its popular Slime (basically, green petroleum jelly) and told him it was washable, he promptly threw it on Mattel's carpet, poured coffee over it, ground it in with his heel, and said, "Are you sure?" (Slime can be washed out of all but a few surfaces. One of the exceptions is shag rugs. Fortunately Mattel's industrial carpet had a short pile, but the addition of coffee to the Slime did not make cleaning any easier.)

The stores prospered. By 1966 sales had reached $12 million, and Lazarus sold his four-store chain to Interstate Stores for $7.5 million. He continued to run the toy operations, by now under the name Toys "R" Us, for Interstate. Even when the stores had been known as Children's Supermarkets, their signs had displaced the Rs backward, causing teachers to complain and well-intentioned citizens to make special trips into the stores to inform store personnel of the error.

Interstate went bankrupt in 1974, and when it reemerged in 1978 it was called Toys "R" Us. At that time the stores accounted for 5 percent of domestic retail toys sales, and Lazarus was put in charge of the entire company. Many of the toy manufacturers had continued to supply the chain with merchandise, extending it generous credit terms while it was going through its reorganization. Lazarus appreciated their faith and, in spite of his tightfisted ways, has over the years returned the favor to a number of toy companies in the same situation.

Toys "R" Us has grown explosively ever since, shedding its nontoy operations and opening more Toys "R" Us stores every year. Although Toys "R" Us is by far the market leader, Lazarus and his managers always want more: more sales, more stores, more market share. Toys "R" Us stays hungry and avoids complacency, if not arrogance.

After the company changed the face of toy retailing forever, it turned to new areas. By late 1989 it had opened seventy-four stores overseas and announced plans to team up with McDonald's to enter the difficult Japanese market in 1991. Even further afield, Toys "R" Us entered the retail children's-clothing business in 1983, and by late 1989 it operated 137 Kids "R" Us stores around the country. Succeeding with the same principles Lazarus used to build his toy chain, Kids "R" Us has attracted the animosity of other children's-apparel retailers.

Soon after it entered the business, several large chains tried to force a number of children's clothes manufacturers, both large and small, to refrain from selling to Kids "R" Us. The company settled its differences with Federated Department Stores years ago, but in 1988 Toys "R" Us sued Macy's for restraint of trade, and action was still pending at the end of 1989. When Lazarus was honored as boys'-wear retailer of the year in January 1989, a number of retail executives who usually attend avoided the luncheon, claiming the press of business and other compelling engagements. Lazarus's feelings were probably not bruised—he is not a gentle competitor himself.

The rest of the toy trade is spread among other national and regional freestanding toy chains, mass merchandisers, wholesalers, catalog showrooms, discounters, department stores, drugstores, variety stores, local chains, special-niche stores, and, of course, mom-and-pop toy stores.

The manufacturers call their customers "The Trade," and the words that follow are often not very complimentary. Buyers and sellers of toys work together closely and help each other, but there is a lack of trust between the two groups that in many cases is justified. Besides, toymakers are a sensitive lot. Evidently a monolithic force bearing down on the land of toys, The Trade crushes the sensibilities of the creative manufacturers. Often portrayed as cretins, these ignorant customers unvaryingly fail to recognize a good—no, make that great—product when they see one. "The Trade didn't want a game from us" (Mattel). "The Trade won't accept a $5 million product from us" (Hasbro). "The Trade is terrible on girls' toys. . . . The Trade didn't understand the product. . . . The Trade thought the category was dead and wouldn't buy it" (Everyone).

The collective term The Trade suggests a unanimity that does not exist. The Trade is really a collection of fierce competitors vying for shares of the tightly contested marketplace. They work on the same seasonality as their suppliers, face the same uncertainties, and are just as anxious about that fourth quarter they must have to make up for the other three.

The second- and third-largest toy supermarket chains are Child World and Lionel Leisure, and frustrated "R" they. Toys "R" Us not only has more stores; it generates far more sales per square foot of selling space. In 1988 Toys "R" Us generated about $335 per square foot of selling space compared with an estimated $210 for Child World and $190 for Lionel Leisure. That translated into about $9 million in sales per Toys "R" Us store versus about $5 million per store for the other two chains. Child World has endured turnovers in ownership and management. Lionel, whose name comes from Lionel Trains, has acquired several chains (including Kiddie City and Toy Warehouse), survived a bankruptcy, and tries doggedly to compete with its powerful rivals, with mixed results. It was the first of the toy supermarkets to dare to enter the Manhattan market, where high rents require high profits, in 1988. In 1988 Toys "R" Us's total sales (which included Kids "R" Us and the company's overseas toy stores) was $4 billion. Child World, with 163 stores, generated $807 million, and Lionel, with eighty-four, generated another $408.9 million.

Lionel is not third in total revenues. That position belongs to Kay-Bee Toys, whose 750 stores are quite a bit smaller: instead of 46,000 square feet, they average 3,500. For the most part, shoppers do not get in the car and drive to a Kay-Bee Toy and Hobby Shop. Throughout the fifty states and Puerto Rico, they stroll through a mall or shopping center, see something that catches their eye, and go in to make an impulse purchase—$780 million worth in 1988.

The trick is pulling in the customers to make that purchase. Tyco's Jim Alley says that going to a Kay-Bee store is like going to a wake. That is because it is full of "stiffs" (toys that failed). Piled high in the front of the store are as many different toys as can be displayed neatly, all at startlingly low prices. Kay-Bee buys "opportunistically" from manufacturers and displays the closeout merchandise prominently in the front of every store—

at closeout prices. In the back is conventionally priced, regular-season merchandise. Kay-Bee is owned by the Melville Corporation, a $6.8 billion specialty-retailing conglomerate whose thirteen divisions include CVS, Thom McAn, and all of K mart's shoe departments.

In competition with Kay-Bee for the manufacturers' closeouts is a unique operation called Wisconsin Toy. Primarily a jobber, the company buys closeout merchandise from manufacturers and sells it to retailers. There are other jobbers, but none so large as Wisconsin Toy. For retailers who want a bargain, Wisconsin Toy's showroom is irresistible—it is the Loehmann's of the Toy Building. Buyers never know what they will find, and what they find today may be gone tomorrow. Like Kay-Bee's, its showroom is a funeral parlor of colorful "stiffs."

"Anything will sell at the right price," explains Phil Cohen, Wisconsin Toy's chairman. His father started the business. The company buys only undamaged merchandise, pays cash, and abides by any stipulations the sellers may impose. A manufacturer may not want the product released until after a certain date, for example, because its regular customers will have it on their shelves until then.

It is a compliment to Cohen that, in spite of their company's opportunistic buying, Wisconsin Toy is respected and appreciated. The company performs a valuable service for the manufacturers and the retailers by removing unsaleable merchandise, which clogs the pipeline for new inventories. The company has recently begun to move into the retailing business, opening over eighty Toy Liquidator stores in factory-outlet malls. Now it resells some of the merchandise it buys.

The other major toy accounts are the huge national mass merchandisers. Wal-Mart has 1,334 stores and K mart 2,164. They do not carry the range of items the toy supermarkets stock. They may stock three thousand and around Christmastime, another two thousand. But they are the three to five thousand most popular items. Target, another discount operation, has only 392 stores, but it is among the top six or seven sellers of toys. The three are very, very powerful.

When the toy companies speak in reverential tones about

"national distribution," they mean the toy supermarkets, the mass merchandisers such as K mart and Wal-Mart, and other large chains, such as Target, Woolworth, and Sears. The mass merchants are tough negotiators. Unlike the toy supermarkets, which have miles of shelves to fill and a reputation for extensive selection to uphold, the mass merchants, the catalog showrooms such as Best Products and Service Merchandise, and the higher-scale chains such as Sears, can take or leave any particular item. They can even expand or contract their toy departments. They want the hot items, but on their terms. Usually they get them, because the thought of 2,164 loudspeakers blaring "Attention K mart shoppers" followed by the name of one of their products is irresistible to toy salespeople, sending them back to their calculators to see whether they can improve the terms just a little more.

According to the terms of the Robinson-Patman Act, manufacturers may not offer the same merchandise at different prices to different customers. Any kind of special deal—volume discounts, advertising allowances, markdown money, trade-in allowances, liberal payment terms—is legal only if it is available to everyone. In reality, there is no one price in the toy business, and no one even bothers to pretend there is. Not all customers are equal: "The bigger the pencil, the better the terms."

Not all vendors are equal either. The toy industry has practiced "dating" for many years. Dating has nothing to do with social intercourse or anything else pleasant, as far as the manufacturers are concerned. Dating is allowing customers to postpone payment; it encourages them to buy now and pay later. The toymakers who began the practice expected it to even out their sales patterns by inducing customers to take some stock earlier in the year. It does that. But customers now expect such long dating periods that the manufacturers spend most of the year in debt to the bank for operating cash. When their customers finally pay them, the manufacturers repay the bank—and then start the cycle all over again.

Customers do pay more quickly if they want something badly, and the manufacturers operate accordingly. Different toys within the same company may command different dating periods according to their popularity, and buyers and sellers are always negotiating. Hasbro may require payment within 60 days on G.I. Joe merchandise and within 120 days on something else. Nintendo requires payment in 30 days and easily receives it.

Everybody in The Trade thinks his competitors are probably getting a different deal, but no one knows the exact terms. They all watch each other constantly. The buyers monitor their competitors' retail prices, and if one seems to be selling an item unusually cheaply, they do not hesitate to wonder out loud why their rival can afford to sell at such a low price. The retailers also monitor each other for the "benefit" of their vendors. Although setting a so-called fair-trade price (a price the manufacturer could once require its customers to charge) is no longer legal, some manufacturers want to protect their customers' profit margins and look askance at discounting. A retailer who spots a competitor "breaking price" will quickly point it out to the manufacturer, suggesting perhaps that the offending customer does not deserve to carry the product.

Trade prices vary widely because so much is negotiable—especially if the customer is powerful. Advertising allowances can be granted in many forms: actual payments, deductions from the invoice, extra merchandise from the manufacturer, or credit against future sales. Advertising allowances are probably the largest concession the trade extracts, but big customers also routinely demand money for cooperative advertising. Co-op advertising may include some television, but it is primarily print. Co-op ads are newspaper display advertisements and circulars that feature a number of different products available at one store or chain; they are financed jointly by the store and the manufacturers of the advertised products. The manufacturer's co-op contribution is "voluntary," but to refuse is to risk losing the opportunity to distribute the item through all those outlets.

There are all kinds of other allowances and concessions. Sales are considered final, but orders are really cancellable until shipped. Return allowances for defective merchandise may be granted if the products (such as electronic talking dolls) are so complex that they are likely to create a high rate of returns. The manufacturers may or may not require their customers to return the actual goods in order to qualify for the return allowance; for example, shopworn unsold goods are not supposed to qualify as "defective." For retailers powerful enough to extract it from the seller, there is also markdown money, money for products that bomb so badly that the retailers have to sell them off below their cost.

Then there are the unambiguously dishonest practices. Desperate companies (or embezzling owners or employees) may offer products for cash—off the books, of course. Or they may ship quantities in excess of those in the sales records. Or they may enter one product in the books and ship a different one.

Cut off from most of these machinations are the small retailers: the niche marketers and the mom-and-pop stores. Some specialize in educational toys, others in imports. A number of the owners are ex-teachers. Like those of the small toy companies, their operations are very personal, reflecting their likes, dislikes, personalities, and values. The stores may stock few or no promotional products, and the ones they do take will be supplied by one of the remaining regional distributors; the big toy companies have no interest in dealing with such small accounts.

The industry usually refers to the distributors, or wholesalers, as dinosaurs because they used to be the toy companies' largest and most powerful customers, and today they are almost extinct. Many of them went out of business, and the ones that remain are far less important. The day of the small toy store is always being proclaimed to be at an end too, and there is no question that the sector has diminished. But personal service, convenience, and specialty marketing ensure that the astute merchandiser in the right location can survive and even flourish.

One niche marketer stands out, better known to the general public than any of the manufacturers. Frederick Schwarz, who founded the store, was the last of the four Schwarz brothers to enter the retail toy business. Henry opened a store in Baltimore in 1849 and supposedly employed the first live Santa Claus at Christmastime. Richard took Boston and Gustav, Philadelphia. It was not until 1870 that Frederick opened FAO Schwarz in New York, but his was the survivor.

The store has switched locations and owners, opened a number of branches around the country, closed a number of branches, and survived several shifts in management philosophy. Through it all, the store's basic identity has remained unchanged. FAO Schwarz has always emphasized imports, high quality, and expensive merchandise. It always features a few spectacularly exorbitant items like its FAO exclusive children's library in 1988. For $6,000 the purchaser received five hundred books and fifty videotapes, suitable for ages one to nine. In 1989 the store offered a hand-painted, gold lamé chair, "embedded with faux gems," for $550. The emporium has a long relationship with companies like Steiff and Madame Alexander, and its customers expect to find those kinds of products there.

In the last few years FAO Schwarz has been led by a dynamic new team of managers with department store backgrounds who merchandise in innovative ways. The managers allow more promotional toys in the store, but since they are provided strictly for the convenience of their customers, the store offers them at noncompetitive (high) prices. The team's primary mission these days is to build and to trade on the store's reputation. They try to lead, to set trends. The store maintains spectacular displays throughout the year and separates merchandise into a series of boutiques.

Recently the store has created excitement by staging events like those at Bloomingdale's, its trendy neighbor. A two-week FAO Expo France, for example, featured personal appearances by the current author of the Babar books, Laurent de Brunhoff; a French chef; a storyteller-illustrator re-creating scenes from *Wheels on the Bus*, along with a number of other attractions. The store was the first to show black-and-white toys for babies.

In terms of dollars, FAO Schwarz will never be a major customer for the promotional toy companies, but the store has such cachet that they all covet space on its shelves.

19

DECEMBER 1987–FEBRUARY 1988
Where Toymen Sleep When They're Not at Home

ALL THE BUYERS AT TYCO'S PRE–TOY FAIR show represented national accounts except one, the buyer from the renowned FAO Schwarz. After he saw the presentation of Dino-Riders, he was so enthusiastic that he called his boss, merchandising vice president Gale Jarvis, to come downtown to Tyco's showroom. He thought she might like to feature Dino-Riders in the window at Christmastime. Gale Jarvis had made FAO Schwarz a place where things happened, and this looked like an opportunity to introduce a new product line.

When she arrived, Neil made an exception to his rule and showed her the product without making her watch the entire presentation. She liked the line but thought an in-store display would be a more effective presentation for it. That would cost Tyco about $50,000.

"No problem," said Neil, who had already spent $100,000 on the pre–Toy Fair show. A display in FAO Schwarz was almost as prestigious as a float in the Macy's Thanksgiving Day parade. It would be priceless publicity. Within the next few weeks Tyco commissioned a New York design company to build three dioramas and a cave to house them. The cave would be a small room, constructed of fake rocks, and visitors would enter it to see the dioramas. The company was known to be reliable, so Neil and Woody left it alone for the next two months.

Finally December arrived. Woody and Neil had planned to be in New York to oversee the dioramas' installation, but it was difficult. They had to spend the day before in Philadelphia, at an all-day long-range planning meeting. When it finally ended, they drove out to New Jersey, packed a pile of samples into Woody's car, and headed for New York. They arrived late, checked into their hotel, and fell into bed exhausted.

While they were sleeping, the previous display at FAO Schwarz was being dismantled, at Tyco's expense. Tyco's construction crew was scheduled to arrive at 6:00 A.M. to install Tyco's dioramas in its place, so that by the time the store opened at 10:00 A.M. the new display would be completed.

Six o'clock A.M. found Woody and Neil standing in front of the store wondering where everyone else was. They were still standing there at 7:00 A.M., and there was still no sign of the construction crew or the dioramas. Finally at 7:30 A.M. the designer cruised up. "Bad news," he reported nonchalantly. "Last night we were picking up your material and it looked like shit."

Woody and Neil stiffened. "We knew then that we had a choice," the designer continued resolutely, ignoring the storm clouds gathering in Woody's eyes. "We could put up a terrible-looking cave, or we could redo it. We chose to redo it. We'll have it ready by sometime later this afternoon or tonight."

Although chilled by the sound of the word *sometime*, Neil managed to force out his usual positive reinforcement. "Terrific. That was good judgment on your part."

The designer departed, and Neil and Woody faced each other. "That's great. What are we going to tell FAO?" Neil asked. "That at midnight, the night before it's supposed to go in, our vendor went to pick it up and didn't like it?"

Woody was inspired. "Let's tell them it fell off the truck and that it's being rebuilt even as we speak. And that sometime today it'll be installed."

Neil thought that was a great idea, so the two of them went upstairs to wait outside the executive offices. There are not many executives in the FAO Schwarz offices at 7:30 A.M., or even at 8:30 A.M., so they had plenty of time to get nervous. They were awed and intimidated by the store's reputation, and they were about to spin its top executives a tale that could be checked with a thirty-second telephone call.

"There's this big hole there," Woody recalled later. "It's December 17, and millions of people are going to be coming through that store. And we think we're going to get our heads handed to us."

But they had decided that being up-front, so to speak, was the best approach, and eventually someone appeared and let them in. The two perched on the couch in the tattered waiting room trying to look casually confident.

Suddenly Gale Jarvis burst through the door, accompanied by the store's president, Peter Harris. She was gracious and friendly and seemed genuinely glad to receive them. "Woody, how are you? It's nice to see you. What are you doing here so early?" she asked.

"Well," he began, "there's good news and bad news." Realizing that with an hour and a half to prepare he could have come up with a more original opening, he quickly hurried on. "Things are going great, but they fell off a truck. And we've got a problem because there's going to be a hole in your store today, and we don't know, it might be ready by three this afternoon, but it's going in tonight, and we'll be there to ride herd, and we're not leaving your store until it goes in."

To this breathless recital the two could only reply, "Terrific."

Woody was proud of his masterful handling of the situation. "I think they were impressed that we told them the truth—as we knew it. And by then we believed it too." It did not occur to either of them that Jarvis and Harris probably had their doubts about Woody's story but sensed that they were better off not knowing.

Having neutralized one battle zone, the pair proceeded downtown to the designer's loft, where they saw immediately that this was no repair job: the entire display was being rebuilt. Later the designer told them he had been unhappy with the vendor's work, so his group had completely reconstructed the entire cave.

That night Woody and Neil were back at the store to oversee the installation. On his way out, one of the store's employees casually mentioned that the windows were ready for them also.

Windows? Woody and Neil looked at each other, stunned. An FAO Schwarz window was the pinnacle of their ambitions, but nothing had been said about windows when they had agreed to do the dioramas . . . or had it? Now that they thought about it, they did recall that when they had met with people from the store a week before, one had said, "You are doing the windows too, aren't you?" But the subject had been dropped, and they had both assumed that the dioramas were the only Dino-Riders display the store expected.

They now learned they were wrong. It was 6:00 P.M., and the FAO Schwarz people were leaving for the night. Someone pointed to some cherry window boxes, about two-by-three feet each. Woody and Neil interpreted that to mean that those boxes were the same size as the windows.

It was like stepping into an anxiety dream. The only difference was that instead of finding themselves seated at a piano onstage at Carnegie Hall or walking into math class unprepared, they were supposed to decorate windows at FAO Schwarz. There was one other difference, of course: *this was no dream.*

Hundreds of thousands of visitors from all over the world flock to New York City at Christmastime. High on their list of sights, along with the Statue of Liberty, the Metropolitan Museum of Art, the Trump Tower, and the Empire State Building, are the windows at FAO Schwarz. And Woody Browne, a very important Tyco vice president and triathlete from New Jersey, and Neil Werde, a marketing director originally from Brooklyn, were supposed to decorate five of them. Tonight.

They were running on practically no sleep. They knew nothing about decorating windows. What they did know was that it would have been easier to fake it if they had had something to put in the space.

Mrs. Browne and Mrs. Werde did not raise their boys to be shirkers, however. FAO Schwarz's newest window decorators marched bravely upstairs, "borrowed" some rocks from the designers, sneaked as many Dino-Riders products off the shelves as they dared, and carried them over to the window area. Then they stood there, puzzled.

There didn't seem to be any way to get to the windows. All they could see were walls with shelves full of Christmas toys. Finally they realized that they were supposed to remove all the toys and rip the shelves from the walls to get to the openings. Remembering all the repair jobs piling up around their own houses, they thought it was pretty funny to be doing carpentry in New York City at 10:00 P.M.

An even bigger surprise lay ahead. When one of them finally poked his head into the first window, he found not a two-by-three-foot area but a display window so huge they could stand in it together. The Dino-Riders and Rulons were two-and-three-quarters inches high. The largest dinosaur was fourteen inches long; most of them were closer to six. The only props they had were a few fake rocks. Somehow they were supposed to decorate five enormous windows with these little pieces of plastic. Just to make it really challenging, it was nighttime. The store was locked, and the building's security guards were so intimidating that Woody and Neil were afraid if they went out, they might not be able to get back in. That meant they were unable to get outside to step back far enough to see how their efforts were shaping up.

Others in their situation might have considered that a blessing. Not Woody and Neil. They began to think they were pretty good. Woody recalled, "We were hysterical. We were exhausted. We were thinking, 'Hey, this is fun. This is wild.' All by ourselves we put together these displays, and we liked them. Then we started patting ourselves on the back. We were really impressed with our work."

Neil agreed. "Two of the five came out, we thought, really pretty well. And the other three, we knew, looked like sin—tiny little figures in these great big windows. But there was nothing we could do. I guess the FAO people thought we were professional or whatever."

By the time they finished, they were so exhausted that they decided to spend what was left of the night right there by their windows. They did not lack for companionship. Surrounded by enough stuffed animals to populate a zoo, they each selected about twenty-five thousand dollars' worth of their personal favorites, piled them into comfortable mounds, and snuggled in for the night. Using the softest ones as pillows, they both fell promptly asleep.

The next morning they took the buyer upstairs to see all the displays. He was delighted. The designers had installed dioramas with moving dinosaurs in three different scenes: a peaceful Valorian camp, the villainous hell of the Rulons, and a battle scene. They looked terrific.

Then they took him outside to see their windows. As they rounded the corner, they came upon the store's permanent window designer and his assistant. The two men were gagging, clutching their throats and screaming comments like "It's terrible. It's shit . . . ugh . . . aargh . . .yech!"

The buyer approached them and introduced Woody and Neil, who announced brightly, "We're the guys who did the windows." The designers were mortified and immediately began to apologize profusely. Filled with holiday spirit, the Tyco "designers" forgave them and magnanimously allowed the FAO designers to alter their handiwork.

Within a couple of hours the real designers had added props and cut down the size of the windows with backdrops, and the Tyco pair considered the results "not bad at all."

"Except for placing the good guys on the bad dinosaurs and mixing up the weapons and not knowing the way the product was set up, they did a great job," Neil concedes generously.

The next week the *Village Voice* rated them among the best Christmas windows in New York City.

On December 26, 1987, two-thirds of a "roadblock" went up when Tyco's two-minute commercial ran on NBC and CBS but not on ABC. (The traffic manager at the advertising agency had failed to get it to that network on time.) Exactly two years from the day of Jim Alley's inspiration, millions of children across the country heard for the first time the words "Harness the Power . . . DINO-RIDERS!"

On February 8, 1988, Toy Fair opened. The entire Dino-

Riders team was so proud of its handiwork that, in Mike Hirtle's words, "We were bursting our buttons."

The Trade liked the product.

A Tyco salesman, mistaken for a buyer, was shown a Dino-Rider knockoff that was already in production.

The press conference featuring Dr. Bob had to be cancelled when the paleontologist failed to appear on the scheduled day. He showed up two days later casually unapologetic and complaining about some mix-up with his hotel reservations.

The company had signed up Marvel Entertainment as a licensing agent, and three licensed Dino-Riders products were being shown already: books at Western Publishing, costumes at Ben Cooper, and lunch boxes at Aladdin.

Jay Garfinkel had taken the eight-minute videotape to the broadcasters' convention, and he thought they might be able to sell a weekly half-hour series.

Woody and Neil were as excited as all the rest, just a little more tired. They had been at the showroom since 6:00 A.M.

EPILOGUE
February 13, 1989

8:00 A.M.

THE CROWDS SURGE IN, BUT THE TOY Building lobby seems strangely empty for the opening day of Toy Fair. Buyers were allowed to register on Sunday, so perhaps that accounts for the shorter lines. Without the crush, some of the excitement is missing.

Every year something changes. This year the Hickory House Coffee Shop went out of business. The Toyland rumor mill reports that it was because Coleco owed it eighteen thousand dollars—or maybe it was thirty-eight thousand dollars.

Some of the hawkers are already out in front of the building. On his way out to join them, a man wearing black tights, red high-topped sneakers, insect antennae, and a red-and-yellow shell on his back stops to pose for a camera crew. Once outside he begins screeching, "Bug Out!" He urges the crowd to visit Ohio Art's showroom and see its new Bug Out game and, incidentally, the game's commercial, in which he stars as the bug.

A man in a caped tweed coat and deerstalker cap, obviously Sherlock Holmes, chews his pipe and chats with a young woman. He interrupts his conversation to hand passersby a red flyer that proclaims, "You can run but you can't hide." The flyer advertises Worlds of Wonder's new game Hide 'N Sneak, an electronic version of hide-and-seek.

A group of young men dressed in red satin baseball jackets and caps emblazoned Yo-Yo Man demonstrates tricks while a young woman hands out flyers and red buttons reading Yo! Readers are urged to enter the state of Yo, as demonstrated by the Yo-Yo Man himself, Tommy Smothers.

The noisiest group is a squad of yokels dressed in overalls and workboots. Apparently opposed to something agricultural, they march in a circle carrying stuffed pigs and placards that read, "Ban Barnyard Commandos," "Lamb Chops Not Karate Chops," and "Boycott Showroom 711N." Pro-ovine and anti-porcine, they chant:

> Pigs are great
> Good to roast
> Send Playmates Toys
> Back to their coast.

Flyers explain that they are H.I.C.K.S.—Horticulturalists Incensed by Commercialized Killer Swine. The gang who brought the world Teenage Mutant Ninja Turtles is at it again. The irrepressible amphibians are back, too, after generating $25 million for Playmates Toys in 1988. This year's edition of the *Toy Times*, available all over the Toy Building, features a photograph of Mt. Rushmore. Right next to Abraham Lincoln, carved out of stone, is a Turtle. The caption explains, "HAIL TO THE TURTLE!—Visitors are flocking to see the newest addition to Mt. Rushmore's prestigious facade, a Teenage Mutant Ninja Turtle. Americans of all ages stand in hushed silence contemplating the Turtles' legendary fight for truth, justice and pizza for all."

Soon the agricultural demonstrators are joined by real protesters. Then the real police arrive and proceed to erect barricades to hold back the protesters so that the Toy Fair buyers and sellers can enter the building. The War Resister League, the Gray Panthers, the National Coalition on Television Violence, Educators for Social Responsibility, and the Stop War Toys Campaign of the New England War Resisters League have all sent members to protest sexist, racist, and war-oriented toys. One wears a George Bush mask and carries a sign reading War Toys Are a Bad Investment. Another is dressed as Santa Claus, except Santa never wore a cartridge belt or carried an M-16 submachine gun. This Santa apparently needs his weapon to guard a card table set up to display his "Toy Manufacturers' Hall of Shame." The honored companies include Hasbro "for 25 years of glorifying militarism with G.I. Joe," Mattel "for 30 years of pimping a passive, plastic Barbie image of women as a role model for girls," Nintendo "for promoting a new obsession with video violence," and Tyco "for militarizing kids' interest in dinosaurs and building toys."

The demonstrations draw some attention from media people, but the buyers generally ignore them. Hasbro, Mattel, and Nintendo accounted for about a third of the industry's domestic sales last year.

At the opening press conference TMA chairman Tom Kalinske says the industry is cautiously optimistic. For the manufacturers, 1988 unit sales were flat, but dollar sales rose slightly. They are finally adjusting to life after megahits. Buyers have been buying conservatively for a year, but the manufacturers have been lowering their break-even points. "What makes many of us feel that the industry's relative slump may finally be over," says Kalinske, "is the fact that in 1987, publicly held toy companies lost $120 million; in 1988 those companies are estimated to show profits of $120 million."

The CEOs of most of the larger corporations are at the press conference as usual. Dick Grey looks happy, as he should. Tyco had a spectacular year. Sales for 1988 were $264 million, up 61 percent, and earnings have risen 70 percent.

Grey chats with Bernie Loomis, who looks like a different person now that he is healthy again, after back surgery. He is in a better mood, too. One of his pet projects is off to a promising start. He thought for years that Western Publishing was missing an opportunity to market its Little Golden Book name ("franchise") more aggressively. He brought Western to Playskool, and together they are launching Little Golden Book Land. Western already has licensees for Little Golden Book Land lunch boxes, pajamas, sleeping bags, costumes, and party goods, but Loomis hopes they will expand even more.

Already making his rounds is Avi Arad. He knows the manufacturers consider him a pest when he checks up on his products, but he wants to see how his creations are displayed. At Lewis Galoob his Bouncin' Babies have been joined by Bouncin' Kids and Bouncin' Ponies. The ballerina doll in Galoob's commercials looks as though she is spinning by herself—in real life she needs help.

At View-Master Ideal, Arad looks at his Heart Strings jewelry kits. The company also bought his large baby doll idea, Baby Bubbles, which gurgles and blows real bubbles. It plans to emphasize Ideal's experience with dolls and has brought back two favorites, Tiny Tears and (complete with potty chair) Betsy Wetsy, so Arad is flattered that the company made his product the centerpiece of the "Ideal Nursery." View-Master Ideal hired the Alberts to design the dolls and create the marketing plan. Since Judy designed clothes for Betsy Wetsy in the 1960s, she especially enjoyed the assignment.

Many of last year's hopefuls exhibit a new assurance. Backward-talking David Fuhrer never lacked confidence, but after touring for a year, he is a more relaxed performer. *Games* magazine chose Backwords as one of the best new games in 1988, and Random House is planning to spend another $1 million promoting it this year.

Kimerlea Osborne, creator of Kool-Aid Kid dolls, has just sold another doll to Goldberger. They will launch the Rad Kids this time next year. After a year of promoting her dolls, she can wear normal clothes at Toy Fair instead of dressing like the doll. In June she is going to appear in *Entrepreneur* magazine representing the state of Tennessee, and the coming year looks even better for the dolls. General Foods plans to display them in 70 percent of the major grocery store chains and use them as a premium for a summer Kool-Aid promotion. Goldberger has extended the line to include a black Kid and a smaller version.

OddzOn Products has sold "millions" of Koosh Balls, which have been on *Toy & Hobby World*'s list of bestselling toys for five months. Knockoffs will not appear in the stores until the end of the summer. Over at the Javits Convention Center the company will join a new group of hopefuls, many of them offering toys designed not just to amuse but to instruct. Cool Toys will donate 10 percent of its Homeless Dolls' gross sales to organizations helping the homeless. Give Peace a Chance is a game for promoting the concept that "we all win if there is world peace." The habits of the Genuine Nun Dolls are so finely sewn that the dolls, although educational, seem clearly intended for adult collectors, not children. "Wee" Share International's "Wee" Sprouts kit allows children to grow their own nutritional salads from Mighty Mung, Alfie Alfalfa, Lucy Lentil, and Radical Radish seeds.

There are also toys just for fun. Boinks are back for the second year; they are simply mesh tubes that can be scrunched up and popped.

The trends for 1989 are not hard to discern. In plush, high-tech is out, high-touch is in. Stuffed creatures are cute and cuddly, but quiet—no talking. They still seem to need a gimmick. Lewis Galoob's Lost 'n Founds bunny, kitten, panda, chimp, and their friends have bottles and bibs and can cry real tears. Hasbro and Mattel both offer lines of plush turtles that transform into other things.

Every company able to get one has a license to create Nintendo games. In 1988 Nintendo and its licensees sold 1.2 billion worth of hardware and games and will sell another $1.8 billion worth in 1989. Six months after Toy Fair, Nintendo will reveal what its competitors will call its Trojan horse strategy. It seems the little gray boxes entering all those American homes are able to access home shopping, stock quotes, and other services, once the network is in place and a modem is attached. Board games are also strong because of the trend toward "cocooning" (staying home). They focus on music and on "social interaction" (guessing games based on wordplay, trivia, celebrities).

In boys' toys, ride-in cars, planes, and military themes are popular. Mattel and Matchbox were so successful with their color-changeable die-cast vehicles that everyone has copied them this year. Galoob has sold 200 million one-and-one-quarter-inch Micro-Machine vehicles in two years, and they are knocked off everywhere as well. Micro-Machine's commercials are fun for adults, too, because they feature Jon Moschitta, the fast-talking actor from the Federal Express commercials. Galoob is still a step ahead of its competition. Enclosed in its Insiders group of Micro-Machines are even tinier vehicles, only one-half-inch long. Mattel, Tonka, Matchbox, Fisher-Price, and Galoob all offer new racing car sets, and by the summer "hyper car" speedy racers will be touted as the hot prospect for Christmas.

In 1988 Kenner's Starting Lineup figurines generated $50 million, demonstrating the power of sports licensing. The lesson was not wasted. Sports stars dutifully appear in showrooms all over the buildings. San Francisco Forty-Niners Joe Montana and Roger Craig sign plush footballs at Dakin. Olympic track star Florence Griffith-Joyner appears at LJN to promote her Flo-Jo fashion doll. Each doll is dressed in a one-legged running outfit and comes packaged with press-on nail decals for little girls to put on their own fingernails. New York Yankee Dave Winfield signs balls at View-Master Ideal to promote the company's MVP Baseball Sports Card Game. Parker Brothers' Talking Baseball game of 1988 may have inspired LJN; this year LJN has collaborated with Topps Chewing Gum to produce Baseball Talk talking baseball cards.

Kenner's 1987 Real Ghostbuster line started the humorous action-figure market that Teenage Mutant Ninja Turtles tapped successfully in 1988. This year Mattel has managed to incorporate two trends into one product line. Anything to do with food seems popular this year, and Mattel has a humorous food-related action-figure line. Kitchen Commandos, led by Burger-dier General and his followers Sergeant Scoop and Private Pizza, are "slugging it out for ultimate control of kitchens across America." Their enemies are the evil Mean Weener and his Refrigerator Rejects, including Taco Terror and Chip-the-Ripper. Vehicles include the BBQ Bomber and Combat Carton, and the Refrigerator headquarters comes equipped with frozen missiles and juice-can bombs.

Nerds and weirdos are in too. Matchbox Toys' Pee-wee Herman has been joined by an Ed Grimley doll at Tyco, by Freddy Krueger (*A Nightmare on Elm Street*) at LJN, and by Ernest P. Worell at Kenner.

The 1989 look in girls' toys has shifted from last year's electric California turquoise, hot pink, and chartreuse to small Victorian patterns and soft pastels. Jungle and safari themes reflect one of the 1988 styles in women's fashions. The most obvious comeback is the large baby doll. Displaced first by Cabbage Patch Kids and then by intelligent electronic dolls, baby dolls meant just to be loved are clearly the thing. Maurene Souza, Hasbro's vice president for girls' toys, is convinced that the girls' arena has gotten more competitive because the companies are conceding the boys' market to Nintendo for now.

Fisher-Price has taken collectibility into a new dimension with its Precious Places miniature Victorian-style village. Instead of offering one dollhouse requiring an endless array of doll furnishings, its Precious Places line creates an entire community of collectible dollhouses. Each building comes with two pieces of sidewalk so that the purchaser will want several buildings just to get started. Decorated in pastels with plenty of flowers, frills, and Victorian gingerbread, the expensive line fascinates buyers.

Trends appear in marketing strategies as well as in products. Tonka, Ohio Art, Matchbox, View-Master, and Ideal all talk about promoting their "franchises," their good reputations, or established brand recognition among parents. They all talk about getting back to their "core businesses." Anniversaries abound: Barbie is thirty, G.I. Joe is twenty-five, and the Viewmaster 3-D viewer is fifty—it was introduced at the 1939 New York World's Fair.

The big turnaround story is Mattel. The company was profitable in 1988: $35.9 million in earnings versus a $113 million loss the year before. After seeing his strategy work, chairman John Amerman is feeling great. Mattel has reduced its overhead, tightened its inventories, lowered the company's break-even point, and renegotiated its financial arrangements. It has also sharpened its marketing, to focus on its "consumer franchises."

"We said to ourselves, we've got great assets at Mattel—classic undermarketed product lines," Amerman explains. "Add them up. Barbie, Hot Wheels, Walt Disney, large dolls, and He-Man. Those are five great franchises that are known around the world. Hasbro, Lego, Fisher-Price have one, maybe two. We have an extremely strong group."

Mattel, which has had the license to make Walt Disney preschool toys for a year, launched the line in 1988 with a small array of products—what Amerman calls a rifle-shot approach. They sold well, so the company is back with more this year. He-Man has been around since 1982 but was having problems. "We left far too much product on retailers' shelves in 1985, and it took us three years to clean it up," explains Mattel's chairman. But Mattel's market research showed that the He-Man character was still appealing, so Mattel has reintroduced He-Man without the Masters. "We have a new line, new product, new approach, new planet."

Hot Wheels and Barbie were the primary focus of last year's marketing efforts, and they took off. The Hot Wheels business rose 80 percent in 1988 and the Barbie business by almost 40 percent—to about $500 million. The company even had a surprise hit with its Li'l Miss Makeup (the Little Baby Hooker, which was stuck over in the corner last year). Mattel had estimated sales at 400,000 units. It sold 2.5 million. No longer a minor product, this year Li'l Miss Makeup has her own room, although she is generous enough to let her friend stay there too. On the usual theory that if a product is good a product line is better, this year Li'l Miss Makeup has been joined by Li'l Miss Dress Up, whose dress is temperature-sensitive so that little girls can decorate it by making designs with water.

This is an important year for Barbie. She is turning thirty. Mattel is trying to exploit the occasion for maximum publicity while keeping the news a secret from Barbie's current customers. It is a difficult balancing act. Tonight the company is celebrating the event, which it is calling Barbie's Pink Jubilee, by throwing an elaborate party for seven hundred customers and media representatives at Lincoln Center's New York State Theater. Mattel has also licensed a line of products called Nostalgic

Barbie, targeted toward adults. The nostalgia is definitely not for the under-twelve set: thirty would make Barbie seem, like, totally old.

As far as Barbie's young customers are concerned, the big news is that Barbie has a new teenage cousin named Jazzie. She comes in Cheerleader Jazzie, Workout Jazzie, and Swim Suit Jazzie, and she has two best friends, Chelsie and Stacie, who can share her Totally Cool Fashions. Her boyfriend, Dude, is the most popular boy in school. It's a funny thing about Jazzie. Not only does she bear a strong resemblance to Hasbro's Maxie (maybe they attend the same high school) but her name, her colors, and even the lettering on her packaging look like Maxie's. All those similarities may create confusion in the stores, but if Mattel is worried that customers may get the two mixed up, it isn't saying. With that resemblance, every dollar Hasbro spends on Maxie may help Jazzie.

Maxie fulfilled her $25 million target for 1988 and Hasbro is expanding the line. Hasbro is also making a run at Mattel's Li'l Miss Makeup, with a line of miniature dolls called Make-Me-Up Darlings. Hearts, musical notes, and cats' whiskers appear on their faces when cold water is applied.

Hasbro, whose showroom is always packed, has an especially well-publicized Toy Fair this year because its Milton Bradley subsidiary has linked up with Donald Trump to produce Trump—The Game. Hasbro also has Dan Rather coming around several times because he is taping a segment on Milton Bradley and Trump—The Game for an episode of "48 Hours" that will cover the toy industry. When the program appears weeks later, some of the game division's executives will complain that there is too much Donald Trump and not enough Milton Bradley.

Hasbro has more excitement than it needs. The company's showrooms share an office building with Viking Press, the publisher of Salman Rushdie's *Satanic Verses*. In the middle of the first week of Toy Fair, just when Hasbro's showrooms are busiest, Viking receives a bomb threat. Thanks to the Ayatollah Khomeini, Hasbro has to clear hundreds of people out of its showroom and lose several hours of prime selling time.

Hasbro's employees will remember Toy Fair 1989 for another reason. It is Stephen Hassenfeld's last Toy Fair: he will die the following summer. In the toy business even a billion-dollar company is a family business, and to most of the employees, who have been with the company for years, it is not just a professional but a personal loss.

Steve Shank has now spent a year heading the industry's third-largest company. Tonka has swallowed Kenner and Parker but left them somewhat whole. Kenner will handle the corporation's promotional business, Parker will take games, and Tonka will concentrate on its "franchise," the Tonka reputation with parents. In other words, the company will try to build My First Tonka into a major preschool brand. The company lost money for the year, $5.8 million on sales of $907.7 million, because of the debt load from the leveraged buy-out, but Shank's strategy looks as though it might work. He meets with the financial analysts at Toy Fair, and he must impress them, for Tonka's stock price will double in the next six months.

Worlds of Wonder is still in Chapter 11 bankruptcy, but it is about to come out. Loren Hildebrand tightened it up, and it has continued to operate. The company has taken one room instead of two at the Waldorf-Astoria and offers a smaller range of products. But the products are demonstrated by professionals, and all the commercials are ready for viewing, which shows the buyers that WOW means business. A few weeks after Toy Fair the company will announce that an investor group is buying the company. Josh Denham, currently president of Wonder Toys, is to be president.

Coleco is finally bankrupt. Its fortunes have been up and down more times than anyone can remember, but the company finally burdened itself with so many losses and so much debt that there was no other way out. It cut its work force from 2,500 in 1987 to less than 700, sold its headquarters and as many of its businesses as it could, lost the Trivial Pursuit license for which it had paid so dearly, and failed in several attempts to renegotiate its debt. With nothing left to pawn, Coleco went to bankruptcy court on July 11, 1988. By then it had lost $240 million for the first six months of fiscal 1988—on sales of $89 million.

The court has allowed Coleco to have a Toy Fair exhibit, which is set up at the Penta Hotel, across the street from Madison Square Garden. Coleco has only a few products, but it still has the Cabbage Patch Kids line. The license was renewed around the same time the company was going bankrupt; the current presidents of Coleco and Original Appalachian Artworks are linked romantically, which cannot have hurt Coleco's chances at keeping the product.

A few months after Toy Fair, Coleco will have to give up at last, and Hasbro will buy it out. Once more Hasbro will get a staple on the cheap: $85 million for Cabbage Patch Kids, with Scrabble thrown in as well.

Tyco is hot. The company has been getting calls from investors, licensers, job hunters, potential acquisition candidates. It is the place to be. This summer the company will grow yet again, when it acquires View-Master Ideal for an outstanding combination of products.

Tyco has a wider range of products than anyone would have believed possible. The star of its radio-controlled line is the Hovercraft, which the company spent two years developing. It scoots over water and sand on an inflatable bag.

Jim Alley's responsibilities keep growing along with Tyco. He now has a marketing director for girls' toys, and the company is offering two large dolls, Oopsie-Daisy, a crawling baby doll, and the Ed Grimley Talking Doll. The company also has a 1950s-themed play set called Dixie's Diner. Set up in Tyco's showroom is a diner, complete with an actress playing Dixie.

Tyco has added ten new dinosaurs to last year's line of Dino-Riders. The new products include a *Stegosaurus* that walks and a *Brontosaurus* that is over three feet long. There is also a *Pachycephalosaurus*, chosen by the designer because the name is so difficult to pronounce.

Backing up Dino-Riders is a half-hour television program, which is part of a ninety-minute syndicated Marvel package that includes "Robocop" and "Spiderman." The Dino-Riders now have a special guerrilla-warfare group called the Commandos, and the program is as violent as all the other action-figure–based programs on television.

Earlier this year Tyco fired its advertising agency, Bozell, Jacobs in Los Angeles, and interviewed several new agencies. Its final choice was . . . Bozell, Jacobs in New York. The Tyco group wanted Garth DeCew to move east, but the agency could not meet his terms. It refused to cover the cost of moving his two-seater airplane—as well as his wife's plane. Besides, his wife has her own business in California. The new commercials for 1989 include an innovative spot featuring the Dino-Riders' weapons. It is "Preparation for Battle."

Neil Werde was mentioned in the *New York Times* in December when he defended Dino-Riders' scientific accuracy. Dr. David Weishampel, the "patches on the elbows" paleontologist Tyco did not choose as its Dino-Riders spokesperson, had complained to the newspaper about several lines of toy dinosaurs. He had singled out Dino-Riders for special criticism.

Dr. Robert Bakker, the paleontologist who got the job, is gone. He parted amicably from Tyco late in 1988 when Tyco designed its *Stegosaurus* to look the way most people think it looked instead of the way the latest research says it looked, which is very different.

At a meeting just before Toy Fair, Dick Grey told the sales force that he expects Dino-Riders to generate about $25 million in 1989. Woody Browne is furious. "It's a self-fulfilling prophecy," he fumes. He thinks the line should sell more than double that. After all, isn't Dino-Riders already a huge success?

In 1988, its first full year, Dino-Riders sales were $35 million, closer to Dick's original expectation of $19 million than to the $60 million Woody and Neil had forecast.

But if the line's international sales are added in—and Woody and Neil like to include them—then total Dino-Riders sales for 1988 were $64 million.

Just as they predicted.

But don't expect them to be surprised.

They knew it all the time.

7:30 P.M.

Some people have more important things on their minds than dinosaurs.

Monday may be the busiest day of Toy Fair, but quite a few people are leaving early. There are going to be some terrific parties this evening, but there is no doubt that the affair of the year is Mattel's black-tie soirée at Lincoln Center's New York State Theater.

Klieg lights beam high into the sky as soon as the sun begins to sink. Emerging from their taxis and limousines, guests find their way to the theater marked not with a traditional red carpet, but with a glittering strip of bright pink.

As they ascend the stairs inside, the women are given wrist corsages of pink roses. The men receive pink boutonnieres. The enormous scale of the room seems to reduce the adults to toy figures, all of them milling about in what looks like a little girl's dream of a ballroom.

Everything is pink. Enormous swags of pink fabric hang from the balconies, secured by giant rosettes. Draped in pink tablecloths, scattered tables offer fruit, cheese, and pâtés. Tuxedo-clad waiters in pink ties and cumberbunds pass pink champagne and pink Perrier water in glasses whose stems are adorned with pink bows.

Two ten-by-thirty-foot screens suspended from the balconies promise entertainment, and seven pink shirred Austrian shades hang below the screens, adding an air of mystery. Across the room, on a pink-framed stage, a string quartet provides soothing background music.

The name for this occasion was chosen with the painstaking care usually reserved for presidential speeches. It could not be called a thirtieth birthday or anniversary—too old, too staid, too matronly. Finally someone had a stroke of lexical genius: "jubilee." It does mean a special anniversary, but it doesn't sound so old-fashioned.

So it is that on February 13, 1989, seven hundred fortunate guests find themselves at Barbie's Pink Jubilee celebration: "Thirty Magical Years of Barbie, 1959–1989."

Entertainment includes five girls reciting rap songs and "doing the Barbie" dance. The two screens light up with slides of Barbie fashions through the years, accompanied by a sound track that includes "9 to 5" backing Barbie's dress-for-success executive wear, "Let's Get Physical" for her workout costumes, and "Puttin' on the Ritz" for her glamorous evening clothes.

The Austrian shades rise to reveal tableaux of Barbie, Ken, and their friends in more of their costumes. One depicts a beach scene, another an art gallery complete with tiny imitation Warhol paintings. The best, as usual, is the evening scene. In the middle is a white scale-model piano, which sets off Barbie in her slinky black evening gown.

After the show a rock band bursts into "Dancin' in the Streets," and the guests began to party. No one seems to notice that one of the fake Corinthian columns near the bandstand is tilting. The elaborate flower arrangement atop it slides off, knocking down a bystander, who has to be taken to the hospital. The guests dance on, oblivious.

Nor does anyone seem to spare a thought for the absent Ruth and Elliot Handler. They are not even mentioned in the evening's speeches.

When the waiters appear with chocolate truffles and pink cookies emblazoned with a chocolate *B*, the party starts to wind down. As the guests begin to leave, that greedy child inside every adult, the one who never quite dies, begins to surface. In addition to pins, corsages, boutonnieres, and scrolls, Mattel has provided a doll for every guest, a special, glitteringly dressed commemorative Barbie doll, one of a limited edition of twelve hundred.

Unfortunately, one just isn't enough for some of the guests— even though taking more means others have to go home empty-handed.

In the coat-check line a woman looks beseechingly at the man next to her. He is clutching two beribboned boxes and stubbornly avoiding eye contact. Finally she speaks. "Can I have one of yours?" she pleads. "I didn't get a doll."

"No," he replies coldly. "I have two children."

Out into the night the guests scurry, the lucky ones hugging their boxes with all the excitement a present can generate. It's been a wonderful party.

Meanwhile, inside each box, an eleven-and-a-half-inch piece of plastic gazes with starry eyes into pink-tissue–lined space. What can she be thinking?

Is she reliving the elegant party? Recalling her thirty years of history? Wishing for world peace?

Not Barbie. If she could speak, there is no doubt that Barbie would talk about her favorite subject.

"Don't you think this dress is totally beautiful? So do I."

APPENDIX:
MEMORABLE MOMENTS
IN TOYLAND

1902	Clifford Berryman cartoon of Teddy Roosevelt and a bear captivates the nation. Ideal's owner secures permission to name the teddy bear.
1916	A. C. Gilbert and others form the first industry association, Toy Manufacturers of the United States of America.
1917	First toy industry lobbying expedition saves Christmas for American children.
1921	Louis Marx and his brother start their own toy business.
1923	Herman, Henry, and Hillel Hassenfeld form Hassenfeld Brothers.
1934–1939	In spite of the Depression, Ideal sells 1.5 million Shirley Temple dolls. Handcar with Mickey and Minnie Mouse saves Lionel. Monopoly saves Parker Brothers. View-Master 3D Viewer is introduced at the 1939 World's Fair in New York.
1945	The Handlers form Mattel. Slinky starts walking down stairs.

APPENDIX:
MEMORABLE MOMENTS
IN TOYLAND

1902	Clifford Berryman cartoon of Teddy Roosevelt and a bear captivates the nation. Ideal's owner secures permission to name the teddy bear.
1916	A. C. Gilbert and others form the first industry association, Toy Manufacturers of the United States of America.
1917	First toy industry lobbying expedition saves Christmas for American children.
1921	Louis Marx and his brother start their own toy business.
1923	Herman, Henry, and Hillel Hassenfeld form Hassenfeld Brothers.
1934–1939	In spite of the Depression, Ideal sells 1.5 million Shirley Temple dolls. Handcar with Mickey and Minnie Mouse saves Lionel. Monopoly saves Parker Brothers. View-Master 3D Viewer is introduced at the 1939 World's Fair in New York.
1945	The Handlers form Mattel. Slinky starts walking down stairs.

1952	Hassenfeld Brothers advertises first toy, Mr. Potato Head, on local television.
1955	*Time* magazine features Louis Marx, "toy king," in cover story.
	Mattel becomes first toy manufacturer to advertise on national television. The appearance of its Burp Gun on "The Mickey Mouse Club" launches the promotional toy business.
1956	Charles Lazarus forms first Children's Supermarket, the predecessor of Toys "R" Us.
1958	Biggest fad in Toyland history, Hula Hoops sweep the world.
	Biggest flop in Toyland history, Christ Child dolls do not enchant the public.
1959	Barbie is born.
1960	Etch A Sketch appears.
1961	First guidelines on TV toy advertising promulgated by the National Association of Broadcasters.
1964	G.I. Joe marches forward.
1966	Twister ties up the nation.
1969	Child Protection and Toy Safety Act sweeps through Congress, enabling the FDA to regulate toy safety and ban unsafe toys.
	Mattel creates a television program based on its Hot Wheels line of die-cast cars. FCC disallows it, deeming it a "program-length commercial."
1972	Consumer Product Safety Act establishes the Consumer Product Safety Commission, which will regulate toy safety instead of the FDA.
1973	Baby Alive eats—and digests—solids.
1976	Hand-held electronic games boom begins.
1977	*Star Wars* toys' I.O.U.s sell out at Christmas.
1978	FTC hearings on television advertising to children.
1980	Strawberry Shortcake launches licensing boom.
1982	Video game boom.
1983	"He-Man and Masters of the Universe" television show launches toy-based program boom.
	Cabbage Patch Kids create riots. Doll appears on *Newsweek* cover.

1952	Hassenfeld Brothers advertises first toy, Mr. Potato Head, on local television.
1955	*Time* magazine features Louis Marx, "toy king," in cover story.
	Mattel becomes first toy manufacturer to advertise on national television. The appearance of its Burp Gun on "The Mickey Mouse Club" launches the promotional toy business.
1956	Charles Lazarus forms first Children's Supermarket, the predecessor of Toys "R" Us.
1958	Biggest fad in Toyland history, Hula Hoops sweep the world.
	Biggest flop in Toyland history, Christ Child dolls do not enchant the public.
1959	Barbie is born.
1960	Etch A Sketch appears.
1961	First guidelines on TV toy advertising promulgated by the National Association of Broadcasters.
1964	G.I. Joe marches forward.
1966	Twister ties up the nation.
1969	Child Protection and Toy Safety Act sweeps through Congress, enabling the FDA to regulate toy safety and ban unsafe toys.
	Mattel creates a television program based on its Hot Wheels line of die-cast cars. FCC disallows it, deeming it a "program-length commercial."
1972	Consumer Product Safety Act establishes the Consumer Product Safety Commission, which will regulate toy safety instead of the FDA.
1973	Baby Alive eats—and digests—solids.
1976	Hand-held electronic games boom begins.
1977	*Star Wars* toys' I.O.U.s sell out at Christmas.
1978	FTC hearings on television advertising to children.
1980	Strawberry Shortcake launches licensing boom.
1982	Video game boom.
1983	"He-Man and Masters of the Universe" television show launches toy-based program boom.
	Cabbage Patch Kids create riots. Doll appears on *Newsweek* cover.

Video game bust.

1984   Hasbro buys Milton Bradley.

Trivial Pursuit sales stun industry.

Transformable robots boom.

1985   Worlds of Wonder is founded and produces the hottest Christmas toy, Teddy Ruxpin.

1987   Worlds of Wonder goes bankrupt.

Tonka buys Kenner Parker.

1988   Coleco goes bankrupt.

1989   Hasbro buys Coleco's assets, including Cabbage Patch Kids.

Second video game boom, led by Nintendo.

1990   *Toyland,* the book, tells all. (Almost.)

SOURCES

ACCORDING TO MARK TWAIN AND OTHER wise men, there are three kinds of lies: lies, damned lies, and statistics. We hope we have not included any lies on these pages. We are fairly confident that we have rooted out the damned lies. Unfortunately, we could do very little about the statistics. We had to use them.

The only thing we can say with complete assurance about industry statistics is that they are all estimates. There is no census of wholesale or retail sales, and there are literally thousands of suppliers and thousands of retailers. In most cases we used the industry and product category figures estimated by the Toy Manufacturers of America. Because we usually employed them to compare categories, illustrate trends, or demonstrate the dimensions of booms and busts, internal consistency was more important than absolute accuracy (which would have been impossible anyway). According to the TMA, its manufacturers' shipment (or industry sales, or wholesale) data are compiled through a process which includes a polling of major U.S. toy and game manufacturers, inspection of public records, and a

313

comparison of trends with the U.S. Toy Market Index (TMI) and Toy Retail Sales Tracking Service (TRSTS).

The Toy Market Index and the TRSTS are based on ongoing quantitative studies conducted by The NPD Group, a Long Island market-research organization. Both reports are sold in various forms to toy manufacturers and retailers, who study them exhaustively. The TMI reports cover a range of demographic and product-specific data (which toys are requested by name by what age child, for example). To construct the TMI, NPD uses data from its ongoing survey of more than sixteen thousand households. Each household keeps a diary recording all purchases, not only toys and games. The Toy Retail Sales Tracking Service reports are based on "consumer takeaways"— what the stores actually report selling—plus what they have in inventory, item by item. The figures are extrapolated from a selected sample of retailers representing 18 to 20 percent of the market.

While TMA estimates of manufacturers' shipments tend to be close to NPD figures, its estimates of retail volume are much higher. NPD estimated 1988 domestic toy retail sales at $9.5 billion without video games, $11.6 billion including them. The TMA estimated 1988 retail sales of toys alone at $12.75 billion. That assumed that the entire $8.5 billion in estimated manufacturers' shipments was marked up 50 percent by retailers and sold at that price. In fact, price margins at retail, especially for the promotional products, tend to be much narrower. In addition, stores put merchandise on sale and offer special prices periodically.

Unit or dollar sales figures on individual products or product lines usually came from the manufacturers.

The descriptions of Toy Fair 1988 and 1989 came from our personal observations.

Most of the anecdotes about the business came from personal interviews. When we used information from published accounts in newspapers, magazines, or books, whenever possible we checked the facts with the people who actually figured in the stories. Whether the anecdotes came from interviews or written articles, we checked figures with the companies concerned if possible. Sometimes the company was no longer in existence, or the people concerned had died or forgotten some of the facts. In those cases we tried to use contemporaneous sources, or close-to-contemporaneous sources.

The publications that furnished the most background information were the *New York Times,* the *Wall Street Journal, Barron's,* the *Los Angeles Times, Business Week, Fortune, Forbes, Time,* and *Newsweek,* as well as the toy trade publications, particularly *Toy & Hobby World* and *Playthings.* We relied heavily on annual reports, 10-K reports, press kits, catalogs, and internal publications from the toy companies. Trade associations and public interest advocates provided us with extensive materials, and staff members from the agencies that regulate or oversee the toy industry were very helpful.

We used a number of books for reference or background. The following selection offers an expanded treatment of some aspect of the toy business or toys themselves for the interested reader. Some are out of print but may be found at libraries.

HISTORY

Fraser, Antonia. *A History of Toys.* New York: Delacorte Press, 1966. Copyright by George Weidenfeld and Nicolson Ltd.

Kaye, Marvin. *The Story of Monopoly, Silly Putty, Bingo, Twister, Frisbee, Scrabble, et cetera* (previously published 1973, as *A Toy Is Born*). New York: Stein and Day, 1977.

King, Constance Eileen. *Antique Toys and Dolls.* New York: Rizzoli; South Kensington: Christie's, 1979.

————. *The Collector's History of Dolls.* First published in Great Britain (London: R. Hale), 1977. First published in the United States of America (New York: St. Martin's Press), 1978.

————. *The Encyclopedia of Toys.* New York: Crown Publishers, 1978.

Lavitt, Wendy. *Dolls: The Knopf Collectors' Guides to American Antiques.* New York: Alfred A. Knopf, 1983.

McClintock, Inez and Marshall. *Toys in America.* Washington D.C.: Public Affairs Press, 1961.

Whitton, Blair. *Toys: The Knopf Collectors' Guides to American Antiques.* New York: Alfred A. Knopf, 1984.

COMPANIES AND PRODUCTS

BillyBoy. *Barbie, Her Life & Times.* New York: Crown Publishers, 1987.

Cohen, Scott. *Zap! The Rise and Fall of Atari.* New York: McGraw-Hill, 1984.

DeWein, Sybil, and Joan Ashabraner. *The Collectors Encyclopedia of Barbie Dolls and Collectibles.* Paducah, Kentucky: Collector Books, 1977.

Hoffman, William. *Fantasy: The Incredible Cabbage Patch Phenomenon.* Dallas, Texas: Taylor Publishing Company, 1984.

Original Appalachian Artworks, Inc. *The Legend of the Cabbage Patch Kids.* Dallas, Texas: Taylor Publishing Company, 1984.

Pennybags, Milburn, as told to Philip Orbanes. *The Monopoly Companion.* Boston: Bob Adams, Inc., 1988.

Shea, James J., as told to Charles Mercer. *It's All in the Game.* New York: G. P. Putnam's Sons, 1960. (Milton Bradley)

Wohjahn, Ellen. *Playing by Different Rules.* New York: AMACOM, American Management Association, 1988. (General Mills/Parker Brothers merger)

ISSUES

Adler, Richard P., et al. *The Effects of Television Advertising on Children: Review and Recommendations.* Lexington, Massachusetts: Lexington Books, 1980. Copyright President and Fellows of Harvard College.

Carlsson-Paige, Nancy, and Diane E. Levin. *The War Play Dilemma.* New York: Teachers College Press, Columbia University, 1987.

Kaye, Evelyn. *The ACT Guide to Children's Television.* Boston: Beacon Press, 1979.

Schneider, Cy. *Children's Television*. Lincolnwood, Illinois: NTC Business Books, 1987.

Sutton-Smith, Brian. *Toys As Culture*. New York: Gardner Press, 1986.

Swartz, Edward. *Toys That Don't Care*. Boston: Gambit Inc., 1971.

———. *Toys That Kill*. New York: Random House, 1986.

Turkle, Sherry. *The Second Self: Computers and the Human Spirit*. New York: Simon and Schuster, 1984.

INDEX

Abbott, Scott, 125

ABC (American Broadcasting Corporation), 53-55, 190, 291

Abdul-Jabbar, Kareem, 254

Abigail, 199

Abrahound Lincoln, 218

Abrams, Marty, 234-37, 242

Abrams/Gentile Entertainment, 236-37

accounting, 28, 70-75, 249

acquisitions. *See* consolidation

ACT (Action for Children's Television), 10, 186, 189, 191-92, 193-94

action figures, 17, 39-47, 77-84, 88-91, 93, 116, 127-31, 132, 136-38, 148-51, 172-74, 182, 200, 210, 264-65, 298, 303-4. *See also* individual products and military toys

Action for Children's Television. *See* ACT

Action Jackson (action figure), 235

Activision (video system), 103

activity toys, 200

ADAM (home computer), 106-8

advertising, 10, 13-14, 28, 30, 45-46, 96, 105, 119-20, 186-202, 211, 310

allowances, 283

air hockey, 94

A.G. Bear (plush), 102

Aladdin, 292

Alben, Russ, 57-58, 241

Albert, Artie and Judy, 8, 156, 165-69, 170, 171, 296

Alchemy II, 251, 257

Alexander, Madame. *See* Madame Alexander

Alf (television character), 17, 112

319

Those Characters From Cleveland.
    See TCFC
"ThunderCats," 193
tiddledywinks (toy), 123
Tiger Electronics, 26
Time, 149, 162, 310
TimeOSaurs (action-figure line), 215
Tin Pan Alley (video game), 94
Tiny Dinos (plush), 216
Tiny Tears (doll), 296
TMA (Toy Manufacturers of
    America), 6, 7, 10, 11, 34, 49,
    131, 191, 196, 203-4, 212, 295,
    309, 313-14
TMI (Toy Market Index), 314
"Today Show, The," 169
Today's Kids, 26
Tolkien, J. R. R., 178
"Tom and Jerry," 195
Tomy America, 164-65
Toni (doll), 144
"Tonight Show, The," 9, 124, 169,
    252
Tonka Corporation, 14, 16-17,
    20-21, 25, 26, 40, 43, 47, 68,
    88-89, 118-21, 217, 242, 247,
    248, 257-58, 260-62, 298, 299,
    302, 311
Tooty Frooty Friends (Potato Head
    figure), 112
Top (Dino-Rider figure), 181
Topps Chewing Gum Company,
    171, 298
Toronto, 8
Totally Cool Fashions (doll
    accessories), 301
Touchables (plush line), 5
Toy Advertising Guidelines, 188-190
Toy & Hobby World, ix, 6, 211, 257,
    297
toy-based programming, 192-94, 310

Toy Book, The, 6
Toy Building (Toy Center South),
    6-7
Toy Center South (Toy Building),
    6-7
Toy Fair. *See* American
    International Toy Fair
Toy Industry Hall of Fame, 7, 49
Toy Liquidator, 281
Toy Manufacturers of America. *See*
    TMA
Toy Market Index (TMI), 314
Toy Retail Sales Tracking Service.
    See TRSTS
toys. *See* individual products or type
    of toy: e.g., dolls; plush; etc. *See
    also* games
toy soldiers. *See* individual products
    and action figures; military toys
Toys "R" Us, 11, 12, 106, 108, 169,
    193, 257, 274-79, 310
Toys That Don't Care, 204
Toys That Kill, 204
Toy Times, 294
Toy Warehouse, 280
Tracy, Dick, 194
trademark violation, 241. *See also*
    counterfeiting; licensed
    products; parallel development;
    parallel marketing; patents;
    plagiarism; security; trademark
    violation
trade secrets. *See* counterfeiting;
    licensed products; parallel
    development; parallel
    marketing; patents; plagiarism;
    security; trademark violation
Traeger, Dave, 238
trains, electric, 85-87, 200
Trakker, Matt (MASK figure), 82-83
Tramiel, Jack, 109